Chapter 4

WORKING IN ONLINE JOURNALISM   61

Chapter 5

USING ONLINE REPORTING SOURCES   83

Chapter 6

WEB PAGE DESIGN   107

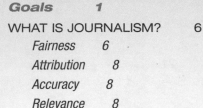

Chapter 1

Chapter 2

Chapter 3

Chapter 7

WRITING AND EDITING ONLINE   143

Chapter 8

USING LINKS IN ONLINE STORIES   169

Chapter 9

MULTIMEDIA AND INTERACTIVITY   191

Chapter 10

LEGAL AND ETHICAL ISSUES   215

Chapter 11

OPPORTUNITIES AND CHALLENGES   237

Appendix A

Appendix B

A few years ago, it became clear to my journalism department, which at the time included broadcast, print and public relations sequences, that we needed to add an online journalism component. I had been teaching broadcast courses, but also had developed an interest in more interactive forms of storytelling through dabbling in early interactive media programs such as Hypercard and AmigaVision.

So, in the summer of 2000 I began to develop an online journalism course, which I taught for the first time in the fall of 2000 using our "experimental" course number, JOUR 495.

I approached the course with the idea that I would take what our students already knew about journalism and help them apply it to the Internet. As an elective course, students in any of the three sequences could take it. Those who did take it reacted positively, and in some cases students who had been on trajectories toward print or broadcast shifted gears and ended up finding places in the online world. After a couple of semesters, the experimental course received its own course number and a permanent place in our curriculum.

I suppose a story similar to this has played out in many other journalism departments. Some, of course, have taken things even further, establishing full sequences and programs in online journalism. But nearly everywhere, programs have added some component of online journalism to their curricula. In some cases, programs have hired journalists from the nascent online world as teachers, but in many more cases it has been journalists from the "traditional" media, like myself, who have adapted themselves to teaching online journalism.

Online Journalism: Principles and Practices of News for the Web is designed to help both kinds of people teach online journalism courses. It approaches the Internet not as a "gee whiz" medium, but as a practical tool for journalism. It assumes that the student has already been introduced to basic journalistic practice and has a general understanding of the structure of the mass media. Consequently, the book seeks to cue this knowledge through adapting it to online journalism practice. The focus of *Online Journalism* is on *content,* and how journalists can use the Internet as a tool to disseminate it.

The book is divided into three main parts. The first four chapters provide an overview of online journalism and discuss its technical foundations. Chapters 2 and 3 discuss some of the technical issues of producing online journalism, including HTML. Chapter 4 provides an overview of what it's like to work as an online journalist and describes how several different online newsrooms operate.

The second part of the book examines the actual techniques of online journalism. These five chapters look at how to use online reporting sources, how to write and edit online journalism stories, how to use and display links to additional information and how to maximize the potential of such online features as multimedia and advanced interactivity.

The final part of the book examines issues that online journalists face today and will face in the future. These two chapters look at how legal and ethical issues that affect journalists apply to online media, and how economic issues and other factors are likely to affect online journalists and media organizations in the future.

Special features of *Online Journalism* include:

- Chapter-opening objectives directing students to the chapter's major points.
- A "What's Next" section to preview important concepts that the student will learn in the next chapter.
- Chapter-end activities to encourage reflection on and application of the chapter concepts. The exercises ask students to explore, assess, and create content.
- An end-of-book glossary for quick reference to important terms.
- An accompanying Web site (http://olj.hh-pub.com) designed to be an integral part of each student's learning experience. The site provides additional original content as well as many up-to-date links to reference sources, examples, online tutorials and other information.
- An Instructor's Manual and PowerPoint presentation available to adopters of this text.

The craft of journalism predated the Internet by hundreds of years. So, it is natural that we would tend to approach the Internet with the attitude that we can adapt it to fit journalism as it has been practiced in the past. This is not a bad start. However, it is also important to understand that the Internet offers the potential to take journalism in new and exciting directions—directions that are more inclusive, more participatory, and more relevant to younger generations. It is in these and other directions that the true potential of online journalism can be realized.

This book is designed as a first step for those people who will some day help this medium reach its full potential.

ACKNOWLEDGMENTS

I would like to thank several people who helped make this book possible. Doug Fever at WashingtonPost.Newsweek Interactive, Jim Debth at CJOnline and Deborah Weiser at WTVG-TV made themselves and their staffs available to me, and I am thankful for their help. Countless others whom I met at conferences and through telephone and e-mail conversations also helped along the way.

Several people reviewed the manuscript at various points in its development, including Bonnie Bressers, Kansas State University; Cecilia Friend, Utica College; Kris P. Kodrich, Colorado State University; Mindy McAdams,

University of Florida; Mike McKean, University of Missouri-Columbia; Donica Mensing, University of Nevada; Kathy Olson, Lehigh University; Jane B. Singer, University of Iowa; Robert Stewart, Ohio University; Jeff South, Virginia Commonwealth University; and Kathleen Woodruff Wickham, The University of Mississippi. I was amazed at the interest they showed in this project, and the fine-tooth comb with which they examined my work. They made great suggestions, and in several cases helped me avert potentially embarrassing mistakes. Of course, any mistakes that remain here—embarrassing or otherwise—are my responsibility alone.

My graduate assistant, Kris Medford, helped immeasurably, including with a lot of the routine work such as getting permissions to use Web images. I would also like to thank students in my online journalism course who gave feedback on a late version of the manuscript. It was quite helpful to get insight from those who will actually be using the book.

Colette Kelly at Holcomb Hathaway Publishers has offered tremendous enthusiasm and encouragement throughout this process, and I am indebted to her for her help. I also thank Gay Pauley at Holcomb Hathaway and Dennis Altshuler, AZLink Internet Services for their help with the production and online aspects of the book, and Aerocraft Charter Art Service for their design and typesetting skills.

The biggest thanks, however, goes to my wife, Cathy, who had to suffer through many months of my work on this book. She has always offered me the encouragement, love and understanding I needed at exactly the time that I needed it.

My mother, Therese, passed away just as I was completing the first draft of this book. Along with my father, she was always there when I needed her, and gave me the guidance and love that has made this and many other things in my life possible. She is still giving me those things, and I dedicate this book to her.

T his textbook's Web site is designed not just as a supplement to the printed book you're looking at now but as an integral part of your learning experience. We have included additional original content on the Web as well as many links to reference sources, examples, online tutorials and other information.

A printed textbook cannot act as a comprehensive resource on the many facets of online journalism. There's really no way it could without having thousands of pages and costing as much as a laptop computer. Instead, this book is designed to introduce you to important topics with the understanding that you are likely to want or need to explore some of these topics in greater detail on your own. For example, your interest in the multimedia authoring software Macromedia Flash might be piqued by Chapter 9's brief overview of the program. You might want to explore Flash in more detail so you can use it in a particular online journalism project. The resources provided on this book's Web site can provide a starting point for such exploration.

The Web site is organized just like the book. The "On the Web" boxes scattered throughout the book chapters offer an overview of the type of material you'll find in that section's Web area. You'll notice that the overviews in the book rarely cite specific information or Web addresses—this is intentional. The Internet is constantly changing—new pages are being added, deleted and moved literally hour by hour. Thus, whenever possible I have avoided citing particular content in these boxes so that the book won't promise something you won't actually find.

The "On the Web" boxes *do* give specific instruction about how to access that section's content on the book's site.

I strongly encourage you to make use of the resources available on the Web site. I have gathered and presented links that I think you'll find useful, interesting and in some cases fun. I will update and add links on a regular basis. Links that have been updated or added in the past month will be marked with an "Updated" icon. I also invite you to share Web sites you find interesting or useful by sending them to jfoust@hh-pub.com. If I post one of your links on the site, I'll provide a credit line acknowledging your contribution.

On the Web

Go to the book's Web site:
http://olj.hh-pub.com.
Then select the appropriate section from the pull-down menu for that chapter.

CHAPTER 1

- To introduce you to the practice of online journalism
- To present the traits that make journalism unique among other types of writing
- To discuss the advantages of online media (i.e., the Internet) for practicing journalism
- To discuss the basic types of online journalism sites
- To provide basic criteria for evaluating online journalism sites
- To outline the organization of this textbook

The **Internet** has been called the greatest advance for communication since the invention of the printing press. It is estimated that nearly 800 million people around the world use the Internet—almost 200 million of those in the United States alone—and that number continues to grow.

Online journalism sites have been an important part of the Internet's growth, and media-related sites consistently rank among the most visited on the Internet. In a 2002 survey, respondents said the Internet was a more important information source than television, radio or magazines, and just as important as newspapers.[1] Thousands of newspapers maintain Web sites—from such "national" and "international" dailies as *The New York Times* and *USA Today* to such small-town weeklies as Mullen, Nebraska's *Hooker County Tribune* and such alternative papers as Detroit's *Metro Times* (see Exhibit 1.1). Nearly every national magazine—and an ever-increasing number of regional and local ones—have Web sites, as do most television and radio stations. Broadcast networks, including ABC, NBC and CBS, have Web sites, as do cable networks, such as MSNBC, CNN and ESPN. These Web sites have an inherent initial advantage because their "parent" media organizations have name recognition and reputations among the public. People trust—or at least know—their local newspapers and television stations and the national media, and they are accustomed to relying on them for news and infor-

Exhibit 1.1   Thousands of newspapers large and small maintain Web sites.

The New York Times

ON THE WEB

UPDATED FRIDAY, JANUARY 9, 2004 4:53 PM ET | Personalize Your Weather

SEARCH   ▸ Go to Advanced Search/Archive

Past 30 Days ▾ ⊙

LOG IN
REGISTER NOW. It's Free!

NEWS
International
National
Washington
Business
Technology
Science
Health
Sports
New York Region
Education
Weather
Obituaries
NYT Front Page
Corrections

OPINION
Editorials/Op-Ed
Readers' Opinions

FEATURES
Arts
Books
Movies
Travel
NYC Guide
Dining & Wine
Home & Garden
Fashion & Style
Crossword/Games
Cartoons
Magazine
Week in Review
Multimedia/Photos
Learning Network

SERVICES
Archive
Classifieds
College
Personals
White Papers
Theater Tickets
NYT Store
NYT Mobile
About NYTDigital
Jobs at NYTDigital
Online Media Kit
Our Advertisers

U.S. Companies Added Few Workers in December

By KENNETH N. GILPIN 2:22 PM ET

The nation's unemployment rate slid to 5.7 percent last month, but businesses added only 1,000 new jobs.

- Stocks Mixed on Weak Jobs Data
- Health Spending Rises to 15% of Economy

Supreme Court Expands Review of 'Enemy Combatant' Cases

By DAVID STOUT 3:57 PM ET

The Bush administration had urged the Supreme Court not to hear the Hamdi case, so the announcement today represented a sharp rebuff.

Senator Tom Harkin, Iowa Power Broker, Endorses Howard Dean

By CARL HULSE 4:47 PM ET

The endorsement hands Howard Dean coveted backing from the most politically influential Democratic lawmaker in Iowa as the state's crucial nominating caucuses near.

- Seeking Women's Votes, Clark Changes Style
- Reality Show to Simulate Presidential Politics
- Complete Coverage: Campaigns

Terror Alert Level Is Reduced

By DAVID STOUT 1:17 PM ET

Homeland Security Secretary Tom Ridge warned that threats will be vigorously monitored even as the alert level was lowered to "elevated."

Tyler Hicks/The New York Times

In The Magazine
Major John Nagl was a leading military scholar on how to fight a resistance. But could he make his ideas work on the ground in Iraq? Go to Magazine

BUSINESS
Ex-Enron Executive's Wife Misses Deadline for Plea

NEW YORK REGION
Jury Awards $8 Million for Smoker's Death

INTERNATIONAL
At Least 4 Killed in Bomb Blast at Mosque in Iraq

MORE HEADLINES

MARKETS

| US | EUROPE | ASIA/AUS |

Dow Jones Industrial Average

10,550
10,500

11   1   3

DJIA	10,458.89	-133.55	-1.26%
NASDAQ	2,086.92	-13.33	-0.63%
S&P 500	1,121.86	-10.06	-0.89%
10-YR TRES.	4.09%		-0.16

© BigCharts.com   4:30 PM ET

- Market Update: U.S. | World
- View Your Personal Portfolio

Stock
Quotes: ⊙   Symbol
                              Lookup

HARRISdirect

Pay ┃ per trade ▸

MOVIES.NYTIMES.COM

Chasing Liberty
The sacrificial first studio release of 2004 stars Mandy Moore as a freedom-hungry first daughter.

- Special Section: Oscars 2004
- Go to Movies

Showtimes & Tickets
Search by Zip Code:

[   ] Go

SPORTS

Rose Embarrassed About Bets

ESCAPES

A New Generation of Hunters

ARTS

Fabergé Eggs Auction

MOVIES

The Art of the Split Screen

Continued.   **Exhibit 1.1**

Mullen, Nebraska

See What's New at the Hooker County Tribune

- Area News Update
- Area Community Update
- Obituaries
- Features
- Sports
- Schools

The Hooker County Tribune has been the local hometown paper serving Mullen and the surrounding area for over 100 years. It is currently owned and operated by Russell and Lanita Evans at 306 NW 1st in Mullen, NE. Current subscribers number 885. The paper is published weekly with a dateline of Thursday each week. - news copy and advertising deadline is Tuesday noon.

Current subscription rates: Mullen and Seneca addresses = $15.00 per year. All other addresses are $18.00 per year.

Office hours: Mon, Tues, Thurs 8:00 - 4:30; Wed, 1:30 - 4:30.

Hooker County Tribune Staff:

- Owner/Editor/Publisher: Lanita Evans, (308) 546-2745
- Office Assistant/Feature Writer: Val Simonson, (308) 546-754
- News Correspondents: Mullen - Betty Brown; Seneca
- Contributing Cartoonist: David Sung
- Contributing Feature Writer: Tammy Hansen Gilbert

Hooker County Tribune
Box 125 · Mullen, NE · 69152
(308) 546-2242
E-Mail The Hooker County Tribune

Back To NebNet Main Menu

Back To Neb-Sandhills Main Menu

From *Hooker County Tribune*. Reprinted with permission.

Exhibit 1.1   Continued.

metrotimes
www.metrotimes.com
metro detroit's news, arts & culture weekly

mf THE INTERACTIVE
GUIDE TO DETROIT

EVENTS
RESTAURANTS
NIGHTSPOTS
MUSICIANS

CONTENTS
Feb. 11 - Feb. 17, 2004
news+views
arts
music
culture
film
food
classifieds
personals
archives

about us
promotions
advertise
careers

COVER STORY

The Black History Quiz

Americana in Black
By W. Kim Heron
Tragedy, triumph & trivia in a **quiz** to make you go hmmmm.

NEWS + VIEWS

Dis in the D
By Curt Guyette
Sharpton fills void left by Kerry, Dean, Clark.

The truth about the caucuses
POLICTICS & PREJUDICES
By Jack Lessenberry
Jack sounds off on **alleged high turnout** and voter burnout.

Eric Reed named retail ad director
FACES
By Michael Jackman
Back from the land of the Hoosiers: **new display advertising head** announced.

Hole of a place
ABANDONED HOUSE OF THE WEEK
Razed home to make way for **urban garden.**

Letters to the Editor
Find out what our readers are saying each week.

NEWS HITS
Confession catch-up
Teens who were subject of Metro Times story fight wrongful murder conviction. (02/11/04)

Rockin' round city hall
Harmony or cacophony: Local musical group adopts Detroit City Council as moniker. (02/11/04)

Tour de abandonment
Local woman to organize tours of forgotten Detroit. (02/11/04)

MUSIC

American dreaming
By Jimmy Draper
Sscion's art-house ballyhoo summons queer spectacles, **Tori Amos** beatings and a love of Love.

---

mf THE INTERACTIVE
GUIDE TO DETROIT

CHOICE PICKS ✪

EVENTS
February 11-14, 2004
The Spirit of Harriet Tubman
At the tender age of 15, Harriet Tubman tried to assist her first runaway slave...
[more]

RESTAURANTS
Restaurant Spotlight
Majestic Cafe
Eclectic **mid-city eatery** gets high marks.
(Eats: 4 stars / Experience 4 stars)

MUSICIANS
Musicians Spotlight
Matthew Dear:
One of Ghostly International's golden boys.

FILM & VIDEO
Destino
(5 out of 5 Stars)
★★★★★

La Commune (Paris, 1871) Part Two
(4 out of 5 Stars)
★★★★

The Company
(3 out of 5 Stars)
★★★

Barbershop 2
(3 out of 5 Stars)
★★★

The Perfect Score
(2 out of 5 Stars)
★★

mation. When the weather turns bad, residents of small towns might be able to log onto their local newspaper's Web site to get an update on school closings. For many people who have moved away from the place where they grew up, the local newspaper still represents "home"; if that newspaper has a Web site, former residents can log on and keep up with local happenings, even from thousands of miles away. The presence of international, national, regional and local media Web sites allows people located anywhere to keep up with happenings almost anywhere else.

The creation of online journalism Web sites requires people with specialized skills. College journalism programs have responded by adding courses and programs to their curricula to train students to create online content. The class you're in right now no doubt has that goal in mind. Graduates who blend the core skills of journalism with the technical knowledge of how the Internet works and the ability to create content for online media can find themselves highly sought after by potential employers.

This book is designed to prepare you to be an online journalist. It assumes that you have learned the basic theories and practices of journalism in other classes and that you are now ready to apply them to online media. The book will review some of those theories and practices—and in many ways expand on them—as it examines the technical issues involved in creating online content and shows you ways to maximize the Internet as a tool for journalism. Technical issues, such as **bits, bytes** and **servers,** are a part of the book, as are technical processes, such as writing computer code and downloading files, but they are both only a *part* of the book. The real goal is to teach you enough about these issues and processes that you can apply them to producing good journalism.

The book is intentionally broad-based: Online journalism as a field is still in its infancy, and it is difficult to predict what it will look like in the future. It is also nearly impossible to describe a "typical" online journalist, or to know if there even is such a thing. How do we compare, for example, a production specialist who works as part of a 10-person team at a large newspaper site to the television reporter at a small-town TV station who is also solely responsible for producing the news portion of the station's Web site? The general answer is that they are both practicing *journalism,* even though it may be difficult to find many commonalities in their day-to-day jobs. For that reason, this book seeks to expose the reader to multiple types of online journalism, practiced in many different settings. Whatever your vision of online journalism or your aspirations for a career in the field may be, this book and its accompanying Web site (see "To the Student" at the start of this book) are intended to provide you with a starting point.

WHAT IS JOURNALISM?

Before we look at online journalism, we should first remind ourselves of some of the attributes of journalism in general. Although there are many kinds of journalism, practiced by many different kinds of people in many different places and for many types of media, some common threads connect—or at least should connect—all journalists.

The early 20th-century journalist Finley Peter Dunne said that the purpose of journalism was "to comfort the afflicted and afflict the comfortable." At its best, journalism can expose inequities and injustices that affect those without money or power, or it can uncover the corruption or other wrongdoing of governments and corporations. In some cases, it can even do both at the same time. Fearless and thorough journalism has toppled presidents, helped to end racially discriminatory practices, and warned the public about potentially dangerous automobiles, medicines and other products.

Yet journalism that does not pursue such lofty goals can still be valuable and effective. For a democracy to function properly, citizens need to be informed about the day-to-day and continuing issues that influence them. People want to know about the things that affect—or will affect—their lives financially, socially and in other ways. Thus, journalism that addresses school vouchers, real estate tax hearings or city council meetings serves an important purpose. To a lesser degree, entertainment or sports journalism also has value, although, unfortunately, some of what is practiced in these areas more closely resembles promotion than traditional journalism.

Journalists are essentially information gatherers: They get information, process it, and then present it in an appropriate form. However, the same could be said of many other professionals, including lawyers, advertising copywriters and stock analysts. What makes journalists unique? Several traits distinguish journalists from these other professionals and, indeed, from other types of writers. The same traits separate online journalism Web sites from other types of Web sites.

Fairness

The core trait of journalism is **fairness,** meaning that journalists approach information without bias and report it the same way. If an issue has two sides, they report both of them; if it has more than two sides, they report all of them. A journalist's job is not to further someone else's point of view or do the bidding of a particular interest, but to remain independent. The old phrase "just the facts, ma'am" aptly summarizes a journalist's responsibility to avoid injecting his or her own points of view into a story or allowing someone else's point of view to dominate the story.

The concept of fairness is not cut and dried, however. For years, conservatives have decried journalism's "liberal bias," while more recently those on the left have countered that the media's bias is in fact to the right. While it is well beyond the scope of this book to settle that dispute, we know that certain journalistic organizations approach the news from either the left or the right. For example, in Washington, D.C., *The Washington Post* has traditionally leaned left while *The Washington Times* has leaned right. Most consumers realize this, however, and act accordingly—likely reading the paper that most closely mirrors their own outlook.

Since the overall point of view of a media organization tends to carry over to its Internet operations, these same biases can be found in online journalism sites. So, you will likely find that washingtonpost.com is more liberal than washingtontimes.com. In addition, many online journalism sites that aren't associated with a traditional media organization cater to one or more political points of view.

Traditionally, the only significant exception to the journalist's fairness credo had been for opinion columnists, who, it was expected, would be giving their opinions in their columns. The Internet has given rise to other possible exceptions, most notably when journalists contribute to **blogs.** As will be discussed in Chapter 4, blogs operate on a more informal, free-flowing model than do traditional stories, allowing and encouraging **bloggers** to give their opinions and state information that may not yet have been verified independently (see Exhibit 1.2). Ethical questions arise when a journalist—who is ostensibly supposed to be fair and objective—drops these traits while contributing to a blog (see Chapter 10).

Blog sites, such as this one by political commentator Andrew Sullivan, **Exhibit 1.2**
are becoming increasingly common on the Internet.

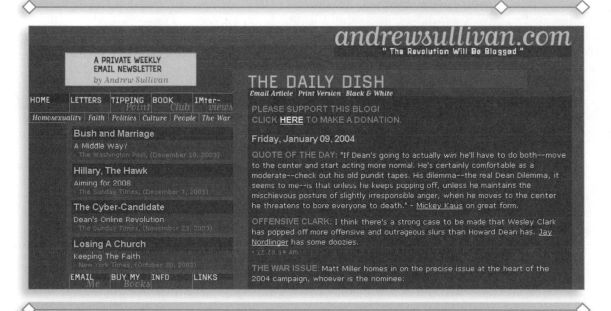

From andrewsullivan.com. Reprinted with permission.

Attribution

The practice of **attribution** is closely related to the concept of fairness. Attribution means that journalists report not only the facts but where those facts came from. This is crucial to allowing readers to decide for themselves how much credence to give those facts. If a study concluding that cell phone use does not cause automobile accidents was financed by cell phone manufacturers, for example, people should give the study's information less weight than if it came from an organization without a financial stake in the issue.

The Internet provides for an entirely new dimension to attribution. For example, if the journalist's information source is an online site, she can provide a **link** to that information in her story. Readers can then not only know where the information came from but actually see it for themselves.

Accuracy

Accuracy means, simply, getting the facts *right*. What is the address of the house that caught fire? How many people died in the fire? Did the fire chief say that a damaged extension cord *caused* the fire or did he say they're investigating the possibility? These are all facts that need to be reported accurately. Good journalists always double-check facts, too, by confirming them with multiple sources. People come to rely on certain journalistic organizations because they trust them, and if journalists betray that trust by reporting inaccurate information, people are likely to look elsewhere for their news.

As will be discussed in Chapter 5, the Internet has become well known for hoaxes and other inaccurate information. Thus, journalists have an even greater responsibility to make sure they check and double-check information, especially if that information comes from an Internet source.

Relevance

Journalism also should have **relevance,** or importance to the audience. A journalistic story should mean something to the people who read it. Often, relevance is established by providing **context** for information. Context is related information that may not be known to the average person, such as the fact that the company that won the right to build the new downtown baseball stadium in a disputed bidding process is owned by the mayor's brother-in-law. Journalists are trained not only to know a lot about the world at large (that's why most college journalism programs require heavy doses of economics, political science and other liberal arts) but to know a lot about the communities in which they live and the topics they cover. The ability—and responsibility—to provide context that makes stories more meaningful is one primary attribute that makes journalism unique.

The concept of relevance is also what dismisses much so-called entertainment journalism. Even though some people may be interested in a pop star's engagement to a movie idol, it is difficult to argue that the information has any real relevance to anyone's life (except the pop star and the movie idol, of course).

Newness

Finally, journalism should have **newness,** providing information that hasn't been given before. The word *new,* of course, is the basic root of *news.* This does not mean that journalists can cover only "breaking" stories, such as house fires and car crashes, but that the stories they report must contain new information. An event that happened years ago can still be "new" if it hasn't been known before—the fact that a city council member was once a member of a white supremacist organization, for example. A story that takes a long time to develop also can be new—such as a yearlong investigation of corruption in a government office, or a six-month analysis of crash-test data for a particular sport-utility vehicle. Enterprising journalists might take a new approach to a story that has been reported before, such as looking at how the much-hyped new major league sports team has affected attendance at such local cultural events as theater and opera.

It is these attributes—fairness, attribution, accuracy, relevance and newness—that separate journalism from other types of information dissemination, no matter what the medium.

ADVANTAGES OF ONLINE JOURNALISM

The Internet has several unique advantages over earlier media (see Exhibit 1.3). These advantages have largely driven the Internet's phenomenal growth over the past decade and in many ways make it a particularly powerful tool for journalism. "Today it can be said that the Internet is a journalist's medium," John Pavlik notes. "The Internet not only embraces all the capabilities of the older media (text, images, graphics, animation, audio, video, real-time delivery) but offers a broad spectrum of new capabilities."[2] While these capabilities will be addressed in greater detail throughout this book, let's also discuss them briefly here.

Audience Control

The Internet's first advantage is that it allows the audience to have greater control over information. For example, one person who goes to a particular Web site may choose to retrieve stories about the new school levy, while another may simulta-

Exhibit 1.3 Advantages of the Internet over other media.

ADVANTAGES	SIGNIFICANCE FOR JOURNALISTS
Audience control	Allows people more power to choose the information they want
Nonlinearity	Allows stories that do not have a predetermined linear order
Storage and retrieval	Stores a vast amount of information and makes it readily retrievable
Unlimited space	Overcomes spatial and temporal limitations of earlier media
Immediacy	Allows information to be published almost instantaneously
Multimedia capability	Enables journalists to include print text, sound, video and other content in stories
Interactivity	Provides for a greater level of audience participation

neously read about the proposed new library. On the Internet, more than with any previous medium, people have the power to choose the information they want and become actively engaged in that information. For that reason, we usually refer to people who consume online content as **users,** since they are actively engaged in seeking information. This is in contrast to terms used for consumers of "old" media—*readers, listeners, viewers*—that reflect more passive activities.

Nonlinearity

A unique attribute of the Internet is that it allows information to flow effectively in nonlinear form, more so than with any previous medium. This means that journalists can design stories that do not have to be accessed in a predetermined linear order. Instead, a story can be structured to allow individual users to experience it differently. For example, a story about a plan to remodel several of the city's dilapidated school buildings may be written so that its various parts can be accessed in any order, independent of one another. Thus, one user might choose to read only about plans for a specific school, while another user could begin by reading about how the school board plans to pay for the project and then move on to another part of the story. An individual story segment would not depend on other segments for user understanding.

Storage and Retrieval

Another important advantage is the Internet's ability to store a vast amount of information and to make that information readily retrievable. If you have used the

Internet to do research, you probably have some sense of the amount of information that can be found online. Entire encyclopedias, archival records of government and industry, and the full text of United States Supreme Court decisions are but a small sample of what is available online, and that pool of information is constantly growing.

Compared to previous media, that information also is easily accessible online. Using a **search engine,** an Internet user can enter a subject, name or place and retrieve the desired information. Web page creators can create links that will immediately take the user to relevant information. For example, in an online story about a court decision that will affect a local school district, a link to the full text of the court's decision could be included, as could links to previous stories about the topic. The Internet's capability to allow such seamless linking among many different sources of data is another of its unique advantages.

Although the Internet is sometimes criticized as providing too much information in a disorganized form, search engines and skillful linking by journalists and others can make searching for specific information less overwhelming (see "Vannevar Bush, the Memex and Journalists" on the following page). No previous medium has even approached the level of information access provided by the Internet. Not only is this an advantage for consumers of online media, but it is also a powerful tool for journalists (as will be discussed in Chapter 5).

Unlimited Space

The Internet also can overcome the spatial and temporal limitations of previous media. Unlike a newspaper or magazine, the Internet has unlimited "space" for information. For example, a print newspaper cannot practically provide the full text of a court decision just discussed because it would be too expensive to print the extra pages. However, that same newspaper could provide a link to the decision in its online version with almost no additional expense. In the same way, the Internet is not constrained by the time limitations of broadcast media such as radio and television. There is no way the local TV news anchor would read the court's decision on the air, but the station could easily provide a link to the decision on its Web site.

Immediacy

The Internet allows information to be "published" almost instantaneously. A text-based online story, for example, can be made available to the audience immediately, with no lag time for printing or physical distribution. This capability allows print-based media like newspapers to overcome the immediacy advantage long held by television and radio. The newspaper's audience no longer has to wait until the next morning for information about breaking news.

Vannevar Bush, the Memex and Journalists

In 1945, Dr. Vannevar Bush published an article titled "As We May Think," in *The Atlantic Monthly* magazine. Bush, who as director of the Office of Scientific Research and Development had overseen the efforts of scientists to help the United States in World War II, said that scientists needed to turn their attention to making the rapidly expanding universe of information more manageable. "Publication has been extended far beyond our present ability to make real use of the record," he wrote.

Bush proposed a machine called the "Memex," which would allow people to connect various pieces of information the way the human mind subconsciously connects related information. Books would be stored on microfilm in the Memex; when the user selected a particular piece of information, other pieces of information related to it would be retrieved automatically. "It is exactly as though the physical items had been gathered together from widely separated sources and bound together to form a new book," he wrote. Users of the Memex would be able to make their own connections (which Bush called "trails") among pieces of information or purchase preconnected information sets.

Although the Memex as Bush described it was a decidedly cumbersome device by today's standards (it consisted of a large desk with various levers, keys, and buttons), Bush in effect was foreshadowing the unique ability of the Internet to connect disparate pieces of information. The trails Bush described that connected information are much like today's links on the Internet.

Bush's article is particularly interesting because he also foresaw the role that journalists could play on the Internet, although he did not mention them by name. Bush wrote of "a new profession of trail blazers, those who find delight in the task of establishing useful trails through the enormous mass of the common record." These experts would connect various pieces of information in a logical and useful way, making the information more accessible to both experts and average people. Today, perhaps no group is better positioned than journalists to provide useful links among the bewildering array of information available on the Internet. Who better than journalists to make sense of the information available online?

On the Web

Read the Vannevar Bush article on this book's Web site:
Under Chapter 1, select **Vannevar Bush, the Memex and Journalists.**

Multimedia Capability

Multiple types of media can be provided over the Internet. As will be discussed in Chapter 2, text, pictures, sounds and video can be provided online. Such **multimedia** capability allows online journalists to have the best of all worlds: the detail of the printed story, the "theater of the mind" imagery of sound, and the emotional impact of the moving picture.

Interactivity

Finally, the Internet provides the potential for a greater level of audience participation, or **interactivity.** By providing chat rooms, bulletin boards or other types of forums (as discussed in Chapter 9), online journalism sites can allow their users to participate in news stories. Users can debate a topic discussed in a story, ask for clarification of issues raised in the story or even provide additional information. Blogs can also facilitate user participation and interaction with journalists.

Not only can such interactivity increase the community's interest in topics of importance, it also can increase the particular news organization's standing in the community by providing a sense that it *listens* to its audience. In this way, online journalism can come to more closely resemble the give-and-take of an interpersonal communication rather than the one-way flow normally associated with mass media.

> ### On the Web
>
> More on the unique attributes of the Internet as well as links to examples of multimedia and advanced interactive content:
> Under Chapter 1, select **Advantages of Online Journalism.**

TYPES OF ONLINE JOURNALISM SITES

Most online journalism sites are associated with previously existing media organizations, such as newspapers, magazines and television stations or networks. These sites normally reflect the basic character of their "parent" media, including geographic coverage area, specializations and—as noted earlier—political point of view. For example, you will find national and world coverage on the CNN.com Web site, and coverage of the Washington, D.C., metro area with a heavy dose of political news on the washingtonpost.com Web site. A few online journalism sites exist only on the Internet, but these are relatively rare. When the so-called Internet bubble burst in the late 1990s, it took down many such freestanding sites with it. Sites like salon.com and slate.com have survived, but they have never been able to build audience levels approaching those of the most popular media sites.

In general, sites associated with larger newspapers and the national television networks provide the most journalistic content. A lot of this content is **shovelware,** meaning it is taken from the newspaper or wire services and simply "shoveled" onto the Web site with little or no modification. This type of content tends not to take full advantage of the Internet's unique attributes, but it does provide users with relatively current information. Also, in many cases, the shovelware becomes merely the starting point for additional features, often called **Web extras,** that are added to the Web site. For example, the site may start by simply posting the story from the morning's newspaper, then add updated information, interactive features and links to other information throughout the day. A primary goal of most journalistic Web sites is to be visited frequently by their users—at least once a day, and perhaps several times throughout the day. Frequently updated content is one way to encourage such repeat visits.

Some Web sites associated with local television and radio stations, on the other hand, are little more than promotional devices—heavy on anchor and deejay biographies and light on original news content. The consolidation in the radio industry has severely reduced news staffing, leading to less emphasis on local news coverage. Thus, radio stations with significant original news content are quite rare. Local television stations fare a bit better, but they usually have much smaller staffs than newspapers. Local television stations also tend not to cover stories as in depth as newspapers, so they usually have less original content to provide online. Not surprisingly, the single area where local television is ahead of newspapers is in providing video clips online; however, these also tend to be merely unedited clips of stories as they ran on the station's newscast—shovelware in video form. But, for someone who missed the station's evening newscast, these online video clips provide a way to see the story as it aired (see Exhibit 1.4).

The differing strengths of newspaper, television and other media has encouraged **convergence** sites, in which two or more media partner to produce a Web site. Typically, a local television station and the local paper join forces to create a site, such as Tampa Bay Online (TBO.com), which is produced in cooperation with *The Tampa Tribune* and WFLA-TV. Media that are owned by the same parent company may also create a Web site together. *The Washington Post* Web site mentioned previously is a partnership between the *Post* and *Newsweek* magazine, which are both part of the same company. The *Post* site also partners with the MSNBC television network and *Congressional Quarterly* magazine. Thus, you are likely to see a mixture of content from these various sources on the *Post*'s Web site.

Convergence allows different media to share not only content but also personnel. Over the past decade, we have begun to see the rise of the so-called **superjournalist,** who gathers information and produces stories for more than one type of media. A superjournalist might cover a story for a newspaper and at the same time gather video footage and soundbites for a story to be broadcast on television or over a Web site. Obviously, to be successful, such superjournalists have to understand how to produce

Television Web sites can provide access to video clips from   **Exhibit 1.4**
news programs that users may have missed.

Farmer Jack Closing Update
Will they change their stores to a stripped-down model?
▣ Watch Video of the Report

Toledo's Priests and Sexual Abuse Policy
Auditors call for revision to punish one-time abusers
▣ Watch Video of the Report

From 13abc.com. Reprinted with permission.

content for multiple media. With the increasing consolidation among the media industries, and the increasing emphasis on online delivery, prospective journalists will have to be prepared to work with a variety of media forms.

EVALUATING ONLINE SITES

As we've discussed, a wide variety of journalism sites can be found on the Internet as well as many sites that provide information but not necessarily journalism. As you begin this course and this textbook, take time to compare some of your favorite Web sites to some of the leading journalistic Web sites, such as CNN.com, washingtonpost.com, nytimes.com, and other sites listed on this book's Web site. Doing so will help you build a better understanding of what constitutes a quality journalism site, so that you'll be better prepared to become a quality online journalist.

As you look at these sites, ask yourself the following questions. The answers to these questions help establish not only the overall quality of the Web site but also whether it should be considered a journalistic site.

Who Is Producing the Site?

Consider the source of the site's content. Is it written by a journalistic organiza-tion or by a corporation, public relations firm or political group? Sometimes the answer to this question will be obvious, but other times you may need to dig deep-er to find out. Clicking on an "About Us" link is a good place to start, but sometimes organizations don't want you to know who is behind the site. For example, a site sponsored by a pro-gun group might want users to think its information is unbiased, when in actuality it's not. When you have the answer to this question, consider whether the producers have some sort of agenda or personal motive: Are they trying to get you to buy something, believe something or vote a certain way? If so, you're probably not reading journalism.

What Is the Content of the Site?

Remember that journalism is usually about issues of public importance—issues that affect people's lives directly or indirectly in important ways. It is hard to argue that a site about collectible teddy bears is journalism, although some people may be very interested in it. If the site is about sports or entertainment, that can be a trickier issue, as discussed previously. In these cases, you need to ask whether the content is promotional in nature—trying to build support for a team, an athlete, a recording artist or a movie—or is unbiased. Does the site consist of merely "fluff" stories, like who won last night's game or who's dating whom, or is it about more substantive issues, such as drug abuse among athletes or violent movies aimed at children? Is the site merely a promotional tool to encourage you to watch a station's newscast or read the printed newspaper, or does it contain useful information on its own? The nature of a Web site's content is one of the clearest indicators of its journalistic intent.

Is the Information Accurate?

Answering this question can be difficult because you may not know whether what you see on the site is actually true. Still, you can look for typographical errors, misspellings, poor grammar and other cues that normally indicate an unprofessional or sloppily produced Web site. Remember that journalism must strive for accuracy and factuality in both large and small issues. That's one reason journalistic organizations have editors to check the work of their reporters. No one is perfect and mistakes are made, but numerous mistakes indicate that what you're reading is not journalism—at least not good journalism.

How Often Is the Information Updated?

Journalism is about what's new, and the Web provides the capability to continually update information. So, if a Web site has not been updated for a long time or contains clearly outdated information, it's not good journalism. A quality newspaper or television Web site should be updated at least once a day, if not more often. Sites associated with weekly or monthly publications or freestanding sites such as slate.com might be updated less often, but they still should be relatively current. You can often find a message line on the Web page that indicates when stories were last updated, as shown below:

UPDATED MONDAY, JANUARY 3, 2005, 1:30 PM ET

What Does the Site Look Like?

I will discuss design considerations in detail in Chapter 6, but for now you can tell a lot about a site just by looking at it. Sites produced professionally tend to have clean, pleasant designs that do not assault the senses or shout, "Look at me!" Most professional news organizations want their Web sites to reflect the character of their organizations and so are not adorned with needlessly moving logos, elaborate animations or other unnecessary additions. Most newspaper sites—for better or worse—look a lot like the printed newspaper. A site that overemphasizes attention-getting appearances or is difficult to maneuver through is not likely to be useful for getting information. Thus, its journalistic integrity has to be questioned.

On the Web

Links to sites mentioned in this section and more about evaluating online sites:
Under Chapter 1, select **Evaluating Online Sites.**

BEGINNING YOUR JOURNEY INTO ONLINE JOURNALISM

Having surveyed the basic landscape of online journalism, we're now ready to start learning to create it ourselves. We will examine the technical issues needed to understand the online world as well as the skills needed to put it to use. We'll also look at how online journalism works—and how it looks—in various forms. Finally, we'll examine some of the broader issues that affect the creation of online journalism now and in the future.

This textbook is divided into three main parts. The first four chapters (including this one) provide an overview of online journalism and discuss some of its technical foundations. Chapters 2 and 3 discuss technical issues of producing online journalism, including **hypertext markup language (HTML),** the computer language used to create Web pages. Chapter 4 provides an overview of what it's like to work as an online journalist and how online newsrooms operate.

The second part of the book examines the actual techniques of online journalism. These five chapters look at how to use online reporting sources, how to write and edit online journalism stories, how to use and display links to additional information and how to maximize the potential of such online features as multimedia and advanced interactivity.

On the Web

Resources for online journalists, including *Online Journalism Review,* the Online News Association and others:
Under Chapter 1, select **Beginning Your Journey . . .**

The final part of the book examines issues that face online journalists today and in the future. These two chapters look at how legal and ethical issues that affect journalists apply to online media, and how economic issues and other factors are likely to affect online journalists and media organizations in the future.

Online journalism as a field is in a remarkable state of flux. It is so new that today's (and tomorrow's) online journalists still have a chance to be the pioneers, largely determining how people will use online journalism well into the future. The "rules" of online journalism are still being written as you read this, and at this point we can only imagine where online journalism will go and what it will look like a decade from now. Few generations are fortunate enough to enter the ground floor of new and exciting media; you are one of those generations.

Welcome to the exciting world of online journalism!

WHAT'S NEXT

The next chapter provides an overview of the Internet and some of the hardware, software, and media associated with producing online journalism. The processes of creating online journalism will build on this technical understanding.

Activities

1.1 Think about where you get your news and information. Is it primarily from print, radio, television or the Internet? Do you use different media for different types of information?

1.2 Compare your local newspaper's print edition to its Web site. How much of the Web site's content is shovelware from the newspaper, and how much of it is original?

1.3 Compare one of the Web sites mentioned in this chapter (washingtonpost.com, salon.com, slate.com, TBO.com) to a site you visit frequently or any popular site (e.g., Yahoo!, ETonline.com, BET.com, AOL.com). Using the criteria and Web sites given in this chapter, explain why the site you visit can or cannot be considered a journalistic one.

ENDNOTES

1. Study: "Net Now More Important Than TV," http://www.cnn.com/ 2003/TECH/internet/01/31/internet.survey.ap/index.html (accessed February 7, 2003).

2. John V. Pavlik, *Journalism and New Media* (New York: Columbia University Press, 2001), p. 3.

CHAPTER 2

GOALS

- To provide an overview of the development of the Internet and the World Wide Web
- To introduce the basic applications that allow information exchange over the Internet
- To discuss the attributes and advantages of digital media
- To survey the basic types, formats and resource requirements of digital media
- To discuss the basic hardware and software considerations related to producing and consuming online journalism

TOOLS AND TERMINOLOGY

Although all journalists must learn to use technical tools of one kind or another, the online journalist faces a particularly daunting array of electronic hardware and software. Moreover, these tools and their accompanying terminology are evolving at a rapid pace, changing—it sometimes seems—daily.

The good news is that you don't have to become a scientist or even necessarily a "geek" to understand and use the basic tools of online journalism. It's likely you use computers and the Internet almost every day, so you've already experienced the basics of online journalism's technical tools. The key now is to look at these technologies with an eye not just toward using them to send **electronic mail (e-mail)** to a friend or to look up the latest sports scores but toward understanding how—and why—they work the way they do.

This chapter will give you an overview of the Internet and the hardware, software and media associated with online journalism. Reading it is not likely to turn you into a computer guru, but it should provide a baseline understanding of the tools and terminology we will be using to experience and create online content.

THE INTERNET AND THE WORLD WIDE WEB

In a little more than a decade, the Internet went from being a mere technical curiosity to a major influence on nearly every aspect of life for most residents of developed countries. The Internet's ability to store and retrieve a massive amount of information in a variety of forms has made it extremely useful for commerce, education, entertainment and, of course, journalism.

Although the terms *Internet* and *World Wide Web* are often used interchangeably, the two terms have distinct—and different—meanings. The Internet is the worldwide **network,** or connection, of computers that allows any **user** on the network to access information from anywhere else on the network. The **World Wide Web (WWW)** refers to the set of technologies that places a **graphical interface** on the Internet, allowing users to explore the network using their mouse, icons and other visual elements rather than having to type obscure computer commands. In fact, it was only with the advent of the World Wide Web in the early 1990s that the Internet, which traces its roots to the 1950s, really began to enter mainstream life.

Early Development of the Internet

In the 1960s, at the height of the Cold War, the United States Department of Defense was looking for ways to create a decentralized communications system that would allow researchers and government officials to communicate with one another in the event of a nuclear attack. The Advanced Research Projects Agency (ARPA) was formed to study the use of computer networks to accomplish this task. By the 1970s, ARPA had successfully connected hundreds of computers to a network that was known as ARPANET. Behind the scenes, however, ARPA engineers had coined another name for this network that interconnected other networks—*Internet*—and by 1983, ARPA's network was formally known as the Internet.

An important innovation that made ARPANET possible was the development of **TCP/IP (transmission control protocol/Internet protocol),** a method of breaking messages into small chunks called "packets" that are "addressed" to specific computers (see Exhibit 2.1). Once these data packets reach their destinations, they are reassembled to re-create the original message. The key advantage of this system is that it allows many different messages to flow to and from many different computers on the network at the same time.

Each computer on the Internet has a unique **Internet protocol (IP)** address that allows other computers to identify it. The IP address is a series of numbers separated by periods, such as 129.1.2.169, for example, which refers to a particular computer at Bowling Green State University. However, since these number strings are difficult to memorize and have no relation to the kind of information contained on the computers they identify, the text-based **domain name system**

Data to be sent over the Internet is broken into packets, which are reassembled   **Exhibit 2.1**
when they reach their destination.

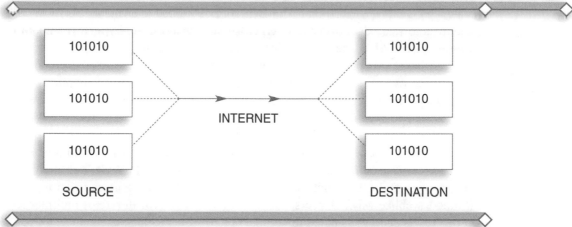

(**DNS**) is usually used to identify computers on the Internet. For example, personal.bgsu.edu is the DNS name assigned to the computer at 129.1.2.169, which houses personal Web pages for faculty at Bowling Green State University.

Text-Based Internet Applications

During the 1980s, the Internet looked nothing like it does today, at least not to its users. WWW technologies had not yet put a graphic face on the Internet, so nearly all communication was accomplished using text-only applications. The **telnet** program, for example, allowed users to log onto and control remote computers, while **file transfer protocol (FTP)** programs allowed users to transfer files to and from remote computers. Although both of these programs are still around, most people aren't aware that they're using them. For example, when you download a program to your computer by clicking a link on a Web page, you're actually activating a "hidden" FTP program built into your browser.

Electronic mail (e-mail), which was also developed before the graphic-based Web, allows one user to send text messages to another user. **Newsgroups** allow users to "post" e-mail messages where others can read them. Literally thousands of newsgroups are available on the Internet, catering to a wide variety of general and specific interests (as will be discussed in Chapter 5). **Chat** allows two or more users to communicate in real time by typing information on their keyboards. E-mail, newsgroups and chat are still widely used today, although they have been significantly enhanced by the addition of graphics and easier to use interfaces. For example, today's popular **instant messaging (IM)** systems, which allow users to send text messages, pictures and other information to one another in real time, are enhanced versions of early chat programs.

Development of the World Wide Web

The World Wide Web can trace its origins to the work of one man at a physics laboratory in Geneva, Switzerland. Tim Berners-Lee wanted to create an easy way for scientists to share data over the Internet, so he developed the **hypertext markup language (HTML).** The primary innovations of HTML are its graphic interface, which allows text, pictures and other elements to intermingle on the computer screen, and its seamless linking capability, which allows users to easily jump from computer to computer on the Internet by simply clicking their mouse on the screen.

As HTML became the standard interface for the Internet, creating the World Wide Web, it was nothing short of a revolution. Now users could connect to the Internet, and retrieve and publish information much more easily, without worrying about arcane computer commands. "Inventing the World Wide Web involved my growing realization that there was a power in arranging ideas in an unconstrained, weblike way," Berners-Lee later noted.[1] The growth rate of the Internet in the 1970s and 1980s paled in comparison to what has happened since 1990.

How the World Wide Web Works

Compared to many computer languages, HTML is relatively easy to understand, since it is text-based (as will be discussed in Chapter 3). Web pages are nothing more than HTML documents that contain text and "pointers" to other types of media, as shown in Exhibit 2.2. A **browser,** such as Microsoft Internet Explorer, Netscape Navigator, or Apple Safari, is used to view Web pages. The browser interprets the HTML coding and then reconstructs the Web page on the user's screen, as shown in Exhibit 2.3.

Exhibit 2.2   HTML documents contain "pointers" to other elements, such as graphics or video clips.

Image File

Sound File

Video File

HTML Document

The Web browser interprets the HTML coding, displaying media files on-screen.   **Exhibit 2.3**

Since much of the value of the Internet is in its ability to allow users to get information on remote computers, a way to access HTML documents located on different computers must also exist. This is accomplished through the use of a **Uniform Resource Locator (URL),** which is normally typed into a browser's "address" window. The browser then takes the user to the document indicated by the URL.

For example, http://personal.bgsu.edu/~jfoust/index.html is a URL that refers to the author's home page. The middle part of this URL is probably already recognizable to you as the DNS name discussed earlier—personal.bgsu.edu—which identifies the computer on which the document is stored. "HTTP" indicates **hypertext transfer protocol,** which is the uniform method of transferring HTML documents over the Internet. Fortunately, all modern browsers will automatically add the "http://" to Web addresses you type, saving you the hassle of the rather arcane punctuation. The end part of the URL in this example tells the browser the exact name and location of the document on the personal.bgsu.edu computer; in this case, the file is located in the folder called "~jfoust" and is called "index.html." File names that end in either ".htm" or ".html" are automatically interpreted by browsers and other programs as HTML documents. Chapter 5 will talk more about URLs and how a journalist can dissect them to help evaluate a site's content.

HTML documents can also contain **links** (which are also called hyperlinks) to other HTML documents, either on the same computer or on different computers. Links often appear on Web pages as blue underlined text, but other types of text and graphic elements also can be used (as will be discussed in Chapter 3). When a user clicks a link on a Web page, his browser automatically retrieves the linked document.

On the Web

The history of the Internet in timeline form, technical information and more about World Wide Web innovator Tim Berners-Lee:
Under Chapter 2, select **The Internet and the WWW.**

DIGITAL MEDIA

An important feature of the Internet is its ability to provide content in a variety of forms. Text, graphics, sound and video are available over the Internet, providing the potential for a much more wide-ranging experience than has been available in previous media.

This is all possible because these media can be manipulated by computers and transmitted over networks such as the Internet. Before that can happen, however, the media must be converted to **digital** form. Thus, it is important to have a basic understanding not only of what it means to "be digital" but of how various types of digital media work.

Understanding Digital: Bits, Bytes and the Like

The entire computer revolution, the subsequent Internet revolution and perhaps future revolutions we haven't even thought of yet rest on a single innovation: digital data. In digital form, information is converted to individual **bits,** with each bit having a value of either zero or one. Because each bit can have only one of two possible values, the digital format is also referred to as a **binary** system.

Bits are normally grouped into eight-digit streams called **bytes.** A thousand bytes make up a **kilobyte,** a million bytes make up a **megabyte,** and a billion bytes make up a **gigabyte.** These terms are usually used to indicate the storage capacity of a computer, as will be discussed in the "Hardware" section later in this chapter.

It is important to contrast digital data with **analog** data, which is stored in continuously varying "waves," as shown in Exhibit 2.4. Analog is how we see

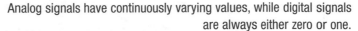

Analog signals have continuously varying values, while digital signals   **Exhibit 2.4**
are always either zero or one.

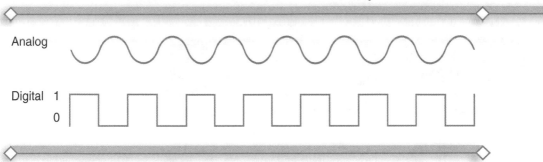

(light waves) and hear (sound waves) and is how radio and television signals were transmitted for more than half a century. Analog's main shortcoming is that it cannot be stored, manipulated or transmitted without some degrading of the original information. Think of making a photocopy of a magazine page, a cassette copy of a song or a copy of a VHS videotape—the copy is never quite as good as the original. Computers, however, because they work with digital information, can store, manipulate and transmit *exact* copies. For example, if you write a term paper using a word processor and copy the file to a disk, that copy will be just as good as the original.

The other advantage of digital is that various types of media can intermingle: text, pictures and sounds can coexist on a single Web page, for example. Once converted to digital, there is essentially no difference between text, sound or video information; to the computer, it is simply digital data. Since the Internet is a digital network, it also means that all these various types of media can flow across the Internet in the same manner.

Types of Digital Media

Although various types of media can coexist on the Internet, one caveat needs to be noted. Different kinds of media have different characteristics—most notably, the amount of digital space they take up. As shown in Exhibit 2.5, media such as audio and video in digital form are far more resource intensive, meaning they require more powerful computers, larger storage and faster Internet connections to work properly.

This section will discuss some of the uses and resource characteristics of various types of digital media. It will also introduce you to the formats used to store digital media in files. A chart summarizing these formats is shown in Exhibit 2.6. You will notice that each format has a unique file extension, which is usually placed onto the end of the file name. Thus, the file extension can be a quick way to tell what kind of file you have.

Exhibit 2.5   This chart shows a comparison of the sizes of a typical text file, graphic image, audio clip and video clip.

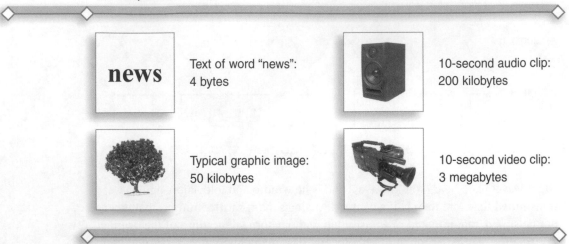

Text of word "news":
4 bytes

10-second audio clip:
200 kilobytes

Typical graphic image:
50 kilobytes

10-second video clip:
3 megabytes

Text. Text refers to letters, numbers and symbols that appear in an online document. Using HTML, text can be displayed in many sizes and styles and is the least resource intensive of all digital media. In the standard **ASCII** (pronounced "ASK-ee") text format, each individual character takes up only one byte of space.

Using standard ASCII text is fine for headlines and body text of documents, but it does not allow such "decorative" effects as sideways text or multiple-color effects. To achieve these effects, text must be converted to a graphic element—in effect, the graphic then becomes a "picture of text," as shown in Exhibit 2.7.

Graphics. In addition to text effects, graphics can include photographs, illustrations, artwork and other visual elements. A graphic can be used to help illustrate a concept (such as how tall a city's new skyscraper will be in comparison to existing buildings) or to provide a more pleasing or interesting visual experience for the reader.

Several formats are available for storing digital graphics. The two most popular in HTML are **GIF** (pronounced "jiff"), which stands for **graphics interchange format,** and **JPEG** (pronounced "JAY-peg"), which stands for **joint photographic experts group.** A third format, **PNG (portable network graphics),** was designed to replace GIF and has been slowly gaining acceptance on the Web. You also may encounter other formats, such as **bitmap (BMP), encapsulated PostScript (EPS)** and **tagged image file format (TIFF).** These formats are normally converted to GIF, JPEG or PNG in a graphics program such as Adobe Photoshop for display on Web pages.

Graphics take up more digital space than textual information does. A typical small JPEG image, for example, might be several kilobytes. Larger graphics

Popular media formats.   **Exhibit 2.6**

TEXT

ASCII (plain text)	.txt

GRAPHICS

Graphics interchange format (GIF)	.gif	Joint photographic experts group (JPEG)	.jpg
Portable network graphics (PNG)	.png	Bitmap (BMP)	.bmp
Tagged image file format (TIFF)	.tif	Encapsulated PostScript (EPS)	.eps
Portable document format (PDF)	.pdf		

AUDIO

Audio interchange file format (AIFF)	.aiff	RealAudio	.ra
MP3	.mp3	Waveform audio file format (WAV)	.wav
Musical Instrument Digital Interface (MIDI)	.mid		

VIDEO

Audio-video interleaved (AVI)	.avi	Moving picture experts group (MPEG)	.mpg
Quicktime	.mov	RealMedia video	.rm
Windows Media	.wmv		

RICH MEDIA

Flash	.fla
Java	.java

This text is actually a graphic image. The size of the graphic is 68 kilobytes,   **Exhibit 2.7**
while the size of the word in text form would be only 14 bytes.

The Daily News

quickly increase in size, and it is not uncommon to see graphics several hundred kilobytes or even a few megabytes in size. However, techniques exist to minimize the size of graphic images (as will be discussed in Chapter 6).

Adobe Corporation's **portable document format (PDF)** is designed for storing print-based documents and making them available online. The advantage of PDF is that it preserves the exact formatting of the original document, including text, graphics and color. For example, a newspaper could make the front page of its print version available to Web users using PDF, as shown in Exhibit 2.8. However, PDF files are quite resource intensive (a single letter-size page might be several hundred kilobytes), and they require the user to download a **plug-in** called Adobe Acrobat to view the page (see "Software" later in this chapter).

Sound. Sound has the potential to perform both "decorative" and informative functions. The use of music or some other sound as "background music" on Web pages was once fairly common, but today's Internet users find it distracting and annoying. More substantively, sound can be used to provide more information about a story: the audio of a 9-1-1 call to police, for example, or a recording of the last radio communication from the space shuttle *Columbia*.

Sound in digital form can exist in a variety of formats. The most common standard formats are **audio interchange file format (AIFF), waveform audio file format (WAV)** and **MP3.** Each format allows sounds to be stored with varying degrees of quality—the higher the quality, the more resource-intensive the file becomes. Using AIFF or WAV, it is not uncommon for brief sound **clips** to be several hundred kilobytes in size, and a three-minute song is likely to approach 100 *megabytes*. The MP3 format, on the other hand, uses a technology called **compression** to make files significantly smaller. A typical three-minute song in MP3 format might average closer to two or three megabytes. Still, this is a significant amount of space, especially compared to text.

These standard formats require users to actually download the entire file to their computers before the sound can be heard. This can produce a significant waiting period, especially with very large files. Newer formats use **streaming** technology, in which users can listen to files as they are downloaded onto their computers. The most popular streaming format is **RealAudio,** which is controlled by the company of the same name and requires downloading a plug-in. RealAudio and other streaming formats are particularly useful because they also allow users to listen to events live. For example, you could listen to the audio of a presidential press conference as it was happening.

A final audio format worth noting is **musical instrument digital interface (MIDI).** Originally designed for computer control of electronic instruments such as synthesizers and drum machines, MIDI can also be used to play music in HTML. Rather than storing actual sounds, MIDI stores information about note pitch, duration and other characteristics that an instrument can then play. Over the

This page from the *Detroit Free Press* uses Adobe's portable document format (PDF)   **Exhibit 2.8**
to display information online that looks just like the print version of the newspaper.

Internet, MIDI files can play music on a user's computer through the small synthesizer built into most **sound cards.**

Video. Video is like the Holy Grail of digital media—creating and distributing it in a way that provides high quality without long waits for the user has remained elusive for Web developers. The problem is that video is by far the most resource-intensive of all digital media. One second of video of the same quality as your television would take several megabytes to store. In addition, in order to maintain uninterrupted flow of the video information, digital video requires transmission methods with very high **bandwidth** (see "Hardware" later in this chapter).

There is no doubt, however, that video can be an extremely valuable tool to online journalism. Some news stories are best understood by being *seen.* Video also provides the potential for users to see events live as they happen and in their entirety—a visit by the president to a local school, for example. Video can provide a supplement to print-based stories, allowing users to view the actual interview with the newsmaker quoted in the print story. Is he lying? Perhaps if you can *see* him answer the question, you'll be in a better position to make up your own mind. For television stations and other broadcast-related organizations, video clips can be stored on a Web site so that users can see past stories they may have missed.

The most common ways of lessening the resource demands of digital video are through compression, decreasing the size of the video **frame** and reducing the number of frames. On both a standard television and a computer **monitor,** visual information is displayed using **pixels,** which are tiny "dots" of colored light. The size of the standard broadcast television frame is 640 by 480 pixels, but cutting that in half to 320 by 240 pixels actually reduces the file size by 75 percent. Of course, the smaller the video frame, the harder it is to see the picture.

The picture you watch on a standard television is actually made up of 30 individual still pictures, or frames, for each second of video. However, by decreasing the **frame rate,** or number of frames per second, the resource demands of digital video can be significantly reduced. For example, reducing the frame rate to 15 frames per second cuts the resource demands roughly in half. The trade-off is that moving video at rates below about 15 frames per second begins to take on a very disjointed, "choppy" appearance because movements are no longer smooth.

Digital video formats include **MPEG** (which stands for **moving picture experts group**), **Quicktime** and **AVI** (**audio-video interleaved**). All rely on compression of one type or another, and all allow for a variety of frame rates and sizes. All also include the ability to store synchronized audio to go along with the video. Streaming formats include RealPlayer's **RealVideo** format and Microsoft's **Windows Media.**

Rich content. HTML itself is not well-suited to highly interactive content. Since it is based on pages (when you click a link, an entirely new page loads), it cannot achieve anything close to the level of interactivity you would find in a video game, for instance. However, higher levels of interactivity can be added to HTML through the use of **rich content** plug-ins. These plug-ins allow the Web pages to contain moving-graphic **animations,** video clips and other media in more interactive form. They also allow smaller interactive items such as rollovers, graphics that change when the user places her mouse over them.

The two dominant rich content plug-ins are Java (which is now built in to most Web browsers) and Macromedia Flash. Both are essentially computer programming languages designed to interface with HTML pages (as will be discussed in Chapter 9). Rich content elements can become very large in file size, reaching hundreds of kilobytes or even several megabytes. Simpler rich content pieces, such as rollovers, usually have much smaller file sizes.

Links. Although not actually a media type per se, links are a crucial part of the online experience. Links allow a user to move seamlessly from Web page to Web page by clicking her mouse on a screen element. That element can be a word, a sentence or a graphic. Links can

> ### On the Web
>
> Why digital is better, resources and technical information about different media types and the raging debate over how to pronounce "GIF": Under Chapter 2, select **Digital Media.**

be used to allow the user to move to the next topic in a story or to access additional information from an outside source. For example, a story about a city's latest crime statistics could include a link to government information about crime statistics in other cities. Links also can be used to activate the downloading or streaming of sound, video or other media elements.

HARDWARE

In computerese, the term *hardware* refers to the physical devices associated with computers: monitors, modems, hard drives, memory chips and the like. As you probably know, hardware tends to come in many shapes, sizes, speeds and prices, and those shapes, sizes, speeds and prices are constantly changing as technology improves.

The prospective online journalist needs to have at least a limited understanding of hardware issues, not only because they affect the creation of online content but because they affect the potential reader as well. For example, an elaborate Web page with spinning logos, graphics and video clips may look great on your high-end computer system, but how will it look to a person with a more "average" computer viewing your page over the Internet? At the same time, we want to avoid, if at all possible, aiming too low by targeting our designs toward outdated equipment. As online journalists, we need to be aware that Web pages must be designed to work properly with a wide variety of hardware and software, because we don't want to limit our audience. Some ways of doing this will be discussed in more detail in Chapter 6.

Bandwidth

The most critical hardware issue involved in creating online content is bandwidth, or the amount of digital data that can flow across a given connection. Bandwidth is most often explained using the metaphor of a pipe for liquid: The larger the diameter of the pipe, the more liquid that can flow through it. The greater the bandwidth, the more digital data that can flow.

The main connections of the Internet—the so-called backbone—consist of high-bandwidth lines. These lines connect powerful computers, usually located in large metropolitan areas, and carry most of the information that flows on the Internet. Even though the backbone is high-bandwidth, the Internet can still experience slowdowns during periods of high use. For example, in the immediate aftermath of the September 11, 2001, terrorist attacks, many users were unable to access news Web sites because so many people were trying to do the same thing. Computer **virus** programs also can slow down the network by making many computers send useless data over the network at the same time.

In practice, however, the most severe bandwidth bottlenecks occur at the site of the home user. A large number of home users access the Internet using a **modem,** a device that allows computers to communicate over telephone lines. Modems have much slower speeds than dedicated network connections and thus have much lower bandwidth. So, home users with modems have to wait longer for pictures to load and may find it next to impossible to reliably play streaming audio or video.

Other options for home Internet access include **cable modems,** which allow Internet access through cable television service, satellite-based Internet services and **integrated services digital network (ISDN)** and **direct subscriber line (DSL)** services that transmit data over telephone company lines. These services allow much faster speeds, but usually at a significantly higher price.

No matter what the connection type, home Internet access is normally provided by an **Internet service provider (ISP),** a company that charges a fee for providing Internet access. In many businesses, users access the Internet through the company's local area network (LAN). The network is a series of computers wired together and controlled by a central server. The server then connects to the Internet using one of the methods described in the previous paragraphs. Most likely, if you live in a dorm or work in the university's computer center, you are also using a LAN for access.

Finally, the Internet increasingly can be accessed without using any kind of wires at all. **Wireless-fidelity (wi-fi)** networks allow computer users to log onto the Internet without plugging into anything, much the way cellular telephones work. The coverage areas for wi-fi networks are growing quickly, and it is likely that wi-fi Internet surfing will eventually be as ubiquitous as wired services.

Computer Considerations

Most new computers sold today are more than adequate for both viewing and creating online content. Like almost anything else, however, more is usually better, so it might be a good idea to invest in more computer if you can. This section addresses the main hardware attributes of computers.

Desktop vs. laptop. This is purely a matter of personal preference. Laptops provide portability, but at a higher cost than comparable desktop systems. It also is usually more expensive and difficult to upgrade individual components of laptops. Obviously, a laptop can be very useful for the journalist who wants to have access to a computer while working in the field.

PC vs. Macintosh. PCs, which are often called "IBM compatibles" or "clones," are based on the original personal computer designed by IBM in the early 1980s. PCs usually run some version of Microsoft's Windows operating system. Macintoshes, usually called "Macs," are made exclusively by Apple Computer and run the Macintosh operating system.

While more than 90 percent of computers sold today are PCs, Macintoshes are applauded for their ease of use and often more inspired physical design. Macintoshes are especially popular with artists and people who work in video production.

For some people, the debate between PC and Mac is almost as serious as religion. In practice, however, little difference exists between using one or the other. Most programs are now designed to look and operate the same on either type of computer, and Microsoft has unashamedly "borrowed" many of the Mac's ease-of-use features for its own operating systems. Transferring files from one system to the other is usually not a problem either. The merits of each system can certainly be debated, but you're better off to just choose your favorite and get to work.

There *are* differences between the two platforms when it comes to how their Web browsers display pages. Macintosh computers, for example, tend to display screen text smaller than does a comparable PC. As you will see in Chapter 6, there are steps you can take to minimize these differences.

Processor speed, memory and storage. Producing most online content does not require a particularly cutting-edge computer. Unless you're doing intense graphics work, or a lot of video, audio or multimedia production, you probably don't need a cutting-edge computer. Most online journalists, in fact, will usually be working mostly with text and thus can get by with a relatively modest system. Online journalists commonly don't get to specify what kind of computer they work on; it's simply provided by the company. Of course, if you're a graphic artist or video specialist, you may be able to negotiate a more powerful system for yourself than that given to most employees.

Still, it's a good idea to understand the basic parameters that determine how "powerful" a computer is. This boils down to the speed of the computer's **processor,** which is in essence the computer's "brain"; the amount of internal memory, which is where the computer stores programs while they are running; and the size of the **hard drive,** which is what the computer uses for more permanent storage of programs and data.

The speed of the processor is normally measured in **gigahertz**—the higher the number, the faster the processor. Memory capacity is measured in megabytes or gigabytes (1 gigabyte equals 1,000 megabytes), and hard drive capacity is measured in gigabytes. If you find yourself needing to choose a computer for online journalism work, perhaps the best strategy is to check the system requirements for the programs you'll be using. Then, try to buy as much above the minimum specifications as you can reasonably afford. There's an old saying among people who build race cars: "Speed costs money—how fast do you want to go?" The same could be said of computers: The more power and capability you want, the more the computer will cost.

Several **removable storage** options are available, including the **floppy disk, CD-ROM, DVD (digital versatile disc)** and **zip disk.** Removable storage devices vary in terms of capacity. Removable storage devices that plug into a computer's **universal serial bus (USB)** port and use computer chips to store data are also increasingly prevalent.

Removable storage is a good idea for keeping copies of previous work and work in progress. Although hard disk "crashes" that destroy data are rare, if you ever do have one you'll be very glad that you've kept extra copies of your work. Removable storage is also useful for transferring data from one computer to another.

Sound and video. A computer's sound card allows it to play sounds through a speaker and to "record" sounds digitally. A variety of sound cards are available, varying mostly in speed and sound quality. Today's standard sound cards are fine for most kinds of online work, but for intensive sound processing, you might want a higher quality one.

Similarly, a standard **video card** is fine for most online work, but if you're editing video you'll want a higher end model. Video cards differ mostly in terms of memory, speed and resolution. Some video cards also allow you to **capture,** or input, video into the computer.

Various sizes of monitors are also available. The smallest monitors sold today on desktop systems have 15-inch screens, while 17-inch, 19-inch and 21-inch

On the Web

More on the Internet's inner workings, the debate over Mac vs. PC, and Moore's Law, which says that the speed of processors will double every 18 months. Plus, a map of the Internet backbone, and sites that let you build your own computer:

Under Chapter 2, select **Hardware.**

models are becoming more common. Flat-panel LCD (liquid crystal display) monitors are more expensive but are often chosen because they take up less space than a standard monitor. The larger the size of the monitor, the higher **resolution** of screen you can use. Higher resolution allows you to fit more on the screen, which means you can have more windows open at the same time.

SOFTWARE

Software is what makes the computer's hardware perform tasks. Your software needs will depend on personal preference and the kinds of tasks you're doing.

Browsers and Plug-Ins

As discussed earlier in this chapter, the browser is what allows you to view HTML-based Web pages. The two main browsers have traditionally been Microsoft Internet Explorer and Netscape Navigator. However, Navigator has been fading in popularity, while Apple's Safari browser has been gaining many Macintosh users. All browsers operate in mostly the same way, although certain users might prefer one over the other. As will be discussed in upcoming chapters, Web pages you design might look a little different in one browser than in another, although these differences can be minimized.

On the Web

A history of the "browser war" between Netscape and Microsoft, plus more information about plug-ins, authoring software and editing software:
Under Chapter 2, select **Software.**

Most computers come with one or more browsers already installed, but companies update their browsers quite often to increase capabilities and fix problems. It's a good idea to connect to the company's Web site to update your browser to the latest version.

Plug-ins allow a browser to display special types of content, such as video, audio or rich content elements. Plug-ins are software-based enhancements that are usually downloaded and installed on the computer. Most companies that create plug-ins create versions for all the popular browsers and make the plug-ins available on their Web sites.

Authoring Software

It is possible to create HTML pages using only a word processing program. However, for Web pages of any significant complexity, you'll probably prefer working with an HTML authoring program, such as Macromedia Dreamweaver or Microsoft FrontPage. These programs are called **WYSIWYG** (pronounced "wissy wig"), which stands for "What you see is what you get." It means that you create Web pages by arranging elements on the page the way you want them and then the program creates the HTML coding to make the page look that way.

Editing Software

Depending on the kinds of Web pages you want to produce, you'll also need various editing software. The most common are word processors for working with text, and image editing programs, such as Adobe Photoshop, for working with graphics. If you're working with sound, video or multimedia elements, you'll need appropriate editing software for those as well (as will be discussed in upcoming chapters).

WHAT'S NEXT

The next chapter will present an overview of the actual process of creating Web pages using HTML and more advanced tools. It will discuss creating Web pages both by manually writing HTML computer code and by using authoring programs such as Macromedia Dreamweaver.

Activities

2.1 Go to some Web sites that have digital video or audio available, and download some of the clips. What do you notice about the time each takes to download? What plug-ins do you need to download the clips? Does the site make it easy to access the plug-ins if a user doesn't have them? How?

2.2 Find out the system requirements for the latest version of authoring, editing or other Web software you'd like to use. Then, go to one of the Web sites that let you build your own computer, and put together a minimum system based on these requirements. Then, put together your "dream system." What's the price difference?

ENDNOTE

1. Tim Berners-Lee, *Weaving the Web: The Original Design and Ultimate Destiny of the World Wide Web by Its Inventor* (San Francisco: HarperSanFrancisco, 1999), p. 3.

CHAPTER 3

- To provide an overview of the basic structure of HTML, including standards for tags and attributes

- To discuss the most often used tags for document structure and working with images and links in HTML

- To introduce the various ways of formatting text in HTML documents, including the use of cascading style sheets

- To introduce the basic operation of HTML authoring programs, such as Macromedia Dreamweaver

- To provide an overview of the process of copying HTML files to the Web

As discussed in Chapter 2, hypertext markup language (HTML) is the computer markup language used to create Web pages. The fact that it is a computer language, however, should not scare you. Unlike many traditional computer languages, HTML is text-based, which means it uses words instead of complex strings of numbers and symbols. In fact, you can use a simple word processing program to write HTML code if you want to.

Although it is relatively easy to understand, HTML has many different aspects. For that reason, it is beyond the scope of this chapter (and this book) to try to teach you everything about HTML. Rather, the intent of this chapter is to present a basic tool kit of HTML knowledge and skills that you can use to create online journalism. Eventually, your knowledge of HTML should be something you hardly ever think about; it should become—like the **Internet** in general—merely a resource you use to create journalism.

This chapter begins with an overview of HTML. It then discusses basic text formatting techniques, including **cascading style sheets (CSS).** Next, the chapter presents an overview of authoring programs that can make creating HTML documents easier. Finally, the chapter discusses the basic process of actually putting HTML documents online. Later chapters will build on these basic concepts by discussing more advanced HTML in the areas of design, writing, links, multimedia and advanced interactivity.

HTML STANDARDS

HTML is not static; it is, like the Internet itself, a work in progress and as such is continually evolving. The World Wide Web Consortium (or the W3C), a group of industry experts and professionals, develops and maintains the standards for HTML to ensure compatibility across producers and browsers. From time to time, new versions of HTML are approved by the W3C. These new versions may add, delete or modify HTML commands, which are called **tags.** The normal process of deleting tags is **deprecation,** which essentially "warns" developers that a tag won't be supported by future versions of HTML and thus should not be used. Tags are normally deprecated because they are no longer needed or because they have been replaced by other tags.

On the Web

HTML standards from the W3C and the latest information about XHTML:
Under Chapter 3, select **HTML Standards.**

The current and final version of HTML is version 4.01. For the future, the W3C is moving toward **XHTML (extensible hypertext markup language).** However, writing XHTML code will be virtually the same as writing HTML code. In fact, the initial version of XHTML, 1.0, is pretty much the same as the final version of HTML, 4.01. The process of converting from HTML to XHTML is evolutionary, and if you understand basic HTML, you'll be well-positioned to deal with the future changes that will come with XHTML.

As an online journalist, you probably won't have to deal with issues of standards very much; instead, it's likely that the technical personnel within your organization will be the ones who have to worry about them. Still, it's a good idea to know *about* the standards and to follow them whenever possible, even though you will occasionally find nonstandard coding and deprecated features in popular Web sites.

BASIC HTML

As an online journalist, you probably won't have to deal with the actual "nuts and bolts" of HTML coding very much. Today's authoring programs do a very good job of creating Web pages while shielding you from the actual technical coding. Still, it's a good idea to develop a basic understanding of how HTML documents are created and how basic HTML tags work. There may be times when you have to "open the hood" of your authoring program to tweak HTML coding when things aren't working quite the way they should, and having a basic understanding of what you'll find there will go a long way toward helping you fix the problem.

If you look at the coding of a Web page, you will see that the HTML looks a lot like a basic text document. You can easily do this by selecting View > Source in Microsoft Internet Explorer (other browsers have a similar command). This will open a new window showing the HTML code for the current Web page, as shown in Exhibit 3.1. You might find it helpful to refer to a particular Web page's coding from time to time as you read this section.

As you can see, the HTML code is just words and numbers. One of the first things you will notice is the use of angle brackets (< and >) to enclose the basic HTML tags. For example, the <p> tag tells the browser to begin a new paragraph. Some tags consist of single letters or words, while others may contain more complex information.

Tags that begin with the slash (/) right after the first angle bracket are called **end tags** because they in essence "turn off" a tag. For example, the <strong> tag tells the

Most browsers allow you to look at the HTML code for Web pages.　**Exhibit 3.1**

```
<html>

<head>
<title>The Jim Foust Home Page</title>
<meta name="GENERATOR" content="Microsoft FrontPage 4.0">
<link rel="stylesheet" type="text/css" href="coms780/stylesheet.css">
</head>

<body background="images/green.jpg">

<h1 align="center"> Jim Foust</h1>
<div align="center"><center>

<table border="0" width="592" cellpadding="0" cellspacing="3">
  <tr>
    <td width="145"><a href="info.html"><img src="images/info.gif" alt="Information" border="0" width="144" height="216"><
    <td width="145"><a href="class.html"><img src="images/class.gif" alt="Class" border="0" WIDTH="144" HEIGHT="216"></a><
    <td width="145"><a href="links.html"><img src="images/links.gif" alt="Links" border="0" width="144" height="216"></a><
    <td width="145"><a href="mailto:jfoust@bgnet.bgsu.edu"><img src="images/mail.gif" alt="mail" border="0" WIDTH="144" HE
  </tr>
  <tr>
    <td width="145" bgcolor="#008080" align="center" height="40"><font color="#FFFFFF">Things
    you may want<br>
    to know about me.</font></td>
    <td width="145" bgcolor="#008080" align="center" height="40"><font color="#FFFFFF">Material
    for students<br>
    in my classes.</font></td>
    <td width="145" bgcolor="#008080" align="center" height="40"><font color="#FFFFFF">Internet
    sites I find<br>
    interesting.</font></td>
    <td width="145" bgcolor="#008080" align="center" height="40"><font color="#FFFFFF">Send me
    electronic<br>
    mail.</font></td>
  </tr>
</table>
</center></div>

<div align="center">
  <center>
  <table border="0" cellpadding="0" cellspacing="0" width="520">
    <tr>
      <td width="166" height="15"></td>
      <td width="364" height="15"></td>
      <td width="56" height="15"></td>
    </tr>
    <tr>
      <td width="166"><img border="0" src="bigvoices.gif" width="120" height="180">
        <p><img border="0" src="videoprod.jpg" width="119" height="152"></p>
      </td>
```

browser to place strong emphasis on the text following the tag (usually by displaying it in boldface), and the tag turns the emphasis off. Thus, the HTML line

This is an important message.

would be displayed in the browser window as

This is an **important** message.

The tags used to turn on commands (such as) are called **start tags.** Not all tags use the start and end format, however. A few tags, such as <img>, which is used to insert a graphic, don't use end tags; these are called **standalone tags.**

Some tags can be modified using **attributes,** which set certain values. An attribute normally consists of a **parameter,** which is the function being set, and the value for that parameter, separated by an equal sign. For example, the tag <img src="carpicture.gif" border="5"> sets two attributes. The "src" attribute tells the browser the name of the image file, and the "border" attribute places a five-pixel border around the image on the page.

Comments contain either notes to Web page developers or technical information. They appear in the HTML document but do not show up on the page itself—the browser simply ignores them. Comments can help to provide information for others who may work on a page later or to remind yourself about what certain parts of a page do. Comments are enclosed by <!-- and --> tags, such as

<!-- This is the news section. -->.

Generally, tags in HTML are not case-sensitive, meaning you can type them in upper or lower case. You should be consistent, however, about how you type HTML tags, attributes and other elements. The generally accepted standard is to type them in all lowercase letters.

The textual content of a Web page is simply typed in the HTML document. Generally, anything not enclosed in angle brackets in an HTML document is actual text that will appear on the page, as shown in Exhibit 3.2.

Structural Tags

Structural tags help organize the basic elements of an HTML document. With rare exception, they do not affect information displayed in the browser window but rather help identify, organize and index the document itself. Readers of Web pages rarely come into direct contact with information presented by structural tags, but such tags are crucial to browser programs to properly display the HTML document.

All HTML documents should begin with the <html> tag. This tells the Web browser (or other programs or people reading it) that it is an HTML document. The last thing in an HTML document should be the </html> tag, which designates the end of the HTML coding. HTML documents are divided into two main parts: the **head** section contains basic structural information about the document,

In this document, the HTML commands have been highlighted. The nonhighlighted portions **Exhibit 3.2**
will actually appear on the browser screen.

```
<html>

<head>
<title>The Jim Foust Home Page</title>
</head>

<h1 align="center"> Jim Foust</h1>
<div align="center"><center>

    <td width="145" bgcolor="#008080" align="center" height="40"><font color="#FFFFFF">Things
    you may want<br>
    to know about me.</font></td>
    <td width="145" bgcolor="#008080" align="center" height="40"><font color="#FFFFFF">Material
    for students<br>
    in my classes.</font></td>
    <td width="145" bgcolor="#008080" align="center" height="40"><font color="#FFFFFF">Internet
    sites I find<br>
    interesting.</font></td>
    <td width="145" bgcolor="#008080" align="center" height="40"><font color="#FFFFFF">Send me
    electronic<br>
    mail.</font></td>
  </tr>
</table>
</center></div>

<div align="center">
  <center>
  <table border="0" cellpadding="0" cellspacing="0" width="520">
    <tr>
      <td width="166" height="15"></td>
      <td width="364" height="15"></td>
      <td width="56" height="15"></td>
    </tr>
    <tr>
      <td width="166"><img border="0" src="bigvoices.gif" width="120" height="180">
        <p><img border="0" src="videoprod.jpg" width="119" height="152"></p>
      </td>
      <td width="364">My Book, <i>Big Voices of the Air</i>, is available
        now through <a href="http://store.yahoo.com/isupress/081382804x.html">Iowa
        State University Press</a>
      </td>
      <td width="56"></td>
    </tr>
  </table>
  </center>
</div>

</body>
</html>
```

while the **body** section contains the main content displayed in the browser. The two sections are designated by the tags <head> and <body>. Thus, the basic structure of an HTML document should be organized as shown in Exhibit 3.3.

Most of the information contained in the head section of the document is quite technical and, for the most part, is beyond the scope of this chapter. One element of the head section you do need to be concerned with, however, is the page's

Exhibit 3.3   The basic structure of an HTML document.

TAG	COMMENT
<html>	HTML document begins.
<head>	HEAD section begins.
[Head information.]	Information in HEAD section.
</head>	HEAD section ends.
<body>	BODY section begins.
[Body information.]	Information in BODY section.
</body>	BODY section ends.
</html>	HTML document ends.

title. Designated by the start and end tags <title> and </title>, the title appears not as part of the Web page itself but at the very top of the browser's window, in the area called the **title bar.** For example, the HTML line

    <title> The Jim Foust Home Page </title>

would show up in the Web browser's title bar as

It is important not only that you include titles in all Web pages you create but that the titles describe what is on the pages. This helps reinforce to users that they are on the correct page. For example, nytimes.com's business page is titled "The New York Times: Business," and its sports page is titled "The New York Times: Sports."

The <body> tag, which should immediately follow the </head> end tag, designates the beginning of the main content section of the document, the portion that will appear in the user's browser window. All of the HTML commands designating what will appear in the browser window and how it will appear will be contained between the <body> and </body> tags. The <body> tag can be used by itself, or it can be extended with attributes to set colors for various parts of the page, as shown in Exhibit 3.4. Note, however, that these extended attributes for

The <body> tag can be modified with several attributes as shown. **Exhibit 3.4**

TAG	DESCRIPTION
<BODY BGCOLOR="red">	Sets the background color of the Web page
<BODY TEXT="black">	Sets the color of text on the page
<BODY LINK="blue">	Sets the color of hyperlink text

the <body> tag have been deprecated, and thus you should avoid using them. The proper way to set the background attributes is by using cascading style sheets (as will be discussed in Chapter 6).

As shown in Exhibit 3.4, some colors can be selected by name in HTML. The 16 colors that can be chosen this way are black, white, aqua, blue, fuchsia, gray, green, lime, maroon, navy, olive, purple, red, silver, teal, and yellow. This is, of course, a rather limited palette, so HTML allows colors to be designated in other ways as well. The most popular way is by using a six-digit **hexadecimal** number to select the color. Hexadecimal (or hex) is a basc 16 numbering system that uses the digits 0 thru 9 and the letters A thru F. A hexadecimal number is identified by the use of the pound sign (#) in front of the number. For example, the color white is designated in hexadecimal by #FFFFFF, so the HTML tag <body bgcolor="#FFFFFF"> would create a white background on the page. Although most authoring programs allow you to select colors without directly typing in names or numbers, it is good to be able to recognize color designations in hex because they are used so often in HTML coding.

On the Web

Online tutorials, references and more information about writing HTML. Also, more information about hexadecimal numbers and how they are used to designate colors:

Under Chapter 3, select **Basic HTML.**

Tags for Graphics and Links

One of the important attributes of the Internet, of course, is its ability to seamlessly combine text, graphics, links and other elements. As noted in Chapter 2, images aren't actually *part* of Web pages but rather are contained in separate files. The <img> tag instructs the browser to find the image file and display it on the Web page. The <img> tag has several possible attributes but the most crucial one is the "src" (source) attribute, which tells the browser what image to insert. For example, if you have a photograph (named "tornado.jpg") of the damage done by a tornado that came through your town, you could place it on your page by including the coding <img src="tornado.jpg">. This assumes that the file "tornado.jpg" is on your local computer in the same directory as the Web page itself. You also can insert images located on other computers by including the complete address to the file, such as <img src="http://personal.bgsu.edu/~jfoust/chemical_spill.jpg">.

The tag for creating links to other HTML documents is the <a> (anchor) tag. Like the image tag, it has several available attributes, some of which will be discussed in Chapters 6 and 8. The most important one is "href," which denotes the page to link to. Like the image tag, the anchor tag can refer to another HTML file in the same location as the Web page that contains it, such as <a href="drug_abuse_sidebar.html">, or to a file somewhere else on the Internet, such as <a href="http://personal.bgsu.edu/~jfoust">. Whatever is enclosed between the start tag <a> and the end tag </a> will become a link to the designated file. For example, if you were doing a story about slamming, the illegal practice of telephone companies changing consumers' phone service without their permission, you might include a link to the Federal Communication Commission (FCC) Web page that discusses slamming. The page is located at http://www.fcc.gov/slamming. Thus, the following HTML would insert a link to that page:

Learn more about slamming from the <a href="http://www.fcc.gov/
slamming">FCC. </a>

That code would show up in a browser as

Learn more about slamming from the FCC.

"FCC," enclosed by the start and end tags, is now a link to the FCC's page on slamming. When users click the link, they will be taken to the FCC page.

FORMATTING TEXT

When you create a journalistic Web page, you want to use different styles of text. For example, you'll want something large and bold for the headline, something smaller for subheads and something even smaller for the main text of the stories. You might also want different styles to use for captions, pull quotes, bylines and so forth. There are three basic ways to format text in HTML:

1. Using preformatted HTML tags
2. Using the <font> and <p> tags
3. Using CSS

Using preformatted HTML tags is the safest and easiest way to format text, but, as you'll see, it offers the least flexibility. Using the <font> and <p> tags can give you more control over text but negates the separation of content and pre-

Separating Content and Presentation

One of the original concepts behind HTML was that *content* would be separate from *presentation*. In other words, the actual information to be conveyed (the words in the scientific paper, for example) would be separate from *how* that information would be presented (the lettering style, size and color).

The developers of HTML envisioned that the content information would exist in HTML documents while presentation information would be controlled by the end user's browser. Initially, HTML provided only a small set of formatting tags, such as the heading tags <h1> through <h6> and <blockquote>. These tags do not specify any font or size information—that is left to individual browsing software to interpret. So, on one browser <h1> may appear as 36-point bold Arial font, and on another it may appear as 30-point bold Times New Roman font.

The great advantage of separating content and presentation this way is that it allows the same information to be easily adaptable to different browsers and devices. It is up to the end user's browsing device to decide how to format different types of text in HTML documents. So, <h1> will format one way on a full-size computer browser screen and another way on a small handheld computer. There is no need to write two different versions of a document for different devices.

Initial versions of HTML provided only for this general kind of formatting—keeping specific information about text display out of HTML code. But as HTML became more mainstream, designers wanted to have more precise control over how text would display on the screen. The HTML standards responded by adding commands (such as the <font> tag) that allowed designers to specify particular font styles and sizes in HTML documents. Obviously, this change negates the separation of content from presentation.

Now, we have come full circle. The latest versions of HTML and XHTML have deprecated most of the specific text formatting HTML tags. Instead, they mandate the use of CSS formatting for HTML documents. CSS usually uses a separate document that contains the specific formatting information for various kinds of text on a page. The HTML document itself contains only general formatting, such as <h2> or user-defined styles. When a browser reads the HTML document, it looks to the style sheet to determine how to display each type of text. For example, the style sheet may say that the <h2> text should be formatted in 12-point bold italic Arial font colored blue. Thus, with CSS, we are once again separating the content from the presentation.

sentation (see "Separating Content and Presentation"). The preferred method, CSS formatting, offers the highest level of flexibility but is a bit more complicated to use.

Using Preformatted HTML Commands

A number of preformatted HTML tags can be used to format text. The advantage of these tags is that they work on all browsers and are easy to use. However, they offer only limited flexibility, and you can't be sure what your text will actually look like on different browsers. The most widely used of these tags are the heading tags <h1> through <h6>. It is easy to format text with these tags—you simply enclose the text within start and end tags, such as

> <h1> This text is in Heading 1 format. </h1>

which formats the entire line of text in <h1> format.

Headings <h2> through <h6> work the same way. Generally, the largest text is displayed using <h1>, while the smallest is displayed using <h6>. However, different browsers and different computer platforms display the heading tags differently. Exhibit 3.5 shows the six heading tags displayed on a PC using Internet Explorer. As you can see, you might use the <h1> format for your story's headline, perhaps <h2> or <h3> for a subhead, <h4> for a byline and maybe <h5> for the body text.

A few other preformatted tags are available, including the <blockquote> tag, which is useful for formatting direct quotations. Although the exact formatting is again determined by the user's particular browser, it usually appears with indents

Exhibit 3.5   The headings <h1> through <h6> displayed on a PC.

Heading 6

Heading 5

Heading 4

Heading 3

Heading 2

Heading 1

on the left and right sides and extra space before and after, similar to the way you would format a block quote in a term paper. To designate the conclusion of a block quote, use the end tag </blockquote>.

As you can see, preformatted tags are easy to use, but you can't actually change the way the text will look on a user's browser. All browsers have built-in specifications they use to display preformatted text, and those specifications are not the same across all browsers.

Using HTML Tags for Text Formatting

To have more control over text formatting, you can use the <p> and <font> tags. We have already seen that <p> is used by itself to start a new paragraph, but it can be extended with attributes to set the horizontal alignment of the paragraph as well. For example:

 Centered text.

 Left-aligned text.

 Right-aligned text.

will produce the display shown in Exhibit 3.6. While the <p> tag itself has not been deprecated, adding these alignment options has. However, for at least the near future, you can use the align attribute of the <p> tag to set text alignment.

Although it is a deprecated command, the <font> tag is still used frequently, and—like the alignment options in the <p> tag—it still works. In fact, you

Text alignment options: block left, block right, and centered.   **Exhibit 3.6**

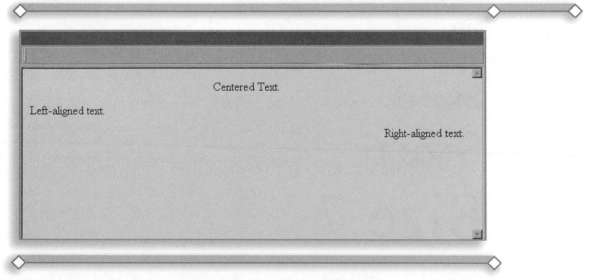

might have trouble finding a Web site that doesn't use the <font> tag in one form or another. Using additional attributes, the <font> tag can set the color, font style and size of designated text. Exhibit 3.7 shows a summary of the <font> tag's attributes.

The size command allows you to choose one of the seven basic lettering sizes available in HTML. The actual sizes of these choices are determined by individual browsers. Setting an absolute value tells the browser to use one of the specific settings from 1 (smallest) to 7 (largest). Exhibit 3.8 shows examples of these sizes displayed in a browser.

Exhibit 3.7   Attributes for the <font> tag.

ATTRIBUTE	EFFECT
color="color"	Sets color of text
face="typeface"	Sets the specific typeface to be used for display of text
size="value"	Sets the size of text

Exhibit 3.8   Text sizing using the "size" attribute for the <font> tag.

Size 1

Size 2

Size 3

Size 4

Size 5

Size 6

Size 7

Some sample formatting code using <font> tags (a) and how the code is displayed in a browser (b). **Exhibit 3.9**

(a)

<p> <font face="Times New Roman" size="5"> This is normally formatted text in Times New Roman font. This entire text block is formatted with the same font. </font> </p>

<p> <font face="Arial" size="6" color="silver"> Here's something a bit more complex. How about different settings </font><font size="+1" color="black"> within the </font> <font face="Times New Roman" size="+2" color="yellow"> same </font> <font face="Arial" color="black">block of text? </font> </p>

(b)

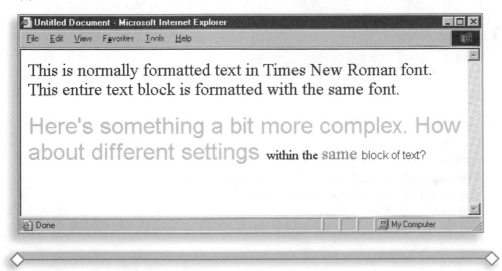

The attributes of the <font> tag can be combined or omitted. If you do not set a color, for example, the text will display using the default color (usually black). The font tag can apply to an entire block of text or just to portions of the text within a block. Exhibit 3.9 shows several <font> tag formatting examples and the resulting display in a browser.

Using Cascading Style Sheets

CSS formatting allows you to set up styles with names; you can then apply those styles as many times as you like within one Web page or a series of Web pages. For example, you might set up a style called "headline" for your headlines, a style called "byline" for reporter bylines and so on. The beauty of CSS is that once you have created the style, you can easily apply it to text on any of your Web site's pages.

CSS style information can be embedded within the main HTML document, or it can be contained in a separate document called an **external style sheet.** Using an external style sheet is more versatile because it allows any number of individual Web pages to link to the same style sheet; then, if you make changes to one or more styles in the style sheet, these changes will be reflected automatically in all of the Web pages linked to that style sheet. For example, a Web site may have a single style sheet to which all pages on the site link; thus, the text formatting for all pages is controlled by a single file.

An external style sheet is nothing more than a text document with the style and formatting information listed as shown in Exhibit 3.10. We don't need to be concerned with the technical format of these style sheet documents because, as we'll see, authoring programs can create them quite easily. If you are interested in creating style sheets by hand, the most widely used text properties are listed in Appendix A.

On the Web

Reference, tutorials and other information on formatting text with HTML tags and CSS, including the text formatting files shown in this section:

Under Chapter 3, select **Formatting Text.**

Style sheets also are particularly valuable because they can be adapted to many different devices. The HTML document can contain code that determines what kind of browser the user has (a process called **browser sniffing**) and then use an appropriate style sheet based on that browser. Thus, for example, there could be one style sheet for users with full-size screens and another for users of handheld devices. You can also create one style sheet for display of a Web page on the screen and another for printing the page.

Exhibit 3.10   CSS style information placed in an external style sheet.

```
.Headline    { font-family: Arial Black; font-size: 24pt; text-align: Left; margin-top: 10 }
.Subhead     { font-family: Arial; font-size: 14pt; font-style: italic; text-align: Left;
               margin-left: 5 }
.Byline      { font-family: Arial Black; font-size: 12pt; font-style: italic; text-align:
               Left; margin-top: 6 }
.body        { font-family: Arial; font-size: 12pt; text-indent: 20; margin-left: 0;
               margin-top: 6 }
.caption     { margin-top: 10; margin-bottom: 10 }
```

USING AUTHORING PROGRAMS

While writing HTML code by hand is a good way to learn how the programming language works, it can get cumbersome, especially for long or complex documents. For that reason, several authoring programs, including Macromedia Dreamweaver, Microsoft FrontPage and Adobe GoLive!, are available to make the job easier. These programs all work on the **WYSIWYG** ("What you see is what you get") principle, which means you start with a blank page and then add elements where you want them. The program then does the "dirty work" of writing the underlying HTML code to create the Web page.

Although it is beyond the scope of this chapter to provide a step-by-step tutorial on using HTML authoring programs, this section will provide a brief overview of how authoring programs work, using Macromedia Dreamweaver MX 2004 as an example. If you're using another version of Dreamweaver, the operations may be slightly different. Dreamweaver is by far the most popular authoring program among professionals, but other programs work in a similar fashion.

Remember as we look at these programs (and as you use them yourself) that they don't allow you to do anything that can't also be done with manual HTML coding. They make it much, much easier to do certain things, but in the end, all these programs do is shield you from having to write the code yourself.

Web Creation and Management

When you start working in Dreamweaver, you must first set up the program's Web management functions. These functions allow you to automate the process of "publishing" your pages to the Web by copying them to a designated file area (see "Putting Your Files on the Web" later in this chapter). Dreamweaver will also keep track of images, multimedia elements and links you use on your pages. For example, if you insert a link in an HTML document to a file called "flowers.html" and then change that file name to "roses.html," Dreamweaver will automatically update the link for you. Dreamweaver also has functions to verify that the links on your Web pages are valid—in other words, that they link to actual Web pages.

For these features to work, however, you must first *define a site* in Dreamweaver. Defining a site, in essence, creates a Web folder that contains Web pages and associated files for media elements. The Web site initially exists only on your computer; it is published to the Internet only when you specifically tell Dreamweaver to do so.

Your first step in defining a site is to create a folder on your computer that will contain the files for your site. You can create the folder on the computer's **hard drive** or on a removable storage medium such as a CD. Give your folder an appropriate name (such as "My_Journalism_Web"). It's a good idea to avoid using spaces in the names of Web folders and file names. Instead, use the underscore character (_).

Now, you can start Dreamweaver and select Site > Manage Sites. Then, select New > Site in the Manage Sites dialog box. That will bring up the main Site Definition dialog box, as shown in Exhibit 3.11. Here, type in a name for your site, and then click the small folder icon next to "Local Root Folder." This will open a window that will allow you to find the folder you've just created on your computer (in this example, "My_Journalism_Web"). When you find it, double-click it; then click "Select" to designate it as the place you'll store files for this site. Close the Site Definition window by clicking "OK."

Exhibit 3.11   Dreamweaver's Site Definition dialog box.

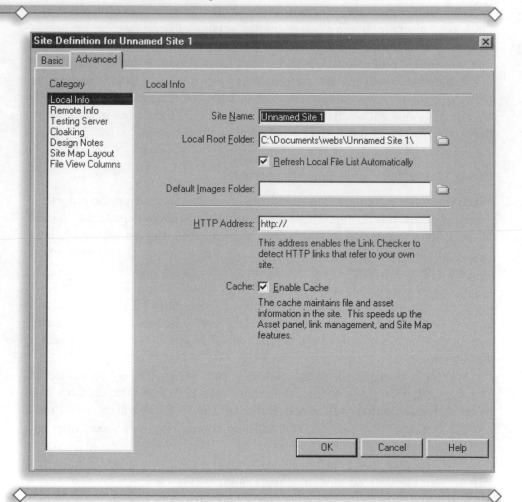

Once you've defined your site, you can then create Web pages that will be contained in the site. As you create pages, you'll save them in the site folder. Dreamweaver will automatically keep track of the files you create as you work with the site. If you create links among files within your Web site, Dreamweaver will allow you to test the links by selecting File > Preview in Browser.

Basic Program Operation

Once you've finished defining your site, you can start creating Web pages. To create a new page, select File > New; then select Basic Page > HTML in the New Document dialog box. Click the "Create" button, and a new blank page will appear on the screen. You create HTML documents by adding items to the blank page—for example, you can click the mouse on the screen and type text, as shown in Exhibit 3.12. You can also add images and links, which we will discuss later in this chapter. As you do this, Dreamweaver creates the HTML coding.

Typing text in the Dreamweaver document window.   **Exhibit 3.12**

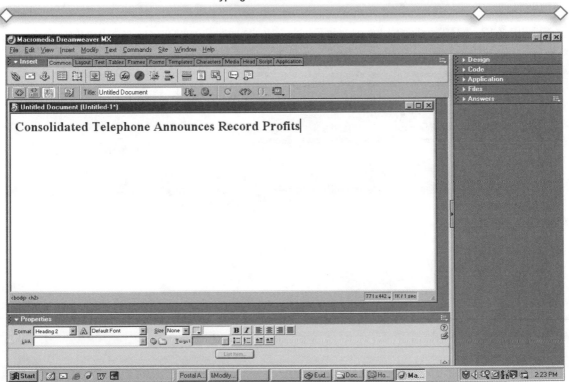

At any time, you can view the HTML code Dreamweaver is creating by select-ing View > Code (see Exhibit 3.13). In the code window, you can manually change the HTML code, and these changes will then be reflected in the main window. It is not usually necessary to edit (or even look at) the HTML code, but it is a valuable feature for times when the HTML may need tweaking. You also can preview what the page will look like in different browsers by selecting File > Preview in Browser. This is extremely important, because the page will often look a little different in the browser than it does in the editing window. You can set up Dreamweaver to pre-view the page in a number of different browsers because different browsers will often display pages differently (as will be discussed in Chapter 6).

By selecting Modify > Page Properties, you can make general changes to your current page. For example, you can type a title for the page (which creates a <title> tag) or change the background color of the page, as shown in Exhibit 3.14. If you want to add a picture to the background of the page, you just enter its file name next to "Background Image."

Dreamweaver is an extremely adaptable program: You can actually change the layout of menu items, creating your own commands and automating cer-

Exhibit 3.13   HTML coding for the page in Exhibit 3.12 shown in Dreamweaver's code window.

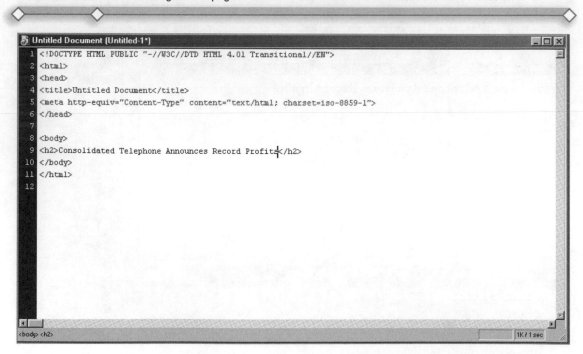

The Dreamweaver Page Properties dialog box.   **Exhibit 3.14**

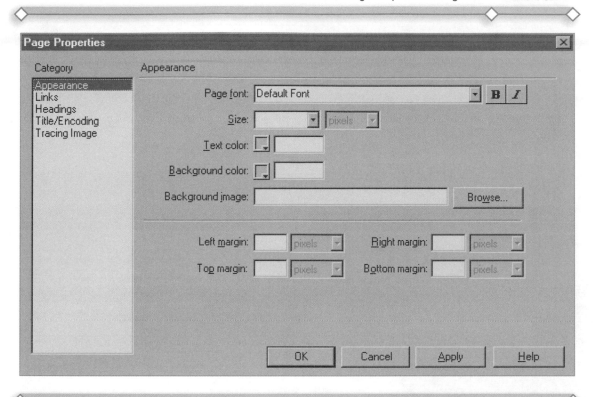

tain tasks (such as inserting an author byline on several Web pages). Dreamweaver can be intimidating at first, not only because it has so many capabilities, but because the program tends to provide several ways of doing the same thing. Once you're comfortable with Dreamweaver, you're likely to appreciate its versatility, but when you're just starting out, the choices can be a bit overwhelming.

The best way to do most things in Dreamweaver is to use its Properties window, which can be accessed by selecting Windows > Properties. The properties window provides easy access to frequently used formatting and other commands, and it changes according to what type of item you select on the screen. If you click your mouse on a graphic element, the Properties window provides tools for manipulating the graphic; if you click on text, it provides text formatting tools (see Exhibit 3.15). All of the commands in the various versions of the Properties window are also available through the menus at the top of the screen.

Exhibit 3.15   Dreamweaver's Properties window changes according to what the user has selected on the screen: graphic element (a) or text (b).

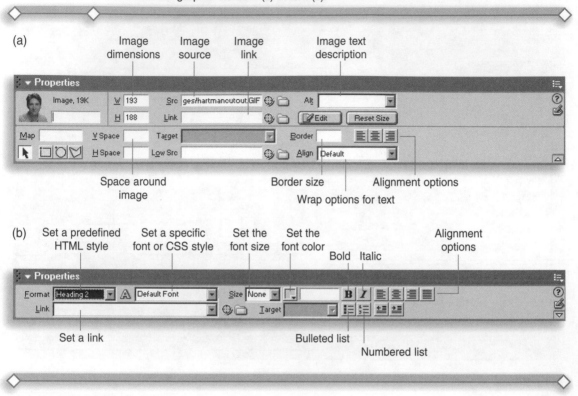

Text Formatting

Once your text is typed on the screen, you can highlight it by dragging your mouse over it and then make formatting changes. Or, you can define your text properties first and then start typing. Through the Properties window (see Exhibit 3.15(b)), you can define text using basic HTML tags (such as headings 1 through 6) or you can specify more exact formatting. These latter formatting options, however, are based mostly on the deprecated <font> features and thus should not be used.

But Dreamweaver also provides extensive support for creating and managing CSS styles. By selecting Text > CSS Styles > Manage Styles, you can create a new style sheet for your document or edit an existing style sheet. Once you've done this, you can create new styles by selecting Text > CSS Styles > New. Here, you can redefine existing HTML tags with CSS or create new styles. The main CSS text formatting dialog box, shown in Exhibit 3.16, allows you to set several properties for styles. After you have created the styles, they are available through the Text > CSS Styles menu or through the CSS Styles window (see Exhibit 3.17).

Dreamweaver's main CSS text formatting dialog box provides access to properties for   **Exhibit 3.16**
font size, weight, style, line height, color and other features.

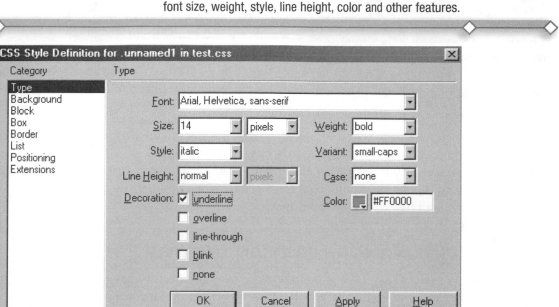

CSS styles you have created can be accessed through Dreamweaver's CSS Styles window.   **Exhibit 3.17**

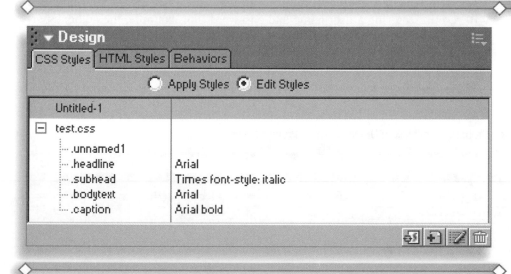

On the Web

Resources and tutorials on using Dreamweaver plus information about other authoring programs: Under Chapter 3, select **Using Authoring Programs.**

Links, Images and Multimedia Elements

Links can be created in Dreamweaver by highlighting the element with your mouse and then typing the link path or file name next to "Link" in the Properties window (see Exhibit 3.18). Or, you can select Modify > Make Link to click to a file's location.

An image is placed on the page by positioning the cursor where you want it to go and then selecting Insert > Image. Once you have placed the image, you can make various formatting changes to it using the Properties window. Video **clips,** audio clips and multimedia elements are placed similarly, using various options under Dreamweaver's Insert menu.

PUTTING YOUR FILES ON THE WEB

For the HTML files you create to be truly useful, they have to be accessible to others. You do this by copying them to an appropriate computer on the Internet called a **server.** Then, others can access the information as long as they know the URL address of the server and the location of the pages. For example, your school may give each student her own file area in which to put Web files, or your class may have a special file area associated with it. If you create pages on your own, you can purchase file space from an Internet service provider.

Once you know the exact location to copy your files, you can configure an **FTP (file transfer protocol)** program to copy the files there. Normally, this will require entering a user name and password. For example, the author's personal pages are stored in a directory called web/docs/public_HTML at personal.bgsu.edu. So, to copy files there, I would configure my FTP program with that directory, my user name and password. Similarly, authoring programs like Dreamweaver have built-in FTP programs to copy files to remote servers,

Exhibit 3.18 Creating a text link in Dreamweaver's Properties window.

as shown in Exhibit 3.19. You configure Dreamweaver's FTP functions using the Site Definition dialog box previously discussed. Here again, authoring programs offer advanced features that can help you manage a Web site. For example, Dreamweaver can publish an entire Web site or only portions you have changed since the last time you published it.

Once you have copied your files to an Internet server, anyone on the Internet can access them—then, you're on the Web!

The FTP options for Dreamweaver's Site Definition dialog box.   **Exhibit 3.19**

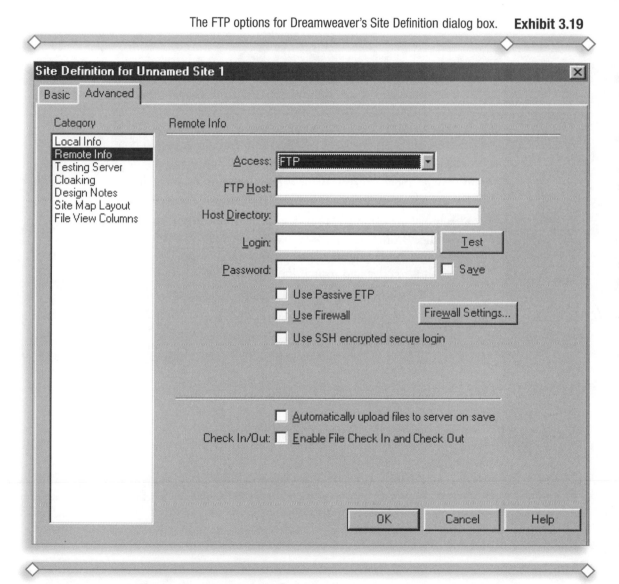

WHAT'S NEXT

This chapter has presented a lot of technical information. It's a good idea to start experimenting with writing your own HTML code so that you can build a comfort level with HTML programming. The next chapter will look at what it's like to work as an online journalist, including how various producers of online journalism create their HTML code.

Activities

3.1 Print out the HTML code of one of your favorite Web sites. Then, use a highlighter to mark the tags and information you recognize. Use some of the resources on this book's Web site to find the tags you don't recognize.

3.2 Create a simple HTML document by hand. Try a resume or perhaps a "vanity" page about yourself, your car, your family or a recent vacation. Experiment with some of the HTML features discussed in this chapter.

3.3 Download the sample HTML text formatting document and linked CSS style sheet from this book's Web site (see page 50). Both documents contain comments explaining how various parts work. Try making changes to some of the styles and formatting, and look at the results.

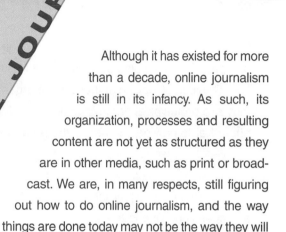

CHAPTER 4

GOALS

- To introduce basic structures of online journalism, including organizations, processes and content

- To discuss the concept of convergence and how it affects online journalism

- To provide an overview of the basic skills and attitudes necessary to be a successful online journalist

- To illustrate the wide range of online journalism organizations by looking at case studies of large, medium and small Web operations

WORKING IN ONLINE JOURNALISM

Although it has existed for more than a decade, online journalism is still in its infancy. As such, its organization, processes and resulting content are not yet as structured as they are in other media, such as print or broadcast. We are, in many respects, still figuring out how to do online journalism, and the way things are done today may not be the way they will be done once the medium reaches maturity. Indeed, it will be difficult even to say *when* online journalism has reached maturity because no one is quite sure what online journalism *should* ultimately look like.

In addition, the **Internet,** more than any previous medium, offers the potential to support many different types of journalism structures, processes and content. Today, we have freestanding journalism sites like slate.com, sites associated with newspapers, sites associated with television networks or local stations, and the so-called **convergence** sites, where multiple types of media organizations combine their news-gathering processes and personnel. We even have sites like Yahoo! News that are more like news processors than news gatherers—organizing, indexing and presenting (usually by automation) news content that comes from other sources. If that's not enough, we have an ever-growing number of **blogs** (see "What About Blogs?" on p. 66), where individuals—journalists or not—can "publish" their own "news" in the form of links, running commentary and essays.

Given all of this, there is no such thing as a "typical" online journalist, and few blanket statements can be made about online journalism organizations or processes. For that reason, the bulk of this chapter concentrates on case studies of three online journalism organizations: WashingtonPost.Newsweek Interactive; CJOnline, *The Topeka* (KS.) *Capital-Journal*'s online operation; and WTVG-TV in Toledo, Ohio. WashingtonPost.Newsweek Interactive is a freestanding online news organization with its own building and hundreds of employees; *The Topeka Capital-Journal* Online occupies the upstairs portion of its newspaper's building and has fewer than 20 employees; WTVG-TV's online operation consists of one full-time and one part-time employee operating largely out of a single room in the television station. The idea of looking at these three organizations is not necessarily to imply that they are prototypical "large," "medium" and "small" online journalism organizations but rather to provide a sense of the broad range of online journalism itself.

Before presenting these case studies, however, I begin with a general discussion of some of the parameters of online journalism. These parameters involve the basic kinds of online journalism sites, production processes and skills needed to be a successful online journalist.

CREATING ONLINE JOURNALISM

One of the initial promises of the Internet was that it would "make everyone a publisher," allowing millions of individual voices to be heard without having to invest in transmitters or printing presses. Indeed, it is possible to publish on the Internet with only a modest investment in a computer, software and an Internet connection. But merely putting a Web page up does not make one a journalist. Because the focus of this book is online journalism, we will concentrate on sites produced by journalistic organizations: those that focus on the traditional processes of gathering, assessing and disseminating news.

Online Journalism Content

The vast majority of online journalism sites are associated with a print or broadcast journalism organization. As such, the online operation is often viewed as an "appendage" to the main news operation, and most of the online content originates from the print or broadcast operation. This situation may some day reverse itself as online journalism grows in stature. For now, however, many organizations simply post their print or broadcast stories on the Internet, creating content that is often referred to as **shovelware.** In other cases, online staff slightly or substantially revise the original content, perhaps supplementing it with **multimedia, links** or other online content, often called **Web extras.**

One of the advantages of online journalism, of course, is that content can be changed and updated often. This means not only that stories can be continually updated as events unfold, but that the overall *character* of the Web site can change throughout the day or week. A growing number of sites use **dayparting** to tailor their content to different readers at different times, creating, in effect, different online editions. For example, a site might feature hard news and business updates during the workday, then concentrate on features, entertainment and other "lighter" content in the evening. The daytime content would be aimed at people in the workplace, while the evening fare might cater to a younger audience looking for things to do in town. For example, Boston.com drops its hard-news edge on weekends, emphasizing instead features, sports and entertainment news (see Exhibit 4.1).

Many sites also strive to update information during the times of day when spikes in readership occur. Such spikes mostly happen in the morning (as people arrive at work), at midday (before they leave for lunch) and in the late afternoon (before they leave for home). If users know, for example, that the site will have something different at lunchtime than it did that morning, they'll be more likely to continue to visit the site several times throughout the day.

The fact that Internet content can be changed so often appeals to journalists because of the immediacy it offers. Most journalists who are working on breaking stories or other time-sensitive topics want to get their material online as quickly as possible. There's no set-in-stone deadline such as print and broadcast reporters face; rather, online journalists have a somewhat continuous deadline—reporters and editors are *always* trying to get updated information posted as soon as it is available and verified. This means that journalists need to be especially diligent about ensuring that their information is accurate and, in a sense, that they are *always* updating their stories. This drive comes from a desire not only to beat the competition but to make sure that readers of the site—who may have come to depend on it for the latest information—will not be disappointed.

Convergence

Convergence is perhaps the most used (and sometimes overused) buzzword in online journalism. It refers, generally, to the combining of media or media organizations. So, for example, we can say that the Internet's fusion of video, text and sound represents a convergence of media.

More significantly, convergence also refers to the merging of media organizations themselves. In other words, a newspaper and a television station may combine their news-gathering resources into a single entity, with journalists producing content for broadcast, print and the Internet. The best-known example of convergence is the combined news-gathering operation of the *Tampa* (Fla.) *Tribune,*

Exhibit 4.1   On weekends, the Boston.com Web site features lighter stories and less of a hard-news edge.

WFLA-TV and TBO.com (Tampa Bay Online). In this case, all three entities work out of a single building, and in some cases a single journalist produces content for all three media. Thus, a newspaper reporter might supplement his print story with an online version, then appear on the television station's evening newscast as well.

For example, consumer reporter Victoria Lim produces content for print, broadcast and online. In many cases, she approaches a single topic from three different angles, concentrating on what each medium does best. Thus, when the Florida governor vetoed crib-safety legislation supported by consumer and health care groups, Lim's television report concentrated on the "nuts-and-bolts" facts. She talked about the legislation and who supported it, and she held an interview with the governor in which he explained why he vetoed it. In the newspaper the next day, Lim's story had a deeper analysis of the governor's veto, disputing many of the reasons he gave for his decision. Online, Lim provided a **streaming** video **clip** showing how parents could check their children's cribs for safety, and links to other information about cribs and crib safety.

Convergence also holds great promise for media owners because it offers potential cost savings. Instead of two full newsrooms (and news staffs), a media organization could maintain a single facility and staff. In the short term, many convergence projects have increased employment, as traditional media organizations have supplemented their staffs with online content producers. However, in the long run, convergence might lead to fewer journalists being hired and fewer reporters performing watchdog and other functions. Either way, convergence is definitely here to stay.

The Internet is commonly a focal point of convergence because it is a place where newspapers, television stations and other "old" media can truly create a combined product. It is important to realize, however, that not all online journalism sites are convergence sites and that not all online journalism is converged journalism.

Content Management Systems

Online journalism organizations normally use specialized software to create and manage their Web sites. In the case of very small operations, an off-the-shelf authoring program such as Macromedia Dreamweaver might suffice, but most sites use more advanced **content management system (CMS)** software. One of the key features of such software is **database control,** which facilitates the management of a large number of individual stories and story elements.

Database control allows the content of pages to be separated from presentation (as discussed in Chapter 3). Individual stories are stored not as complete Web pages but rather as just textual information and formatting tags. For example, the headline might be tagged as "headline" and the story itself as "body." When the software calls up an individual story from the database, it automatically presents it in the proper format based on predefined formatting rules and the story tags.

What About Blogs?

A New Form of Expression, But Is It Journalism?

A relatively recent phenomenon (even by the standards of the Internet) has been the growing popularity of blogs. A blog—the term is a shortened form of "Web log"—is like an electronic journal or diary. The author of the Web log (the **blogger**) can include text, pictures or other media elements as well. A particularly important aspect of any high-quality blog is links to other information.

Blogs come in many forms. Some really are like diaries, essentially chronicling the life and thoughts of a particular person. Others deal with a specific topic or issue, such as free trade, the environment or reality television. As this is being written, the Eaton Web Portal, a site that lists blogs, shows more than 13,000 blogs, including 1,444 about "fun," 114 about "librarians," 685 about "sex," and 783 "weird/alternative." Your check of the Eaton Web Portal will no doubt show even higher numbers.

Virtually anyone with access to a computer can blog. Blogging sites like weblogger.com and blogger.com offer simple tools for creating blogs, shielding the writer from having to create HTML code. These and other sites also offer space for people to publish their blogs.

For some, blogs represent the true promise of the Internet, allowing millions of voices to be heard on a nearly infinite array of topics. For independent bloggers, there are no gatekeepers—publishers, editors or bosses—to tell them what to write or make them change what they've written. The blogger's point of view need not be changed to fit any prevailing customs or even logic. Blogging offers the potential to create entirely new forms of discourse, making room for a level of participatory community that has not been possible before. Some say that blogs are the model of what journalism will resemble a generation from now, as many points of view create a "marketplace of ideas" unfiltered by media corporations or editors. Writer and columnist Andrew Sullivan, whose blog site, andrewsullivan.com, is one of the most popular on the Internet, says journalists "have longed for" a mode of unfiltered expression like the one blogs provide.

The downside to the fact that anyone can blog is, of course, that anyone can blog. Some blogs contain valuable information, interesting and informed points of view and compelling narratives; others are little more than incoherent rants. The danger of blogs is that not everyone can tell which is which.

Nonetheless, mainstream journalism organizations are beginning to embrace blogging to a limited degree. A number of journalists have begun their own blogs, either as part of the media organizations they work for or as independent sites. This has raised serious ethical questions about whether the free-flowing world of blogging is at odds with a journalist's objectivity and fairness (this will be discussed in Chapter 10). Still, specialized reporters have created blog sites that can provide readers with

What About Blogs?, continued

valuable information outside the realm of the traditional column or news story. Two examples are Dan Gillmor's daily technology blog on the *San Jose Mercury News* Web site and Aaron Barnhart's "TV Barn" site about television shows. Gillmor is a technology columnist for the *San Jose Mercury News,* while Barnhart is a television critic for the *Kansas City Star.* Both of their sites offer additional news, information and links about their areas of expertise.

Beyond blogging, we are now also seeing the rise of mobile blogs, or **moblogs.** The proliferation of cellular phones with text, imaging and Internet capabilities has made it possible for people to instantly post text and photographs to the Internet from anywhere. Moblogging, too,

presents both potential opportunities and ethical questions for journalism. Imagine, for example, that a moblogger gets images of a spot news story, such as an accident or shooting, that our journalistic organization's reporters couldn't get. Should we use them? Should we provide an area on our Web site where mobloggers can post their own spot news coverage?

On the Web

Links to blogging sites, more information about blogs and sites that let you create your own blogs. Also, cyberjournalist.net, a site with links to journalists' blogs:
Under Chapter 4, select **What About Blogs?**

For example, the headline might be displayed in 18-point bold text and the **main story** text in 12-point normal text. The key here is that once the overall site design has been determined, the software automatically "plugs in" individual stories.

The backbone of the content for many online journalism sites, of course, comes from the "parent" media organization—the printed newspaper or the television newscast, for example. Most content management systems are designed to integrate with the software used in the print or broadcast newsroom. Thus, when the final version of the print newspaper is being sent digitally to the printing plant, it can also be sent to the online CMS, which automatically reformats the content to online form and posts it to the Web site. Most CMS systems can also input and format content from other sources, such as wire services, and integrate it into the Web site.

More advanced formatting features can be programmed into the CMS. For instance, the software can extract the headline and the first paragraph of each story and display it on the site's home page. The headline can be made a link to the entire story, and the first paragraph can act as an overview of the story. In other cases, the software can automatically insert wire service stories and links that will be continually updated. Exhibit 4.2 shows an example of current Associated Press (AP) stories displayed on the main page of the *Toledo Blade*'s

Exhibit 4.2 Associated Press information is automatically updated on the *Toledo Blade* Web site.

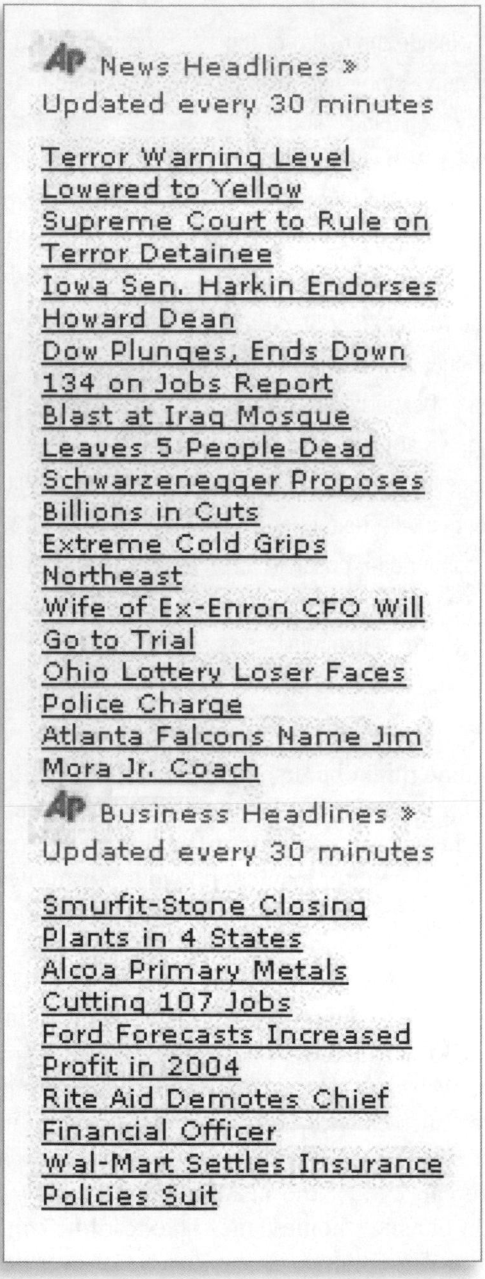
AP News Headlines »
Updated every 30 minutes
Terror Warning Level Lowered to Yellow
Supreme Court to Rule on Terror Detainee
Iowa Sen. Harkin Endorses Howard Dean
Dow Plunges, Ends Down 134 on Jobs Report
Blast at Iraq Mosque Leaves 5 People Dead
Schwarzenegger Proposes Billions in Cuts
Extreme Cold Grips Northeast
Wife of Ex-Enron CFO Will Go to Trial
Ohio Lottery Loser Faces Police Charge
Atlanta Falcons Name Jim Mora Jr. Coach
AP Business Headlines »
Updated every 30 minutes
Smurfit-Stone Closing Plants in 4 States
Alcoa Primary Metals Cutting 107 Jobs
Ford Forecasts Increased Profit in 2004
Rite Aid Demotes Chief Financial Officer
Wal-Mart Settles Insurance Policies Suit

From toledoblade.com. Reprinted with permission.

Web site. CMS software also can provide output designed for cellular telephones or other handheld devices (as will be discussed in Chapter 11).

Despite the automated nature of much CMS production, the systems also allow manual creation of content as well. For example, a page editor could modify one or more pages manually to create a certain look or to update content.

Online News Processes

As noted at the beginning of this chapter, no "typical" online news production process exists. In general, however, the process is an amalgam of print and broadcast methods and terminology. Online journalism tends to be very collaborative, with teams of people working on individual stories. In this regard, online is more like broadcast than print. Online also borrows job titles from broadcast, using, for example, the term *producer* for people responsible for various aspects of online projects.

Online media mixes together people with technical skills and people with journalism skills. This is not unlike traditional media, where, for example, the printing press operator or videotape technician might know a lot about equipment but not necessarily have journalism skills. However, in the online world, a closer intermingling of the journalists and the "techies" tends to occur. In many cases, in fact, people without journalism training find themselves in journalistic positions simply because they understand the technical aspects of online production. This is not altogether bad, as most journalism skills can be learned on the job, but ideally the people producing online content should be trained journalists who also understand how the technical processes work.

Beyond understanding technical issues, the online journalist has to be adaptable and willing to learn new jobs. Jim Debth, the new-media director for CJOnline, says he looks for people "with good news judgment and the ability to learn something quickly." As online

> ## *On the Web*
>
> More about shovelware, dayparting and content management systems. Plus, the debate over convergence: Will it create jobs or destroy them? Under Chapter 4, select **Creating Online Journalism.**

production processes change, journalists need to be able to learn how to use new software and new computer systems. Twenty years ago, it may have been OK for a budding journalist to concentrate only on the words of a story and not learn how to use technology to produce or disseminate his work, but that isn't the case today.

As you read the next section of this chapter, you will notice that the people involved often possess combinations of journalistic and technical skills. You might be surprised at the many different things online journalists need to know to do their jobs. Although there truly is no such thing as a typical online journalist, nearly all of them combine technical and journalistic skills and learn to do a variety of different jobs.

ONLINE JOURNALISM ORGANIZATIONS: THREE CASE STUDIES

This section looks at three online journalism organizations: WashingtonPost. Newsweek Interactive, *The Topeka Capital-Journal Online,* and the Web operation of WTVG-TV in Toledo, Ohio. As you will see, the organizations differ greatly from one another yet share a common goal: gathering and disseminating news and information.

Our examination of these organizations focuses on the journalistic aspects of Web production, not issues related to promotion and advertising. We are most concerned with where the journalistic content comes from, how it gets on the Web site and what form it takes.

WashingtonPost.Newsweek Interactive

WashingtonPost.Newsweek Interactive (WPNI) is a wholly owned subsidiary of the Washington Post Co., which also owns *The Washington Post, Newsweek* magazine, several television stations and the CableOne network. Among other things, WPNI is responsible for publishing the Web sites for *The Washington Post* (see Exhibit 4.3) and *Newsweek.* Our focus here is *The Washington Post*'s Web operation, which is housed on several floors in an office building in Arlington, Virginia, a suburb of Washington, D.C.; the *Newsweek* site is created by a separate team working in New York.

Editorial staff. Executive editor and vice president Doug Feaver oversees the *Post*'s Web operations. He has worked at the *Post* since 1969, spending time at the business and metro sections of the print edition before coming to WPNI in 1997. He originally was a liaison between the print and online operations but eventually became editor. Feaver says he became involved in the Web operations largely because he "wasn't afraid of computers." The *Post* Web site has partnership agreements with several organizations, including MSNBC and *Congressional Quarterly,* meaning the organizations can share content and cross-promote one another.

WPNI has about 230 employees, more than 50 of whom are involved in creating journalistic content. The structure of the online newsroom mirrors to an extent the structure of the print paper; online editors for sports, business, national, metro and other sections oversee their respective sections on the Web site. There are also additional editorial personnel for the Web site's technology (technews.com) and politics (OnPolitics) sections.

Everything available in the print edition of *The Washington Post* is also available online with the exception, due to licensing agreements, of some syndicated columns. The first edition of the next day's paper is sent in digital form to WPNI

From washingtonpost.com. Reprinted with permission.

at about 11:00 each night. The proprietary content management system used by WPNI automatically sends stories to their appropriate online sections. A final edition of each day's paper comes to WPNI early each morning; changes are again automatically fed to the appropriate online section. Throughout the day, the WPNI newsroom receives updated stories from the main newsroom as they are being worked on and sometimes publishes them on the Web site. Feaver says that concern about "scooping" of the print paper by the Web site has never been much of an issue at the *Post*. On occasion, the online version has held off publishing an exclusive story from the next day's paper, but that situation is rare. As Feaver notes, most stories will be picked up by evening newscasts before the next day's paper comes out anyway. Also, since the printed paper is not widely distributed outside the D.C. metro area, many reporters see the Web site as a chance to have their stories available to a larger, national audience.

Although the content management system handles a lot of the actual formatting of stories, the online editors also can change their sections manually. For example, the online sports editor might add updated news from the AP or a video clip.

The paper's home page receives by far the most attention throughout the day. A home page editor is always on duty, manually updating the page by changing the position of stories, adding updates and wire copy, and cycling stories from other sections of the paper to the home page. The goal is to never let the home page remain static for more than an hour; at times when important stories are breaking, it is usually updated much more often. Although the rest of the site's pages are formatted mostly by the software system, the home page is coded in HTML by hand to give editors more design flexibility.

The attention given the home page by WPNI helps illustrate the general importance of home pages to online journalism sites. A large percentage of users simply "check on" the home page several times throughout the day, not bothering to go any farther into the site's content. If something important is happening, users assume they will find it on the home page. Thus, stories that appear on the home page are judged to be more important, or potentially more compelling, than stories that don't. Consequently, newsroom personnel sometimes have heated discussions about what stories belong on the home page and how they should be placed. Because the Web provides nearly unlimited space, it's a case not of lesser stories being discarded but rather of just not appearing on the home page. "While the Web is infinite, the home page is very finite," says Tracy Grant, a former managing editor at the *Post*.

Other content is also updated throughout the day. The *Post's* "Department of Continuous News" is charged with making sure the rest of the site also remains dynamic throughout the day. Thus, reporters usually file more than one version of their stories online, and as many stories as possible from the following day's print paper first appear in shorter form on the afternoon edition of the Web site. Proponents of the continuous news push see this preposting as an advantage for reporters because it gives them "a head start in picking a lead and structuring the stories." Some staffers, however, are a bit more cynical, calling the initiative the "Continuous Work Department."[1] Either way, producing content for the Web has become a part of life for nearly every *Post* reporter.

The focal point of the WPNI newsroom is the newsdesk, a semicircular area with chairs and workstations for several people (see Exhibit 4.4). Normally, the editor in charge, the home page editor, the nation/politics/world producer and the photo editor sit at the newsdesk. During the wars in

The newsdesk is the focal point of *The Washington Post*'s online operation.   **Exhibit 4.4**

Afghanistan and Iraq, a war producer also worked at the newsdesk. WPNI employees liken the newsdesk to the bridge of a battleship, because its "stations" are staffed by different people in shifts. The same person, for example, might work as home page editor for a few hours and then return to work as a section editor away from the newsdesk.

A bank of television monitors in front of the newsdesk shows feeds from cable news networks and broadcast stations. One monitor cycles through a series of news-related Web sites—BBC news, CNN, *The New York Times, The Chicago Tribune, USAToday,* etc.—displaying each page for a few seconds. Workers at the newsdesk communicate with the main *Post* newsroom (located in downtown Washington, D.C.) via telephone, **e-mail** and **instant messaging.** At noon each day, a teleconference links the WPNI newsroom with the downtown newsroom for a discussion of stories each group is working on (see Exhibit 4.5).

Specialized staff. Graphics and multimedia content are created by specialized staff members who work with newsdesk personnel but also have a fairly high degree of autonomy. "There's a high trust factor," says senior video editor Chet

Exhibit 4.5   A daily teleconference connects personnel from the WPNI newsroom with the main *Washington Post* newsroom.

Rhodes. "We're not just an 'order them up' operation. We're journalists first, but we've learned how to edit and push the buttons." Rhodes and his staff are responsible for recording video and audio information and putting them on the Web site. In the multimedia facility, Rhodes can record video from MSNBC, the Associated Press and other sources (see Exhibit 4.6). On occasion, *Post* reporters file video or audio feeds, as reporters in Iraq did during the war that started in 2003.

Giovanni Calabro, WPNI's graphics manager, is in charge of creating graphics to supplement editorial content. Sometimes, WPNI staff use graphics from the print edition as a starting point, but often they create such images as maps and diagrams from scratch. Calabro uses graphics programs, such as Adobe Photoshop, and also creates "a huge portion" of the news content in Macromedia Flash (see Exhibit 4.7). Normally, graphics staff work with editorial staff to create content that will help tell the story. "They [the editorial staff] come to the table with assets and say, 'What can you do with this?'" he says. "There's a high degree of cooperation. You don't hear a lot of 'this belongs to me' around here."

Chet Rhodes works on video feeds in the WPNI multimedia facility.   **Exhibit 4.6**

Tom Kennedy, managing editor for multimedia, supervises the creation of visual content, such as photography, for the *Post* Web site. A former photo editor for newspapers and *National Geographic* magazine, Kennedy sees the Internet as "the most interesting facet of the business." Among other duties, he supervises the creation of a daily photo gallery containing the work of *Post* photographers. His goal, he says, is to "help create content with a strong narrative arc, regardless of the medium."

A five-person Live Online team manages chat and message board features. WPNI features somewhere between 30 and 60 hour-long chat sessions each week, with *Post* reporters, news makers, experts, entertainment figures and others. Questions from users are submitted in advance, and then Live Online staff edit and choose the best questions, although they normally don't share the questions with the chat participants before the chat. Users can submit follow-up questions as the chat is going on, but these, too, go through Live Online staff first. This vetting process creates a more orderly (and informative) chat session. The completed sessions are then archived, making them available to users for later reference.

Exhibit 4.7   WPNI graphics manager Giovanni Calabro works on a graphic for a news story.

Senior manager for production Mark Walley works to make sure the *Post* Web site looks and functions correctly. A makeshift usability lab is used to test how the site's Web pages look on different browsers and different computer platforms (see Exhibit 4.8). Walley also provides support for editorial and advertising staff who want to use advanced programming such as Java or Flash.

WPNI philosophy. Feaver says that the *Post*'s online mission is similar to the mission of the newspaper itself: to cover the Washington, D.C., area like no one else and to explain the governmental decisions that are made there to the nation and the rest of the world. The online version is especially well-suited to the second goal, increasing the reach of the *Post* well beyond the capital beltway. About 80 percent of the site's 5 to 6 million unique visitors a month come from outside the D.C. metro area. A large percentage of those users, says Feaver, are people at work.

The most popular stories on the *Post*'s Web site tend to be important, continuing stories, such as the war on terrorism. The Clinton-Lewinsky scandal was the site's first big story, and its audience also spiked during the 2000 presidential election controversy and the 9-11 terrorist attacks. Users also tend to flock to the horoscope pages, advice columns and stories about the Washington Redskins football team.

Mark Walley tests the usability of WPNI Web pages on a variety of computers and browsers.   **Exhibit 4.8**

"There's no question that online news is for real," Feaver says. "9-11 was a defining moment when online was second only to broadcast in how people got their information, and we've managed to keep much of that audience." However, he says, online journalism will have to adapt and explore new ways of covering stories to reach its full potential. "Online has got to be more than just a repurposed newspaper," he says. "The way we present journalism will change, but we don't know how. If we succeed as a medium, we will have a new medium. We won't just be a new version of TV or print."

Feaver says that the most successful online journalists are able to adapt their core skills to new situations. He prefers people with strong humanities or journalism backgrounds who are not afraid of technology and are willing to learn new things. "If they can read and write and think, we can teach them how to use the tools," he says.

CJOnline

CJOnline (CJO) is the Web operation of *The Topeka Capital-Journal* (see Exhibit 4.9). Topeka, the capital of Kansas, is a town of about 170,000. The CJO staff consists of 17 people, split about half and half between content and technical or sales positions. Jim Debth, new media director, oversees the site's operation. For much of his life, Debth worked as a classical trumpet player, before getting into the newspaper business in 1989. That year, he joined the *Cedar Rapids (Iowa) Gazette* and helped it establish one of the country's first audiotext services, which provided telephone-based interactive information. Later, he helped the paper start a computer bulletin board system (BBS) and a web portal, FYIowa.com. Before coming to CJO in 2002, he worked in New York City for a company that wrote content management software.

CJO occupies part of the second floor of the newspaper's downtown building. About 80 percent of CJO's content comes from the print version of the paper, nearly all of which is available online. A local television station (KSNT) and radio station (WIBW) are partners with CJO and regularly provide video or audio information for the site. The stations also occasionally feature *Capital-Journal* reporters on their newscasts.

Tim Richardson is CJO's main reporter and the newsroom link between the print and online versions of the *Capital-Journal*. His desk is in the main newsroom downstairs. At the paper's daily budget meeting, where story ideas are discussed, Richardson looks for stories that could be enhanced online with additional media elements. He often sends portable tape recorders along with reporters and asks them to record their interviews. He then makes parts of the interviews available online. A staff videographer also shoots spot news and other stories.

A number of stories from each day's paper are thus supplemented with information online. Links to previous stories about the same topic are included, as are links to related information available online. If he has it, Richardson includes audio links to interviews or sound bites from meetings or other events.

In many cases, CJO provides an opportunity to make more of a story available than appears in print. For example, sometimes stories that end up being cut for print appear in their original, longer versions online. The site also features photo galleries, where staff photographers can show more of their work on particular stories. Throughout the day, Richardson also updates stories or writes spot or breaking news stories.

CJO has received a lot of attention for its **shells**—Web pages with links to additional resources (see Chapter 8). Its Kansas Legislature shell, for example, provides links to a wealth of Web-based resources about legislators, the capital, issues and the legislative process. "We're the seat of state government in Kansas; that's the one thing we have a monopoly on and that we can cover better than anyone else," says Debth. "No one's going to do this better than us." Similarly, its Rock Kansas page, about the state's music scene, and Hawkzone page, about University of Kansas sports teams, have been held up as models for the potential of online linking. "It's not just finding stuff on the wire," Debth says. "There are other sources out there."

CJO is a relatively small operation that has established a good reputation among online journalists. "We're out in front on a lot of things," says Debth. "We hang our hat on the fact that we put up great content."

The Topeka Capital-Journal Online Web site.   **Exhibit 4.9**

Breaking News   Local   US & World

Police nab man after second car chase
Police investigate armed robbery to store
Urologist's death remains a mystery

Updated
2:18 p.m.
MORE ▾

SUNDAY SPECIAL
6 months for $24
SUBSCRIBE

January 09
News / Weather
Sports
Entertainment
Features
Archives
Subscribe
Classifieds
County Legals
Ads / Coupons
Keyword / Search

News

Districts hope to receive help from Legislature

Shoestring budget

News   Sports   Features   Special

🌬 30° Topeka, KS

Local
GOP: Abolish state agency
Insurance commissioner to propose legislation
Mother helps son's spirit resonate through book

Kansas
Outlook for winter wheat crop grim
KU official to lead Hispanic group

Business
Canine cowboys at work
Utilities plan to split bills

Learn more at www.wr.com

Westar Energy.

Choose Your News!
Register now for the FREE CJOnline Email Edition!

Topeka **HomeFinder**
Your next home is just a few clicks away.

IN-DEPTH SECTION
City Government:
Time for a change?
• Read the proposal
• Voice your opinion
• Follow the events

A New Session... A New look
KANSAS LEGISLATURE
THE TOPEKA CAPITAL-JOURNAL
Monday, January 12

Careers
Sign-in
Register
Job Matching
Job Search

BIG 12 CHAMPIONS

Pre-order your copy of the 2003 K-State Football Book documenting the Wildcats' Championship Season!

In-Depth   CityGuide   WebGuide

Story compilations

City Government
P-Cards
Neighborhoods
Ad Astra
'51 Flood
'66 Tornado

BlueCross Sale
Phelps
Westar
Target
Sensational
Crimes
Powerful People

Today's Print Ads   **Kansas CarZone**

Top Jobs   **View All Top Jobs**
Health Lawrence Memorial Hospital Mobile ...
Self-Sufficiency Coordinator Broad function...
LPN People. Strength. Commitment. If you'v...
Outside Sales Executive Auto Glass Center is l...
Sales College not work for you, but still wa...
Driver Midway Wholesale CDL-B Delivery Dr...
General Emp. Start a new job NOW! Excellent...
Progressive mental health facility taking appl...
Welding Opportunities Caterpillar Work Tools C...
LAN Manager, KU Dept. of Medicinal Chemistry. ...
School Bus Drivers $9.40/hr 4 h...

Contact CJOnline
About CJOnline
Privacy Policy
Advertising Info

Copyright © 2003
The Topeka
Capital-Journal

Forums   Survey

"McClinton is smart. I have had a chance to talk to him as well. I am somewhat troubled by the charges against him. I don't know if they are true or not, but I don't know if such a controversial choice is what was really needed. But he could do the city good. It does mean 2005 will be interesting."

Respond to this comment
Post a message on any topic

Top Homes   **View All Top Homes**
In Silver Lake, 2100sf rancher, 3 car gar, 3BR...
3BR, 2BA, SW maintenance free home in Quail Co...
Westwood Colonial 1900 Arnold, 3Br, 1.75Ba Ton...

Top Autos   **View All Top Autos**
1996 FORD CONTOUR 5 spd, 4 DR, CD, AC, PS, PB,...

WTVG-TV

WTVG-TV is the local ABC television station in Toledo, Ohio, the 68th-largest television market in the United States. WTVG is owned and operated by Disney Corporation, the parent company of ABC. The station's Web site, 13abc.com, is essentially a one-woman operation; that woman is Deb Weiser, director of Internet services.

Weiser was working in a university publications department in 1994 when the university decided it needed to start using the Internet for marketing and promotion. The university's chief information officer asked if anyone in the publications department wanted to help. "I was the only one who wasn't afraid of the technology," Weiser says, and so she began working on the university's Web pages. Although at the time she knew very little about the Internet, she worked with the university's computer science department to learn how to write HTML code. By the time she left the university to join WTVG in spring 2000, she had become manager of Web services and had redesigned the entire Web site.

When Weiser came to WTVG, the station had no Web site. At the time, the station's general manager had rather modest goals for the station's Web presence, envisioning about 20 pages (today, the site has nearly 1,000 pages). Within two months, Weiser had the WTVG-TV site up and running.

Today, nearly all of the news content on the WTVG Web site comes from the station's daily newscasts. On occasion, however, Weiser will rewrite AP stories to include on the site. She is tied into the newsroom's computer system and can monitor stories that news staff are working on throughout the day. Weiser selects the most compelling stories from the morning, noon and early evening newscasts and adds them to the Web site, writing headlines and summary paragraphs for each story (see Exhibit 4.10). The small "13 ABC" logo under the headlines denotes original station content. For some stories, such as when a group of tall sailing ships visited the city, she produces shells with links and additional information.

Weiser uses Macromedia ColdFusion to manage the Web site, although she created the initial design templates by manually writing the HTML. Other Disney-owned stations use a proprietary content editing program with automated templates, but Weiser likes the flexibility that hand coding gives. She also uses Java and animated GIFs for some of the site's ads and other content. The site includes a modest number of video clips, which Weiser digitizes off-air from a computer in her office. She also digitizes material from original source tapes on occasion.

Weiser also manages the Web site's contests. The site invites users to apply for free tickets to local events and other prizes, with winners chosen at random. Weiser then makes sure winners get their prizes.

The personnel in the newsroom have varying levels of enthusiasm for the Web site, Weiser says. Some reporters and producers are very excited about having content on the Web, while others are less enthused. The station's news

The WTVG-TV Web site.   **Exhibit 4.10**

From 13abc.com. Reprinted with permission.

On the Web

Links to the Web sites profiled plus information about what it's like to work at other online news operations:
Under Chapter 4, select **Online Journalism Organizations: Three Case Studies.**

director, who often communicates with Weiser about stories, doesn't mind if the Web site "scoops" the newscast on most stories. "If we've got news," Weiser says, "the sooner we can get it to the public the better—whether it's on the Web or on the newscast."

Weiser believes that local news and information is what brings people to the WTVG Web site. "Our emphasis is local news, and that's what people want. People come to our page for local news—and the contests." Also among the most popular pages is the live graphic showing current weather radar.

WHAT'S NEXT

This chapter completes our overview of online journalism and some of its technical foundations. The next section examines some actual techniques of online journalism. Chapter 5 begins this examination by looking at how journalists can use online information sources for their stories.

Activities

4.1 Look at some of the Web sites of local or national journalism organizations. Do the organizations have partnerships with other organizations? Would you call these convergence sites?

4.2 Imagine that you're a journalist for a converged television/print/online news organization. What kinds of equipment would you carry with you to cover news stories?

4.3 Visit a locally produced journalistic Web site. How does it compare to the three sites featured in this chapter? Which site does it most closely resemble?

ENDNOTE

1. Michael Getler, "Department of Continuous News," *Washington Post,* July 13, 2003, p. B06.

- To examine the general process of using online sources for journalistic stories

- To discuss the use of e-mail, newsgroups and listservs as potential tools for journalists

- To provide an overview of Web page–based information, including general reference sources, specialized sources for journalists, search engines, directories, online journalism sites and databases

- To explore basic techniques of evaluating online sources using both technical and journalistic skills

The Internet is, without a doubt, the largest repository of information the world has ever known. Yet, the Internet itself is merely a conduit to millions of individual sources of information, some of them relevant and reliable, some of them not. The challenge for the journalist is learning to separate what is valuable from what is not. In many ways, this task is no different from what journalists have always done—with the telephone, by in-person meetings with potential story sources or by poring through historical archives or legal briefs. Some of the sources work out; some of them don't.

The Internet offers a potentially valuable source of information not only for online journalists but also for those working in print or broadcast journalism. Going online to check facts, look for sources or find background information has become an everyday occurrence in nearly every newsroom in the country. But for the online journalist, Internet sources can be particularly valuable because the sources themselves can actually become *part of the story.* The online journalist can provide links to Internet sources that allow readers to see the raw data the reporter has relied on or to pursue a story in more detail. Good journalists have always cited their sources in their stories; now, they can not only cite them but also let readers see the source *for themselves.* This ability to let readers retrace the reporting process or embark on their own explorations of stories makes online journalism truly unique; it is a capability that no other medium offers.

This chapter presents an overview of some of the online sources available to journalists and how to use them. It is not a primer on how to be a reporter—it's assumed you have learned those basic skills in other classes. I will be examining only a subset of the broader topic of **computer-assisted reporting (CAR),** which encompasses many skills that involve using computers to enhance journalism. The focus here will be on providing an overview of the kinds of sources available online, with the ultimate goal being to find information and links that can be used in online journalism stories.

The chapter begins with a discussion of how to approach the Internet as a reporting source. It then briefly examines **e-mail** and **newsgroups** as a reporting tool. The bulk of the chapter is about using Web sites as information resources. I begin by looking at some of the main types of Web-based information resources and then discuss ways to evaluate Web sites. This chapter is about finding and using online sources that will make your stories fuller, more contextualized and—potentially—more relevant and interesting. Chapter 8 addresses presenting these sources to the user in ways that are compelling and useful.

THE INTERNET AS A REPORTING SOURCE

The Internet is simply a new source for journalists—no more, no less. In that way, it is no different from the telephone, which is only of value if the journalist knows what number to call, what questions to ask and how to use the answers to those questions. The basic process of finding information online is no different than finding other kinds of information. One of the first questions a journalist should ask herself is, "Who is likely to have the information I need?" The answer to that question may be a source that is accessible online, but it might not be. The Internet is not a replacement for traditional news sources or reporting processes; it's merely a supplement to them—albeit in many cases a very good one. Journalists still need to make phone calls, meet with sources in person and—yes, it's true—visit libraries and other repositories of printed information when appropriate. Sometimes, in fact, an Internet source functions simply to lead a reporter to one or more traditional sources.

The *Associated Press*'s "Guidelines for Responsible Use of Electronic Services" includes a paragraph about making use of sources on the Internet. It

provides, in a nutshell, an overview of the natural skepticism with which journalists should approach online sources:

> Apply the strictest standards of accuracy to anything you find on electronic ser-
> vices. The Internet is not an authority; authorities may use it, but so do quacks.
> Make certain a communication is genuine before relying on it as a source for a
> news story. More than one person may share an e-mail address, and e-mail
> addresses and Web page sponsorship can easily be faked. Ask yourself, "Could
> this be a hoax?" Do not publish on the wire any electronic address without test-
> ing to see that it's a working address, and satisfying yourself that it is genuine.
> Apply, in other words, your usual news judgment.[1]

Or, as ABC *World News Tonight* anchor Peter Jennings puts it more succinctly:
"The Internet is a great research tool, but when it comes right down to it, the thing
that bothers me is I'm never quite sure if I'm talking to a goat."[2]

Some ways of evaluating online sources will be discussed at the end of this
chapter. For now, the point is that journalists should treat information they get
from the Internet the same way they would any other information that they find:
with caution.

The Internet is notorious as a medium for hoaxes, speculation, half-truths and
inaccuracies. Good and bad information spreads with the same lightning-fast
speed on the Internet. For example, when a humor Web site made up supposed
Chinese translations of American movie titles (*Batman and Robin,* for example,
was translated as "Come to My Cave and Wear This Rubber Codpiece, Cute
Boy"), *The New York Times* published the translations as if they were real. Later,
after the *Times* had admitted its embarrassing mistake, Peter Jennings read another false translation on *World News Tonight* (thus becoming something of a goat
himself). And it didn't even stop there: the titles continued to circulate on the
Internet, and media outlets continued to report them as true.[3]

Matt Drudge, who runs the site DrudgeReport.com, is probably the poster
boy for the potential pitfalls of Internet information. While Drudge does have
some good sources and often gets stories correct before anyone else, he also has
been known to post information on his Web site before it has been subjected to
journalistic scrutiny. This, in and of itself, is not a big problem as long as readers realize that his content is at times merely speculative. However, Drudge's
site is one of the most-read sites for journalists, and too often other media outlets pick up Drudge's information and present it as factual before checking it
out for themselves. As Philip Seib points out in his book *Going Live: Getting
the News Right in a Real-Time, Online World,* "merely delivering raw information is not journalism."[4]

If approached with the same caution used with other types of sources, however, the Internet can be an extremely valuable information source. Bill Dedman, a
Boston Globe reporter who is one of the leading authorities on online reporting,

Exhibit 5.1   *Boston Globe* reporter Bill Dedman conducts an online reporting seminar.

won a Pulitzer Prize by using databases to show how mortgage lenders practiced racial bias. He says journalists "need to have an expectation that you can look things up on the Internet" (see Exhibit 5.1). In other words, using the Internet should become a part of the basic repertoire with which you approach any story. That repertoire, the basic reporting process, begins with determining what your story is actually *about,* then deciding what information you need to make it work. At that point, the Internet becomes one more place you can look for that information. As you work on the story and gather information, of course, the focus of your story might change based on what you learn, but the Internet can remain a potentially valuable information source.

E-MAIL RELATED SOURCES

You probably spend at least part of every day reading and writing e-mail messages either to individuals or to groups. For many types of communication, e-mail is easy and convenient; unlike the telephone or an in-person visit, it allows both the sender and the recipient to work around their own schedules. It also provides an inexpensive (or even free) way to communicate with people located far away.

Using E-mail

Because e-mail has become so ubiquitous, some reporters are tempted to use it in place of telephone calls or visits to story sources. However, e-mail "interviewing" of sources should be used only as an absolute last resort, in cases where using the telephone or paying a visit to the source would be impossible (not just inconvenient). For all its virtues, e-mail is a decidedly one-dimensional way of communicating: It gives you only words on the screen, with no voice inflection or visual cues to supplement those words. To the reporter, these limitations are extremely significant when it comes to judging the honesty of sources. Although you may not always be able to tell if someone is lying by watching his facial expressions or carefully assessing his tone of voice, both of these cues are important to reporters striving to learn the truth. In an e-mail message, they simply are not there.

E-mail also does not allow the kind of give-and-take with sources that often leads to the best quotes and information. You *can* resend an e-mail message to the source with follow-up questions, but the spontaneity that comes with telephone or in-person interviews will be lost. Rather than being "on the spot," the source will have plenty of time to think about how to answer your follow-up questions. Often, sources will ignore tough or controversial questions that come via e-mail, simply because they can. Refusing to answer a question on the telephone or in person, on the other hand, requires an active response on the part of the source (hanging up on you or saying "I have no comment," for example).

Although you should never use e-mail in place of telephone or in-person interviews, e-mail communication can be a useful supplement to them. E-mail can be a good way to establish contact with a source in order to arrange an interview. Particularly with reluctant sources, an initial contact via e-mail presents a nonthreatening way to establish a line of communication. Using e-mail to ask an uncertain source to talk to you allows him to think about it. In this situation, the fact that the source doesn't have to provide an immediate answer can often work to your advantage as the person might decide to talk to you after having time to think it over. Once you have interviewed a source, e-mail can provide a convenient way to check facts or to ask for other routine information you may have missed in the interview. For these reasons, it's always a good idea to get the e-mail addresses of any sources you interview.

Newsgroups

Newsgroups, as discussed in Chapter 2, are essentially "bulletin boards" of e-mails about particular topics. As a reporter, you need to be particularly skeptical of information posted in newsgroups. Often, people will post messages with false or unverifiable e-mail addresses, so there is no way to know who the message actually came from. Many newsgroups are havens for false information and the spreading of rumors as well. You should *never* report information you find in a newsgroup without verifying it through another reliable source. That said, however, some newsgroups can be good sources for background information on topics or can help you locate sources to interview in person, especially for obscure or underground topics. For example, some reporters used the newsgroup alt.dss.hack to do stories about the illegal theft of satellite TV signals by hackers. These reporters spent some time reading the newsgroup to learn background information about how the hackers operated and eventually made contact with leaders whom they later interviewed for their stories. The newsgroup was not the only source they used, but it was a valuable initial source for learning background and making contacts.

Such participation by journalists in online forums, however, also raises ethical questions. For example, is it OK for a journalist to pose as a "regular person" and ask questions about a topic on a newsgroup? In many cases, potential respondents might react differently if they knew that what they said could become part of a news story. The answer to this ethical question might depend on the importance of the topic, how likely it is that people would respond differently to a journalist and whether the journalist's employer has a policy on such things. In many cases, the journalist might be able to find the answer to her questions by simply exploring the newsgroup postings more closely, thus making the ethical question moot.

Some newsgroups that cater to journalistic topics can be excellent resources for information. In these groups, you can find out how other reporters have approached stories or ask for advice on journalism-related topics. For many journalists, in fact, perusing the latest information in newsgroups like these is a part of their daily routines. Google's "Groups" search tool, available from the site's **home page,** is a good tool for finding newsgroups that deal with a particular topic.

Listservs

Listservs provide another way for journalists to use e-mail. A listserv sends out identical e-mail messages to everyone who subscribes to it. For example, the United States Environmental Protection Agency maintains more than 80 listservs on such topics as toxic waste, air pollution and pesticides, and the Human Rights Campaign has a listserv with press releases involving gay, lesbian, bisexual and transgender equal rights issues. Once you've subscribed to a listserv, you will automatically receive any information it sends out; some listservs send out information every day, while others are more sporadic. The process of subscribing varies by the listserv, but you usually just send an e-mail that contains the word *subscribe* to a designated e-mail address. To stop receiving e-mails from the listserv, you send an e-mail that says *unsubscribe*.

Of course, you need to consider the source of the information transmitted via listservs. Some listservs are run by government agencies, while others are run by businesses or others with a particular agenda or point of view. Listservs are usually most valuable to journalists for keeping up with current topics or providing a starting point or other ideas for a story.

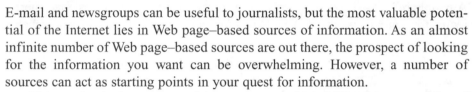

On the Web

E-mail resources, newsgroup search tools and listservs of interest to journalists:
Under Chapter 5, select **E-mail Related Sources.**

A growing number of media outlets also offer e-mail updates on particular topics a user chooses. For example, a news Web site might allow you to sign up for news about business, technology or weather. When stories about these topics are posted to the Web site, you will receive an e-mail alert.

WEB PAGE–BASED SOURCES

E-mail and newsgroups can be useful to journalists, but the most valuable potential of the Internet lies in Web page–based sources of information. As an almost infinite number of Web page–based sources are out there, the prospect of looking for the information you want can be overwhelming. However, a number of sources can act as starting points in your quest for information.

This section looks at some of these sources, which fall into the categories of general reference sources, specialized sources for journalists, search engines, directories, online newspapers and databases. My examination of these sources is by no means exhaustive; in fact, in most cases I will look at only a few examples that represent the many choices available. As always, the best way to learn these sources is to use them on your own in practical searching situations. This section is intended merely to get you started.

General Reference Sources

Sometimes you just need to find the answer to a simple question: Who was the 23rd president of the United States? What's the mayor's home phone number? How do I get to the board of elections? How many ounces are in a cup? A number of online resources can help you find the answers to questions like these.

Online encyclopedias and almanacs contain biographical, historical, scientific and general interest facts. Some, such as the *World Book* and *Encyclopaedia Britannica,* allow only limited access without a paid subscription. However, the full text of the *Columbia Encyclopedia* is available online.

Internet-based telephone directories are particularly useful because they allow you to search the entire country, a region or a particular city. If you don't know a person's full name, you can enter as much information as you know (for example, the person's last name and a state) and then do a search. The search will return telephone numbers and street addresses in most cases. Of course, these online sources won't help you find unlisted numbers, but they do allow you to find both individual telephone subscribers and businesses.

Mapping programs provide street maps of particular areas or driving directions from one place to another. They can even estimate how long the trip will take and, in some cases, alert you to road construction or other potential hazards along the way. The best-known of these programs is Mapquest (see Exhibit 5.2), which also allows you to "zoom" in or out on a particular location.

Other handy (and sometimes fun) sources include *Columbia Journalism Review's* inflation adjuster, *Roget's Thesaurus, Bartlett's Familiar Quotations,* the *American Heritage Dictionary,* ConvertIt (calculators for various measurements) and the *CIA World Factbook.*

Specialized Sources for Journalists

A couple of Web sites deserve special mention because they are designed specifically for journalists. ProfNet and the National Press Club provide searchable

Exhibit 5.2 Mapping programs like Mapquest allow you to download maps and driving directions.

From MapQuest.com, Inc. Reprinted with permission.

databases of experts on a variety of topics, allowing journalists to find authoritative sources for their stories. Bill Dedman's excellent site, PowerReporting.com, is a one-stop source for a wide variety of useful journalistic sources (see Exhibit 5.3). PowerReporting.com has links to sources for various news beats, search tools, media organizations, government agencies, companies and people finders. It also has "quizzes" and reference information that can test and build your knowledge of online searching strategies.

Bill Dedman's PowerReporting.com is an excellent resource for journalists looking for information online.   **Exhibit 5.3**

January 9, 2004

- Top 100 sites
- Newsroom training
- People finders
- Beat by beat
- Company research
- Government info
- Nonprofit research
- Reference shelf
- Search tools
- Alerts for journalists
- Journalism shoptalk
- Fair Lending
- Home run manas
- Help
  - Contact
  - Credits
  - Site map
  - Search
  - Suggest a link
  - Set as home page

Media news headlines
The Death of Journalists in Asia -- but Not the Death of Asian Journalism...
Asia Media

PM takes journalist to task...
Bangkok Post

Editor's view: the case for flexibility...
Business Europe

News powered by
Moreover Technologies

POWER REPORTING
RESOURCES FOR JOURNALISTS

Welcome to Power Reporting!
Thousands of free research tools for journalists.

COLUMBIA JOURNALISM REVIEW
AMERICA'S PREMIER MEDIA MONITOR

Power Reporting is a partner of Columbia Journalism Review.

Test your skills on the Newsroom treasure hunt or try the tutorial on Web searching.

Beat by beat	Companies	People finders	Reference shelf	What's New
Aging	SEC Edgar	Phone books	Book search	
Agriculture	Secs. of state	Reverse directories	Dictionaries	**Journalism**
Arts	EDGAR people	Biographies	Encyclopedias	Alerts
Business	Hoover's	E-mail search	Maps	Associations
Census_2000	Patents	News archives	Quotations	Awards
City/suburb	OSHA inspections	Public records	Archives	Blogs
Computers		Domain names		Books
Crime & law	**Nonprofits**		**Government**	Cartooning
Disasters	GuideStar	Experts	Agencies	Critics
Economics	NCCS	ProfNet	FedStats	Diversity
Education	BBB	Doctors	Find Law	Editing
Environment		Lawyers	FirstGov	Education
Family		Authors	GPO Access	Ethics
Food	**Search tools**	Area Codes	PACER Courts	FOI
Guns	AltaVista adv.	ZIP Codes	International	Freelancing
Health	Google adv.	Campaign donors	U.S.	Graphics
History	Google directory	AutoTrack ($)	States	History
Housing	All the Web adv.	KnowX ($)	Cities	Humor
International	ResourceShelf			Institutes
Military	Direct Search		**Training**	Jobs
Politics & policy	HotBot	**Media**	Seminars	Links
Race	Britannica	AP news	Treasure hunt	Magazines
Religion	Journalism lists	NYTimes	Search tutorial	Management
Science	News archives	Boston Globe	CAR bookshelf	Newspapers
Sports	Nexis ($)	All papers	CAR syllabi	Online
Terrorism		CNN	Managing CAR	Photography
Transportation	Search tools chest	MSNBC	Internet rules	Radio
Weather	Yahoo advanced	Romenesko	Sample files	Television
Work				Writing

Search Engines

Search engines can help when you don't know where to find the information you want online or whether it even exists. Many different search engines are available, but they all work similarly. They compile a gigantic list of information contained on Web pages using "robots" that periodically search the Web. Then, when you type in something you're looking for, the search engine looks in its list for the information and gives you the results, as shown in Exhibit 5.4. No search engine can find everything on the Web, and no search engine is entirely up-to-date. However, as you probably have discovered, they can be very useful when you know how to use them.

One mistake that many people make with search engines is to think in terms of topics instead of the actual information they're looking for. Search engines essentially know nothing about topics—they merely try to match words and phrases. If you type in "chair," for example, a search engine is likely to give you information about chairs you sit on, chairs of committees and chairs of academic departments.

Dedman says the key is to "visualize the result" of your Web search. In other words, think about what a successful end to your search would look like. What words *will actually be on the page* of the Web site that provides the answer to your question? What words *won't* be on the page? The key is to search for the right words, not necessarily the topic. For example, if you wanted to find a complete list of the children of presidents, your first inclination might be to use search terms like "presidential children" or "presidential offspring." This would eventually get you what you're looking for, but you're also likely to have to sift through a lot of irrelevant information. A better strategy would be to start with the names of presidential offspring you already know—Jenna Bush, Chelsea Clinton, Amy Carter—and then use those *names* as your search terms. Remember, search engines don't know anything about topics; they merely match terms.

Boolean connectors, such as AND, OR, and NOT, can help you perform more specific searches. Although my examples will show the Boolean connectors in all capital letters to make them stand out, most search engines are not case-sensitive. If you're getting odd results, however, you may need to verify that.

When used between two terms, the AND connector tells the search engine that *both* terms must appear on the Web page. So, the search *dogs AND cats* will return only Web pages on which both the word *dogs* and the word *cats* appear. By default, most search engines assume an AND connector between search terms if you don't type one. So, the search *dogs cats* is in effect the same as the search *dogs AND cats*. But again, make sure the search engine you're using does it this way.

The OR connector tells the search engine to look for pages on which *either* word appears. The search *dogs OR cats* would thus return any page that had either of the two words on it (this means you'd get a much longer list than with the first search).

Searching for information using the Google search engine: entering the search item   **Exhibit 5.4**
and viewing the results.

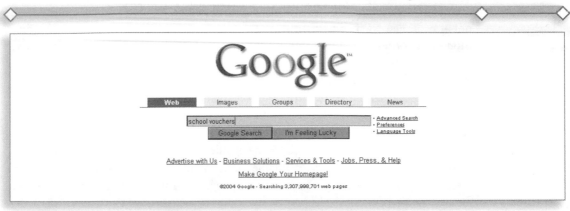

From Google. Reprinted with permission.

The NOT connector excludes the words following it. Thus, the search *dogs NOT cats* will return only those pages that have the word *dogs* on them and do not contain the word *cats*. In other words, any Web page with the word *cats* on it would not appear. The NOT connector is useful when you are searching a relatively common name or term and you *don't* want the common results. For example, if you want to search for information on someone named Michael Jordan who is not the famous basketball star, you might search *Michael Jordan NOT basketball.*

Enclosing search terms in quotation marks tells the search engine that the terms must appear side by side as you've typed them. So, the search *"George Herbert Walker Bush"* will return pages on which the names "George," "Herbert," "Walker" and "Bush" appear side by side in that order. The search *George Herbert Walker Bush,* on the other hand, would also return pages on which these names in any combination appeared—for example, a page with the names *George* Clooney, *Herbert* Hoover, Junior *Walker* and Barbara *Bush.*

Some of these results also can be achieved without using Boolean connectors or quotation marks by using a search engine's advanced search page. Here, you can also activate other advanced search functions, such as searching only pages in a particular language or pages within a specific domain.

The more you use search engines, the better you will become at doing efficient searches. If you're getting too many results, you need to narrow your search—think about using AND or NOT or enclosing the terms in quotation marks. If you're not getting enough results, try using OR. If you're getting the wrong results, you may need to rethink your search terms. Check your spelling, for one thing, or think about other ways the information you're looking for might be presented on a page.

Directories

In some cases, using a **directory** can be a faster path to the information you're seeking. A directory is a Web site in which Web content has been organized by topic; the most popular one is Yahoo!. As shown in Exhibit 5.5, Yahoo! allows you to start with broad categories (entertainment, education, science and so forth) and then "burrow down" into specific topics. For example, clicking the "Science" link presents a page with many subcategories, including chemistry, oceanography and physics. These links, in turn, lead to further subcategories.

The advantage of directories is that the information is already organized for you. The only trick is finding the proper subcategories that lead to it. It is not unlike using the computerized card catalog in your school's library—you just need to find out which shelf contains the books on your topic. One disadvantage of directories is that they access a much more limited slice of the Internet's information. Someone has already exercised editorial judgment in deciding that the information is worthy of being included in the directory. Since cataloging Internet content in

The Yahoo! Web directory.   **Exhibit 5.5**

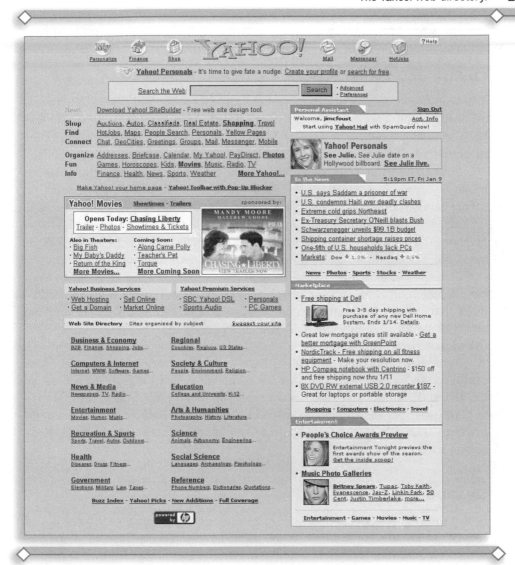

this way takes time (and, in most cases, human effort), there is no way a directory can keep up with the information that is constantly being added online. Still, directories can often be a useful tool for finding a specific fact or reference source.

It is also important to point out that the Google and Yahoo! sites offer *both* search engines and directories. For example, clicking the "Directory" link on Google's home page will take you to a directory, and you can use Yahoo!'s search function by typing search terms in the "Search the Web" window (see Exhibit 5.5). In practice, however, Google is much better known for its search engine, and Yahoo! is best known for its directory and other information services.

Online Journalism Sites

The Web sites of journalistic organizations also can be helpful resources at times, especially to students. Never before have so many examples of quality journalism been so readily available to students. Of course, neither have so many examples of not-so-good journalism been available. Once again, you have to be the judge.

You can sometimes find useful background information or ideas on how a story might be approached on these sites. Seeing how someone covered a story about a sexual harassment suit at a factory halfway across the country might give you ideas on how you could approach the same kind of story locally. Such a story might also give you the names of people (a nationally known attorney specializing in sexual harassment cases, for instance) whom you could contact for your own story.

The search capabilities vary among journalistic sites; some sites do not even have a search function, or their search features don't work very well. Some sites don't have much archival material available, and others charge to retrieve archived stories. But on some sites, you can access quite a bit of previously published material.

Looking at how other journalists have approached stories may become less useful to you as your career progresses (although perhaps no less entertaining). Legal and economic issues also can prevent you from using **links** to these stories in your own story (as will be discussed in Chapter 10). Still, at least at this point in your career, it's great to be able to see so many examples of how other journalists have written their stories.

Databases

A **database** is a collection of digital information organized into parts called **records** and **fields.** For example, if you wanted to create a database for your baseball card collection, you might note the player, number and year for each card as well as its condition and value. Each card's information would be a record, and each piece of information within that record (player, condition, value and so forth) would be a field. The value of databases is that they allow you to search, organize and analyze information by records and fields. For example, if you wanted to find out how many of your cards were in "excellent" condition, you could get a listing by querying (asking) your database.

Addressing the skills and techniques of database use are beyond the scope of this textbook, especially since our focus is on finding information online that we can link to in our stories. Just be aware that databases are becoming increasingly prevalent on the Internet and that they are particularly valuable as a potential tool for journalists who can analyze and find compelling stories within the data. For example, *The Philadelphia Daily News* analyzed Department of Transportation, court and other databases to chronicle a dramatic drop in the number of tickets written by city police officers. *The Miami Herald* used the Florida Traffic Crash Database to show how puddles were making a new section of highway one of the most dangerous in the state.

U.S. federal government agencies provide some of the most valuable online databases, although state, local and other governments are putting information online as well. The U.S. Census Bureau's Web site is a treasure trove of demographic information (see Exhibit 5.6). The Federal Aviation Administration's National Aviation Safety Data Analysis Center (NASDAC) provides searchable databases for aircraft registrations, accidents and near collisions. As shown in Exhibit 5.7, NASDAC's Near Midair Collision database allows you to search by

The U.S. Census Bureau Web site. **Exhibit 5.6**

Exhibit 5.7   The Federal Aviation Administration's NASDAC database search tool allows you to find information by one or more categories.

National Aviation Safety Data Analysis Center

Accident/Incident Database System Query Form   ?

| Submit | Reset |

Narrative Text

Report Nbr

Registration Nbr

Event Start Date
(DD-MMM-YY)

Event End Date

State

Airport Name

Operation Type

Event Type

Flight Phase

Operator Name

Aircraft Make Name

Aircraft Model Name

Aircraft Series

type of aircraft, state, airport, aircraft operator and other fields. Other government agencies, such as the Securities and Exchange Commission, Federal Reserve Banks, Federal Election Commission and National Traffic Safety Board also make databases available that hold potential journalistic value.

Like using search engines, the keys to successful database searching are knowing what you want the result to look like and understanding how you're most likely to achieve that result. Most databases are designed to allow a **query** by one or more data fields. Depending on your purposes, you might enter your query in one field or several. For example, if you wanted to find out how many midair collisions occurred at Memphis International Airport, you would select that airport as part of your query. If you wanted to know how many of those incidents involved

On the Web

Links to sites discussed in this section, tips on using search engines and databases and how Yahoo! got its name:
Under Chapter 5, select **Web page–based Sources.**

Boeing 747 jets, you would add those criteria to the query under "Aircraft Make" and "Aircraft Model." Similarly, you could find only incidents within a certain time range by specifying dates in the start and end fields.

EVALUATING SOURCES

You have already seen that evaluating the source of information found on the Internet is particularly important. To do this, you should use the same types of skills journalists would use to evaluate any source. You should ask yourself if the source seems truthful, is relevant to the story, has an ulterior motive or particular point of view that affects what he or she says, is qualified to speak to the topic of the story, and other questions. On the Internet, however, establishing the answers to these questions can be trickier because it sometimes requires technical skills that face-to-face or traditional printed sources do not.

This section is designed to help you evaluate Web page–based sources of information, although some of the techniques could be applied to e-mail or newsgroups as well. These techniques, even when used together, are rarely enough for you to establish the reliability or usefulness of a source. Instead, they usually are just a starting point for deciding how—or if—you will use a source: Will you rely on what the source says as "fact"? Will you repeat the source's information but caution the reader of its origin? Will you choose to ignore the source? Will you verify the source's information with another source? Will you include a link to the source in your story? These decisions should be made only after carefully vetting the source. Knee-jerk decisions—either for or against using a source—can be very risky: You might include inaccurate information in your story or ignore a source that could have been quite valuable.

Evaluating Top-Level Domains

Chapter 2 discussed the use of **Uniform Resource Locators (URLs)** to access information on the World Wide Web. You will remember that URLs use the **domain name system (DNS),** a text-based addressing scheme, to identify different computers on the Internet. Dissecting the different parts of the URL can offer clues as to who is providing the information on a given Web page. The URL for the Web page you are viewing can be found in a small window at the top of your browser.

The first item to look for is the address's **top-level domain (TLD),** which identifies the type of entity that is publishing the Web site. For a simple URL address like http://www.cnn.com, the TLD is the final period in the address and everything that follows it, .com in this case. To find the TLD in a more complex URL, you must first ignore everything that follows the first single slash (/) in the address, as shown in Exhibit 5.8(a). That leaves a simple DNS entry; again, the TLD is the final peri-

Exhibit 5.8   Determining the TLD of a complex URL is a matter of first ignoring everything following the first single slash (a) and then extracting the TLD as you would normally (b).

(a)   http://personal.bgsu.edu/~jfoust/personal/carfiles/probegt/engine mods/klze.html

(b)   http://personal.bgsu.edu

od and everything that follows it, as shown in Exhibit 5.8(b). As you know, some addresses to Web pages can be very long—sometimes stretching beyond what will fit in the browser's address window. However, using this technique will always allow you to determine the address's TLD, no matter how long and complex the URL.

Once you have isolated the TLD, you can then get a general idea of the type of entity responsible for the Web site. As shown in Exhibit 5.9, in the United States, specific TLDs are assigned to different types of entities. Colleges and universities, for example, get .edu addresses, while nonprofit organizations get .org.

Web sites located in countries outside the United States use **country-code top-level domains (ccTLDs).** In these cases, the top-level domain merely indicates the country where the Web site is located. For example, the University of Wollongong in Australia uses the domain name uow.edu.au, with ".au" designating that the site is located in Australia. For such sites, you can often look just to the left of the TLD for the information found in United States TLDs—for example, the ".edu" in uow.edu.au.

Government entities. A .gov, .mil or .us TLD indicates that the information comes from a government agency in the United States. That doesn't necessarily mean that it is automatically credible, but at least you know that it comes from an official source. You can treat Web sites with an .int TLD, such as the United Nations, similarly.

Educational institutions. The .edu TLD indicates that the source of the information is someone associated with a college or university. However, determining whether it is an official of the university (such as the president or provost) or a student takes a bit more digging (as will be discussed in the "Personal Web Pages" section later in this chapter). Universities produce two general types of information that are useful to journalists. First, the university may release news or information about itself, such as a plan to raise tuition by 20 percent. Second, since universities are generally centers for the creation of knowledge, professors may release information about their research. For example, a professor in a political science department may publish her research findings showing that 80 percent of the state's 18- to 21-year-olds are not registered to vote. Either of these

Top-level domains in the United States are assigned based on the type of enity publishing   **Exhibit 5.9**
the Web site.

.aero	Air-transport industry sites
.arpa	Internet infrastructure sites
.biz	Business sites
.com	Commercial sites
.coop	Cooperative organization sites
.edu	Educational institution sites
.gov	Government sites
.info	General usage sites
.int	International sites
.mil	Military sites
.museum	Museum sites
.name	Individual's sites
.net	Networking and Internet-related sites
.org	Sites for organizations
.pro	Sites for professions

stories has potential interest for a journalist, but both must be treated as if they had come as print documents from their respective sources. A call to the university's public relations department or to the political science professor would be a good first step in confirming (and building on) the Web-based information.

Commercial and nonprofit organizations. Although they represent somewhat different entities, the .com, .biz, .info, .org and .net TLDs should be treated the same by journalists. Determining the real source of such Web sites—and their inherent credibility—can be more challenging than with other domains. Commercial entities are a bit easier perhaps because they are normally more out in the open about their intentions: They want to sell you something. But nonprofit organizations (.org) also have an agenda, and—commonly—financial support from commercial entities. Always check into the membership, board of directors and supporters of nonprofit organizations, and make certain you factor their particular biases into any information you find on their Web sites.

It's actually quite easy to find the registered owner of a Web site. To start, just go to the InterNIC Web site, which is the central repository for domain registration information: http://www.internic.net/whois.html. Type the name of the Web site you want to check in the box. Type in only the last part of the DNS name—what follows the next-to-last period. For example, don't type "www.nra.org," just "nra.org". Make sure the button next to "Domain" is selected, and then click the "Search" button, as shown in Exhibit 5.10. The contact information for the owners of the Web site will appear.

Personal Web Pages

When evaluating the content of a Web page, be aware that merely establishing what the TLD is may not be enough. Some organizations—particularly colleges and universities—allow individuals to publish Web pages on their computers. Faculty members and students may be given space on the university's servers. These pages can usually—but not always—be identified by the presence of a tilde (~) symbol in the URL. For example, in the author's home page

http://personal.bgsu.edu/~jfoust/homepage.html

the ~ before my name indicates that the page is associated with an individual, not the university itself. Thus, I may post extremely interesting or even relevant information on my Web page, but I will be doing so for myself and not representing my university.

Most commercial and government organizations have strict rules against employees or others publishing personal pages on their Web sites. For that reason, personal Web pages indicated by a tilde are usually found only in .edu domains. However, some **Internet service providers (ISPs)** will give Web space to individual subscribers and denote these individuals with tildes in the URLs.

As a journalist, you need to be particularly skeptical of personal Web pages. Any information found on a personal Web page should be thoroughly checked and double-checked before it is published.

Other Evaluation Criteria

You also can look for other clues that will help you evaluate a Web site's content. These are quite simple and would also apply to most print documents. For example, you should

- Examine a page carefully for grammar and spelling. Chances are if the information is being provided by a reputable source, it will be free of spelling errors and improper grammar.

To determine who owns a site, type the site's address into the search window at InterNIC, **Exhibit 5.10**
which will reveal the ownership and contact information for the site.

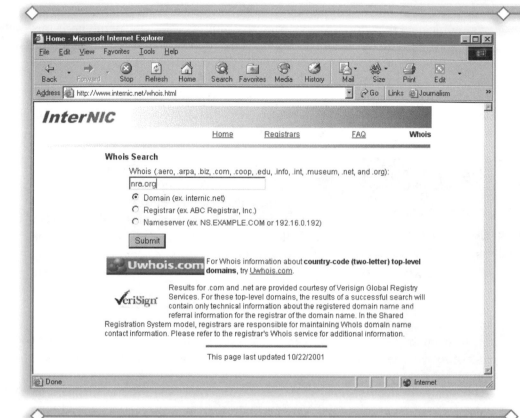

- Look at the overall design of the page. Does it convey the impression of a reputable organization?

- Check the date. You should determine when the page (and the site itself) was last updated. Most reputable sites include a date stamp, for example, "Last updated January 15, 2004, 5:15 p.m."

- Look for an "About Us" or "Contact Us" section of the Web site. These sections often include valuable information about who is behind the site and what the site's purpose is.

Being Careful: External Links and Hackers

Even if you try to be thorough about evaluating Web-based sources, you can run into some pitfalls if you're not careful. First, always be aware of the links you're clicking on a Web page and where they are taking you. You may think that a link is taking you to another part of the same Web site, but in reality it may be taking you to a completely new site. Thus, make sure you check the URL for the *exact page* from which you're getting your information. Just because you started on the Environmental Protection Agency's page five mouse clicks ago doesn't necessarily mean you're still on that organization's page. Most reputable organizations are fairly careful about linking to outside sources without first warning you, but you also need to be vigilant about keeping track of your location.

On occasion, the URL or other information on a Web site may have been corrupted by hackers. Although some people who merely experiment or tinker with computers also call themselves by this name, many people delight in wreaking havoc on computer systems and users. Computer **viruses** and Internet "worms," which can slow computers to a crawl and damage data, are the most common works of nefarious hackers, but hackers also do other illegal things. For example, they have been known to replace the content of a reputable Web site with other content or to redirect users to a different site entirely, sometimes as a joke or to spread a political message. In 2000, hackers changed the content of a United Nations Web site by adding to it Bruce Springsteen song lyrics with the caption "children of the darkstar." In 1999, hackers redirected users of Hillary Clinton's Senate campaign Web site to a Web site run by her rival Rudolph Guiliani.

On the Web

More about URLs, TLDs and hackers. Also, resources at the University of California-Berkeley for evaluating Web pages: Under Chapter 5, select **Evaluating Sources.**

Thankfully, such hacking is relatively rare. Still, you need to maintain an extra layer of skepticism (and common sense) about what you might find on a reputable Web site. If your local congressperson's site contains pictures of scantily clad lingerie models, for example, you would probably do well to first suspect the work of a hacker. That doesn't mean you don't have a story, however; it just means your story is about what the hacker did.

WHAT'S NEXT

Now that we have looked at the technical issues involved in Web production, the structure of online journalism organizations and the basics of finding information online, we're ready to talk about actually *producing* online journalism sites. The next four chapters will address Web design (Chapter 6), writing for the Web (Chapter 7), using links (Chapter 8) and adding multimedia and interactivity (Chapter 9). Chapter 8, especially, will build on this chapter as it discusses choosing and presenting links to information in online journalism stories.

Activities

5.1 Think about some of your current story ideas in terms of what information you might be able to find on the Internet. What kinds of information are you looking for, and how might you best find it online? Try to find at least three relevant sources for each story. How have you evaluated these sources?

5.2 Try answering the questions in the "Web Treasure Hunt" at the PowerReporting.com Web site. You can find a link to it on this chapter's Web page.

5.3 Consider this URL: http://www.moveon.org/volunteerphotos.html/#leafleting. First, isolate this URL's top-level domain. Then, see if you can find out who is behind this Web site by using InterNIC. Can you find a telephone number to contact the owners of the site?

ENDNOTES

1. PowerReporting.com, http://powerreporting.com/rules.html.

2. *The Salt Lake City Tribune,* http://www.sltrib.com/2003/Sep/09152003/92598.asp.

3. Christopher Callahan, *A Journalist's Guide to the Internet: The Net as a Reporting Tool,* 2nd ed. (Boston: Allyn and Bacon, 2003), p. 21.

4. Philip Seib, *Going Live: Getting the News Right in a Real-Time, Online World* (Lanham, MD: Rowman & Littlefield, 2002), p. 53.

CHAPTER 6

GOALS

- To discuss the basic design structure used in most online journalism sites
- To introduce the principles that guide visual design for the Web
- To discuss how to present text, color and graphics on Web pages effectively
- To provide an overview of how HTML tables and cascading style sheets can be used to create design grids for Web pages
- To discuss how differences among Web browsers and computer platforms affect Web page design

WEB PAGE DESIGN

Designing Web pages is part science, part practical skill and part art. That last part is what scares some people, especially those who consider themselves decidedly *not* artistically inclined. But the good news is that even though some of the most visually stunning Web pages on the Internet could be considered works of art, you don't have to be artistically inclined to create attractive and useful Web pages. In fact you can go a long way toward good Web design by simply *not* violating certain aesthetic rules. Your pages may not look like works of art, but at least they can be attractive and easy to use.

Like many of the concepts discussed in this book, the principles of design covered in this chapter are intended merely to introduce you to the most important things you need to know. This chapter is not intended to be a comprehensive source for Web page design. Since our focus is on creating online journalism, we don't need to know a lot about innovative or envelope-pushing design theories; we simply need to learn ways to effectively present journalistic content. Certainly, this chapter cannot make you an artist if you don't already have artistic ability. For that reason, it concentrates on the aesthetic principles and practical skills of design that anyone can learn and carry out.

This chapter begins with a discussion of the basic design structure used by most online journalism sites. It then looks at basic design principles, many of which have carried over from print design. Next, it presents an overview of effective ways to present text, color and graphics on Web pages. Finally, it shows how Web pages can be laid out using HTML (hypertext markup language) tables in an authoring program. In some places, the chapter builds on the basics of HTML and cascading style sheets (CSS) discussed in Chapter 3.

BASIC ONLINE JOURNALISM DESIGN

Before we discuss some theories and aesthetic design principles in general, we need to look at the basic design of online journalism sites that exist today. This is not to say that the existing design aesthetic is the best way or that you necessarily need to constrain yourself to this way of thinking, but simply that this is the way most online journalism sites are designed *today*. This basic structure, as we will see, presents both constraints and opportunities for designers.

Layout Grids

Designers call the basic layout structure of a page—be it a print document or a Web page—the **grid,** a series of lines and boxes into which the content fits. The grid of most online journalism sites resembles the general layout of the front page of a newspaper. As shown in Exhibit 6.1, online journalism sites

Exhibit 6.1   The basic grid design used by most online journalism sites.

THE DAILY NEWS

Link

Link

Link

Link

Link

Link

Link

Link

Link

normally consist of an identifying element across the top of the page (similar to a newspaper's **nameplate**), links to other sections of the Web site down the left-hand side of the page (usually called the **navigation bar**) and a main content section to the right. Although critics contend that this reliance on a standardized design stifles innovation and the full use of the online medium, users have come to expect this type of design and are generally comfortable with it. Also, the basic design still allows for a good deal of customization, creativity and expression.

Exhibit 6.2 shows the nytimes.com, CNN.com and espn.com Web pages, each of which adheres to this basic design. You can see, however, that in actual execution each site presents a unique character, or "personality." *The New York Times* page has a more conservative visual design, while CNN adds a bit more color and graphics. ESPN goes further still, using more color, a more dominant main headline and bolder graphic elements. Few users would mistake *The New York Times* Web site for ESPN's, but if a user were familiar with one of them, she would be able to adapt to the new one with relative ease.

Page Dimensions

Another concept carried over from newspapers is the idea of designing **above the fold.** This concept mandates that the top half of the newspaper's front page contain its most important information and most attractive elements so that when people see the top half of the front page (perhaps at a newsstand or in a vending machine), they will be attracted to the newspaper and be more likely to purchase it. Web pages, of course, are not folded, but most are longer than the typical user's browser window. Thus, Web pages should be designed with the most important visual elements appearing at the top of the page, so that when users come to the page, they don't have to scroll their browser window down to see the most important information. As you can see, each page in Exhibit 6.2 is designed so that the user can immediately see the most important elements on the page without having to scroll down.

As discussed in Chapter 3, different users have differently sized computer screens. For this reason, Web pages must be designed to function well on as many different screen **resolutions** as possible. Make a page too large, and it will be difficult for users with small screens to see all of it; make a page too small, and users with bigger screens will have large "dead" areas in their browser windows. As a compromise, today most pages are designed assuming that the user will be viewing the page with at least 800 x 600 **pixels** of resolution—roughly the equivalent of a 15-inch monitor. Once you make allowances for the browser's window frames and other menu elements, that leaves about 750 x 420 for actual top-of-page content. Thus, the dimensions of the "above the fold" part of the page should be no more than 750 x 420.

Exhibit 6.2   The home pages of CNN (a), *The New York Times* (b) and ESPN (c) show how the basic grid structure can be adapted to different sites.

(a)

From CNN.com. Reprinted with permission.

(b)

Exhibit 6.2 Continued.

(c)

Usability

The concept of **usability** encompasses the visual design of pages and the logical presentation of information, but it also speaks to how pages *connect* and relate to one another. Usability, at its essence, is about how easy it is for the user to navigate to achieve his desired goals. In the case of online journalism, that means finding the desired information quickly and efficiently.

In a nutshell, usability is about answering two related questions for the user: (1) Where am I? and (2) Where can I go? The first question involves making sure it is immediately clear to users what page they are on. Most online journalism sites do a good job of this—at least on their home pages—using dominant nameplate-style designs at the top. The second question is in large part a function of **link** design and presentation (discussed in Chapter 8). Generally, however, you always want the user to have a clear sense at all times of what options are available. Note in Exhibit 6.2 that each site's navigation bar reflects the main areas available on the site.

Beyond the home page, the structure of the site needs to be understandable to the user. When the user clicks into a new section of the site, it should be clear where she is now. As shown in Exhibit 6.3, for example, when users click the "Technology" link on the main CNN Web page, they are taken to a page that is clearly labeled. The large "Technology" heading at the top lets users know exactly where they are.

The home page of a site should function as a landmark for the user. In other words, it should be a place the user can *always* get back to if she gets lost. Most online journalism sites accomplish this by making the site's main logo a link back to the home page. For example, in Exhibit 6.3, the CNN logo is a link that will take the user to the CNN home page. Most users, too, have come to expect that clicking any site's logo (be it an online journalism site, a commerce site or any other type of site) will take them to the home page.

> ### *On the Web*
>
> More about basic site design and usability, including tips from usability guru Jakob Nielsen. Also, links to sites discussed in this section:
> Under Chapter 6, select **Basic Online Journalism Design.**

PRINCIPLES OF DESIGN

Just as the basic online journalism layout grid borrows from its print predecessors, so do the basic principles of online design. As print and online are both chiefly visual media, it is not surprising that the basic visual aesthetics would be similar. In fact, if you have had a newspaper design or desktop publishing course, these basic principles will probably be familiar to you.

Exhibit 6.3 The CNN Technology page clearly indicates to the user where she is.

From CNN.com. Reprinted with permission.

Unity

Unity means that the overall design of the page creates the impression of a coherent whole. All of the design elements—text, graphics, color, the grid itself—should work together as if they were a single element. Generally, everything on the page should look as if it *belongs* with everything else. The user should be able to quickly grasp the page's basic content without being overwhelmed by a lot of seemingly disparate elements. Although unity is important to print designers, it is critical to Web designers because users are able to leave a Web page easily. Many experts say that a Web page has only a few seconds to establish itself as valuable in the eyes of the user—if the page is not seen as worthwhile, the user will leave and perhaps never come back. Unity can make those critical first few seconds positive for the user.

Although the CNN.com page shown in Exhibit 6.2 contains many different elements, it is unified by the repetition of blue color hues, the repeating "tabs" to denote different sections on the bottom half of the page and the use of consistent fonts. The overall grid design also establishes unity, as content is neatly contained in three columns, which are of unequal width at the top of the page and of equal width at the bottom. *The New York Times* page in Exhibit 6.2 utilizes a four-column grid over its entire length, except for a small box near the center that spans the two middle columns. This box functions as a divider between the primary page elements (above the fold) and the secondary elements.

You can go a long way toward creating pages with good unity by keeping to a structured grid design. Create an overall design grid for the page (such as that shown in Exhibit 6.1) and then align your elements to the grid. Exhibit 6.4(a) shows a page with poor layout: Each element seems to "float" on its own, and there is no overall unity. Some elements are aligned to the left of the page, some are aligned to the right and some are seemingly aligned to nothing at all. An improved version of the page, shown in Exhibit 6.4(b), establishes a grid with four columns at the top and two columns below. The page's elements are then aligned to these grids, creating a more unified design. It also looks "neater" than the previous design, which usually indicates good unity.

Contrast

Although the overall effect of the page should be unity, within the page different elements should be easily distinguishable from one another. This is crucial to making a page easy to use—the reader must be able to quickly find what he is looking for, be it the navigation bar, the top story or the sports section. As we will see later in this chapter and in Chapter 7, Web page readers tend to **scan** pages rather than reading word by word. Pages must facilitate scanning by making individual elements distinguishable from one another quickly and easily.

Exhibit 6.4   A poorly formatted Web page (a) and an improved version (b) adhering more closely
to an aligned design grid.

(a)

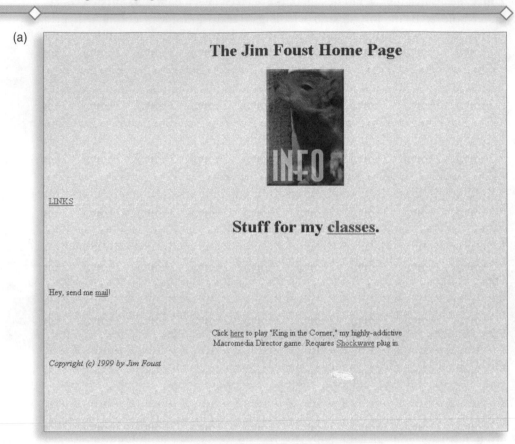

Contrast can be created by using different colors, varying text sizes, bold text and pictures and graphics. It also can be created by the positioning of individual elements; an element located "away" from another one, for example, is likely to be contrasted from it.

On the CNN page shown in Exhibit 6.2, the navigation bar on the left is contrasted from the rest of the page by its bold blue coloring. The main story is also contrasted by a lighter blue background (as opposed to the white background of the rest of the page) and the use of a large photograph and bold headline. On the bottom half of the page, contrast is created by the bold headings and individual graphic tabs for the sections as well as by the small pictures.

Unity and contrast may seem at first to be conflicting principles, but they're really not. Unity has to do with the user's impression of the page: Does it look

(b)

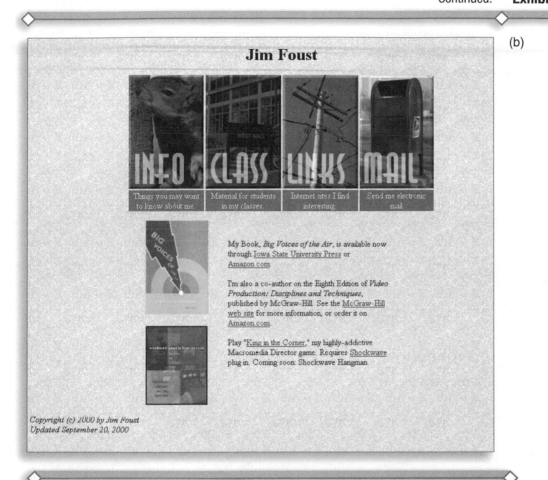

Copyright (c) 2000 by Jim Foust
Updated September 20, 2000

like a cluttered mess or a neat and coherent whole? Once past this initial impression, contrast helps the user separate the individual elements of the page to find what he wants. Achieving unity *and* contrast at the same time can be a challenge, but both are important to good visual design.

Hierarchy

Not only should a page have contrasting elements, it should also establish a **hierarchy** of those elements' importance. In other words, the page should be designed so that the most important elements on the page stand out. On the ESPN page shown in Exhibit 6.2, the most important element is the story about the hockey series. This importance is forcefully established by the large picture and bold headline for that story. The eye is drawn quickly to this element on the page. If the user is interested in that story, she is likely to look at the story's additional elements (below the picture), but if not, she will look at the rest of the page. Either way, the page draws in the user by establishing a dominant, "attractive" element.

Hierarchy can be established by the use of pictures, bold colors and large or bold text. In print design, it has been an accepted standard that a large picture will always be the element that people look at first. However, a study done by the Poynter Institute found that on the Web, people are most immediately drawn to text elements.[1] For that reason, both text and pictures are often used on the Web to establish the dominant section of a page.

The hierarchical structure continues on a well-designed page past the initial dominant element or elements. The other parts of the page should be designed in relation to their relative importance. On the CNN page shown in Exhibit 6.2, once past the dominant main story, the next tier is the "More Top Stories" section and then "The New Iraq" and—possibly—the navigation bar. Remember, the user with a typical-sized monitor will be seeing only the top half of the page at first. Elements of less importance to the user—such as the copyright notice—are small and placed at the bottom of the page (not visible on the exhibit), far down both on the screen and in the visual hierarchy.

Consistency

Consistency means that the same design element is used within a single page and across all pages in a site. The discussion of unity addressed using the same font styles for similar elements on a page—all links in the same font style, size and color, for example. This applies both to a single page and to pages across a site. Compare for a moment the CNN home page shown in Exhibit 6.2 and the CNN Technology page in Exhibit 6.3. Note that the pages repeat the main design elements—the navigation bar, the heading, the basic page structure, the colors and the fonts.

On the Web

The good, the bad and the ugly of Web design, including the site Webpagesthatsuck.com. Hope that your designs never end up there!
Under Chapter 6, select **Principles of Design.**

Consistency is important to establishing and maintaining the "identity" of your Web site. You always want users to remember whose site they're visiting. If they click on another section of your Web site and the page looks completely different, they are likely to wonder whether they have left your site. Consistency is also valuable because once users learn your site's basic page structure, they are able to move around freely within the site without having to relearn new designs.

Consistency can be achieved more easily by using **templates** in Macromedia Dreamweaver or other authoring programs. Templates are Web pages that contain design and other elements that will be repeated over several pages. For example, a template could contain the overall design of the page—a main area for the story, a headline area at the top and a navigation area with links on the left side—but without the actual text. To create the actual page, you start with the template and just fill in the content; in this way, each page need not be created from scratch. Templates also can contain links to style sheets, further automating the process of formatting text. Templates allow authoring programs to work much the way **content management systems** (discussed in Chapter 4) do—you simply fill content into predefined page structures.

USING TEXT

Despite the Web's great potential for delivering a **multimedia** experience with sounds and visuals, words are still the most important element of online communication. For that reason, not only must we choose our words wisely (as will be discussed in Chapter 7), we must also *present* those words effectively. Chapter 3 showed some ways HTML code and CSS can be used to format text in different ways; this section will examine some of the aesthetic principles of text presentation.

Font Classifications

As you know, HTML allows you to display lettering on Web pages in different font styles. For Web page design, font styles are divided into four categories: **serif, sans serif, novelty** and **monospace.** Serif fonts, as shown in Exhibit 6.5(a), have small protrusions—called serifs—on the tips of the letters. Sans serif fonts do not have these protrusions, as shown in Exhibit 6.5(b). Novelty fonts are stylized representations letters, as shown in Exhibit 6.5(c). Monospace fonts (which can be serif, sans serif or novelty) are designed so that every letter or character in the alphabet occupies an equal amount of horizontal space, as

Examples of the four main types of fonts—serif (a), sans serif (b), novelty (c) and monospace (d)—and a comparison of proportional and monospace fonts (e).   **Exhibit 6.5**

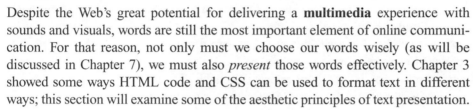

(a) Serif

(b) Sans Serif

(c) Novelty

(d) monospace

(e) slimming

slimming

shown in Exhibit 6.5(d). Compare the two lines in Exhibit 6.5(e): the top line shows the word *slimming* in Times New Roman font, while the second line shows the same word in monospace Courier New font. Notice how the letters in the top line are given differing amounts of horizontal space based on the width of the letter—a thin letter like "i" gets less space than "w" or "m." On the bottom line, each letter has an equal amount of total space; thus, two wide letters side by side are closer to each other than two thinner letters. Non-monospace fonts are called **proportional,** because the spacing given to each letter is proportional to the letter's width.

Serif fonts are by far the most popular for long passages of text in print media. In fact, you would probably have a hard time finding a newspaper or magazine in which the main body text was not set in some type of serif font. It is generally believed that the serifs on the letters subtly "guide" the eye from letter to letter and word to word, making it easier to read long text passages.

On the Web, the serifs on serif fonts are often lost because of the computer screen's low resolution as compared to print. Especially in small sizes, the serifs can begin to look jagged or disappear altogether. For that reason, sans serif fonts are used just as often for longer text passages on the Web. Novelty fonts should *never* be used for long text passages and, in fact, should probably never be used at all. Unless you have a really good reason—perhaps to achieve an artistic effect on a page's headline—you just shouldn't use novelty fonts. They are hard to read, and even though you may think they are clever, the user is likely to find them annoying. Similarly, monospace fonts are awkward to read because of the inconsistent spacing between letters and thus should also be avoided.

Another consideration in selecting fonts is what fonts are likely to be installed on your users' computers. If you specify a font on your Web page that is not installed on a user's computer, that user will see the text in a different font (which may throw off your page's formatting) or, worse, not see the text at all. Although technologies are being developed that will eventually overcome this problem by embedding the actual fonts in Web pages, for now you need to assume that your page will not properly display unless the font you specify is installed on the user's computer.

If you're in doubt about a certain font, it's a good idea to specify more than one. For example, HTML and CSS allow you to list multiple fonts, instructing the browser to display the text in the first font it finds installed on the user's computer. This is a good habit to develop, as it ensures that your pages will display as you intend them to on the maximum number of different computers. For example, specifying a font as "Times New Roman, Times, serif" allows computers with either Times New Roman or Times font installed to display the text properly. If neither font is available, the browser will try to choose an appropriate generic serif font, which may not be ideal but will be better than nothing. The formats for specifying multiple fonts in HTML and with CSS are

```
HTML:  <font face="Arial, Helvetica, sans-serif">
CSS:  {font-family: Arial, Helvetica, sans-serif}
```

Most authoring programs allow you to choose groups of fonts automatically.

The Times/Times New Roman (serif) and Helvetica/Arial (sans serif) font styles are by far the most popular ones used in Web pages. Either is appropriate for headlines, captions and body text. Verdana is also a popular sans serif font, because it is found on most PCs and Macintosh computers. Generally, you should use no more than two or three different font styles on any Web page; using too many fonts can give a page an undesirable "ransom note" effect.

Text Alignment

As discussed in Chapter 3, there are three main types of text alignment: **block left, block right** and **centered.** Generally, block left alignment is the best bet for long text passages. It is by far the easiest alignment to read on multiple lines, as you can probably see for yourself by attempting to read the different alignment samples shown in Exhibit 6.6. Centered text is suitable on occasion for headlines or subheads but should not be used for anything longer than a phrase or sentence. Block right alignment should be used even more sparingly, if ever.

A fourth type of alignment, **justified,** is available through CSS formatting (see Exhibit 6.6). Although perhaps the most popular alignment option in print, justified text is not used often on the Web. To make both the left and right margins line up, justified text inserts small spaces between words and letters; in print, these spaces are largely imperceptible to the reader, but with the computer screen's lower resolution, the spaces are often quite noticeable. Thus, use justified text sparingly on the Web, if at all.

Line Length

Another important consideration for text readability is **line length,** the horizontal length (width, actually) of text lines. Short line length can create an awkward ping-pong effect for the reader, as shown in Exhibit 6.7(a), while long line length makes it hard for the eye to follow all the way to the end of the line and then reenter the text in the proper place for the new line, as shown in Exhibit 6.7(b). A moderate line length, as shown in Exhibit 6.7(c), allows a more comfortable reading experience for the user.

Optimum line length is a factor of font size and style. Print designers generally say that the best line length for a given font and size is determined by typing "one and a half alphabets":

abcdefghijklmnopqrstuvwxyzabcdefghijklm

Exhibit 6.6   Text alignment options: block left (a), block right (b), centered (c) and justified (d).

(a)

In the 1960s, at the height of the Cold War, the United States
Department of Defense was looking for ways to create a decentralized communications system that would allow researchers and
government officials to communicate with one another in the
event of a nuclear attack.

(b)

In the 1960s, at the height of the Cold War, the United States
Department of Defense was looking for ways to create a decentralized communications system that would allow researchers and
government officials to communicate with one another in the
event of a nuclear attack.

(c)

In the 1960s, at the height of the Cold War, the United States
Department of Defense was looking for ways to create a decentralized communications system that would allow researchers and
government officials to communicate with one another in the
event of a nuclear attack.

(d)

In the 1960s, at the height of the Cold War, the United States
Department of Defense was looking for ways to create a decentralized communications system that would allow researchers and
government officials to communicate with one another in the event
of a nuclear attack.

The length created by typing these 39 letters is considered the best line length for readability. You can use this same technique for online work. Similarly, using the rule of thumb of 10 to 12 words per line will achieve a similarly efficient line length. Remember, line length doesn't *always* have to be the absolute optimum—doing so would severely limit page design options—but it should not go too far one way or the other, especially for longer text passages.

Examples of line length that is too short (a), too long (b) and about right (c).   **Exhibit 6.7**

(a)

In the 1960s, at the height
of the Cold War, the United
States Department of
Defense was looking for ways
to create a decentralized
communications system that
would allow researchers
and government officials
to communicate with one
another in the event of a
nuclear attack.

(b)

In the 1960s, at the height of the Cold War, the United States Department of Defense was
looking for ways to create a decentralized communications system that would allow
researchers and government officials to communicate with one another in the event of a
nuclear attack.

(c)

In the 1960s, at the height of the Cold War, the United States
Department of Defense was looking for ways to create a decentralized
communications system that would allow researchers and government
officials to communicate with one another in the event of a nuclear
attack.

Text Techniques to Avoid

A few text-related design issues are fine for print but should not be used on the
Web. First, avoid line-to-line hyphenation on Web pages because hyphenated
words stretching over two lines are difficult to read online. It's OK to use hyphenated words, such as *top-notch* or *world-class,* just not words that are hyphenated
over two lines. Second, avoid the use of underlining, except for links. On the Web,

On the Web

More information and resources on using text, including font samples and the history of fonts: Under Chapter 6, select **Using Text.**

users have come to expect that anything underlined is a link; thus, they are disappointed when they click a nonlinked underlined word and nothing happens. Finally, avoid italicized text as much as possible. Italicized text tends to look "jaggy" on-screen and thus is both sloppy looking and difficult to read. It is still OK to use italics for such items as book or movie titles and the occasional subhead or pull quote, but you should avoid setting any long text passages in italics.

USING COLOR AND GRAPHICS

Color and graphics can be important design tools for creating visually interesting Web pages. Unfortunately—especially in the hands of amateur designers—they can be overused or used improperly, actually harming the overall attractiveness and usefulness of a page. Used judiciously, however, color and graphics can create a more engaging and compelling experience for the Web page user.

Color Considerations

Colors should be selected based on their relationship to one another and to the Web page's intent. Most journalistic Web pages choose relatively subdued color schemes, in keeping with their overall mission of providing serious, important information. Splashes of bold color may appear in logos, nameplates or ancillary parts of the page, but overall journalistic Web pages are free of splashy color.

Color combinations are particularly important when it comes to text display. Although readability studies have shown that nothing is easier to read than black text on a white background, light background colors occasionally can work well. Also, judicious use of color for the text itself can create emphasis, such as the accepted practice of making linked text blue. When selecting colors for text and backgrounds, make sure high contrast exists between the text color and the background color: normally, a dark color for the text and a light color for the background. If the contrast is insufficient, as shown in Exhibit 6.8(a), the text will be difficult to read. Similarly, as shown in Exhibit 6.8(b) poorly chosen background graphics on Web pages can make text difficult to read.

Although literally thousands of colors are available on a typical computer, for Web design you should constrain yourself to the so-called **browser-safe palette.** This group of 216 colors is recognized by both Macintosh and PC platforms, so it will display properly on both machines. Most authoring programs allow you to select your colors directly from the browser-safe palette. Using colors outside this palette can lead to improper display on certain computers.

Poor color contrast (a) and distracting backgrounds (b) can make text difficult to read.   **Exhibit 6.8**

(a)

New Stadium Approved

(b)

Couldn't find a place to park today? You're not the only one...

by Steve Saxon

She sits and she waits. Her eyes dart back and forth; she is looking for the perfect opportunity. She makes her move and breathes a sigh of relief. She finally got it.

It sounds like Jenger Downey is playing in a heated match of checkers or chess. But no, those games pale in comparison to her challenge. Downey is trying to find a parking spot on the Bowling Green State University campus.

Graphics and Storage Space

As noted in Chapter 2, the two most popular graphic formats used on the Web are **GIF** and **JPEG.** GIF is particularly well-suited to high-contrast artwork (such as logos), while JPEG usually works best for images with subtle tonal variations (such as photographs). Either format will work for any type of image, but the key consideration is making the graphic take up the least amount of storage space possible so it will download quickly.

A graphics program such as Adobe Photoshop allows you to create, manipulate and save graphic images in different formats. Although a comprehensive tutorial on using graphics programs is beyond the scope of this chapter, we will discuss some basic functions that can help make graphic images as small (in terms of storage space) as possible.

After an image has been scanned on a scanner or created with a digital camera or other device, it can then be opened in a graphics program. All images should be properly cropped, or cut, so that only the most compelling part remains. **Cropping** is itself something of an art form, carrying over from print journalism, where photographers used to actually cut their photographs by hand. In most cases, however, cropping is fairly straightforward: You want to make sure you preserve the essence of what's important in the photograph, but no more. This is especially critical on the Web, where the additional, unneeded parts of the picture will take up space and slow the download times. For example, Exhibit 6.9(a) shows a photograph with extraneous information around the edges. In Exhibit 6.9(b), the image is opened in Photoshop and the portion to keep is "boxed in" using the program's selection tool. Once the part to keep is selected, choosing the Image > Crop menu selection instructs the program to discard the outer area, leaving the image shown in Exhibit 6.9(c).

Exhibit 6.9 A photograph with extraneous information (a) can be opened in a graphics program (b) and cropped (c).

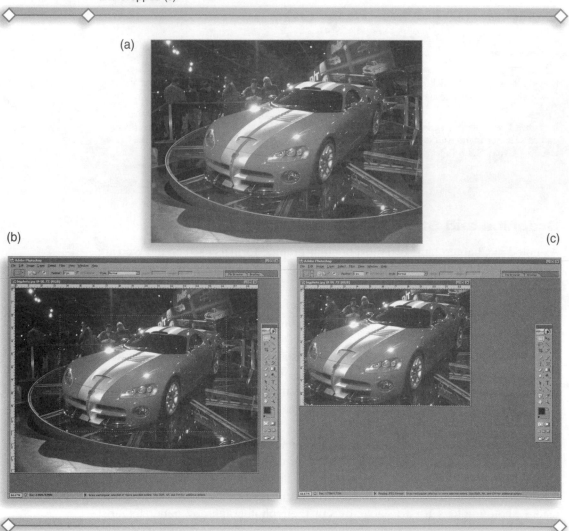

(a)

(b)

(c)

You also want to properly set the image's resolution, or level of detail, measured in **pixels per inch (ppi).** At higher resolutions, an image has more detail but also consumes more storage space. In print, images are usually created in at least 600 ppi resolution, but for Web work there is no need for resolution above 72 ppi, since that is the highest available screen resolution on all types of computers. As shown in Exhibit 6.10, in Photoshop you can set the image's resolution in the Image Size dialog box, accessed under the Image menu. You should also use the Image Size dialog box to set the image's dimensions appropriately for how it will appear on the finished Web page. Rarely are images—even dramatic and compelling photos—displayed on online journalism Web pages any larger than about 3 inches by 3 inches, and most images are closer to 2 inches by 2 inches. Remember, storage space (and subsequently, download time) is always a key consideration.

Viewing an image's resolution and size information in Adobe Photoshop. **Exhibit 6.10**

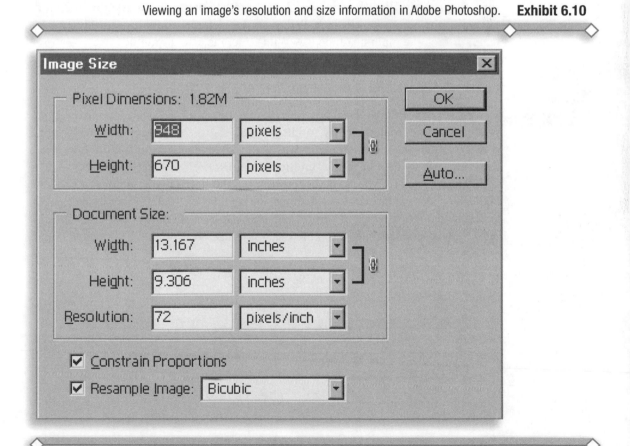

Adobe product screen shot reprinted with permission from Adobe Systems Incorporated.

Graphic Design Elements

In addition to helping to tell stories visually, graphics can be used online to enliven the design of Web pages. The nytimes.com, CNN.com and ESPN.com Web pages shown earlier in the chapter provide several examples. The CNN page, for example, uses small graphics for the tabs on the lower half of the page and for several buttons ("Search," "Push," "Personalize" and "Vote").

Since the text formatting capabilities of HTML are limited (even when using CSS), creating special textual effects often requires that text be converted to a graphic element. This takes up more storage space (remember, a graphic takes much longer to download than text), but it is sometimes necessary to properly display a textual logo or other element. In Exhibit 6.2, for example, the names of all three Web sites are actually graphics. On the ESPN page, in fact, the main headline ("A Wild Ride") is also a graphic.

On the Web

More on colors and the browser-safe palette, Adobe Photoshop and other graphics programs and text graphics:
Under Chapter 6, select **Color and Graphics.**

USING TABLES TO DESIGN WEB PAGES

We know that HTML was not initially intended for advanced page design. Because it was created chiefly to allow scientists to share their research papers over computer lines, little thought was given to advanced design issues, such as the ability to divide a page into multiple columns.

A feature that HTML *did* have, however, was the ability to create **tables,** or charts to display technical information, as shown in Exhibit 6.11. A table allows a Web page to be divided into sections of vertical columns and horizontal rows, with the content in each table **cell** separated from the other sections. Over time, HTML's table com-

Exhibit 6.11   An HTML table used to format a technical chart.

	Ferrari Stradale	Ford GT	Porsche 911 GT3
Engine Type	DOHC V-8	DOHC V-8	DOHC Flat 6
Displacement	219 cu. in.	330 cu. in.	220 cu. in.
Power (hp @ rpm)	425 @ 8500	500 @ 6000	380 @ 7400
Torque (lb-ft @ rpm)	274 @ 4750	500 @ 4500	284 @ 5000

mands have evolved to allow not just these square-grid charts but more advanced page formatting. Thus, tables have become an important tool for page design.

Because the HTML coding for tables is quite cumbersome, this section will discuss creating tables using an authoring program. You *can* write the HTML for tables by hand, but the actual process can be quite arcane. Rather than spending a lot of time dealing with HTML table commands, it would be better to focus on the results we can achieve. Using an authoring program, in this case Macromedia Dreamweaver, will allow us to do this.

Before we look at tables, however, we should first briefly address **frames,** another HTML feature that allows the browser window to be divided into different sections. The advantage of frames is that they actually allow different sections of the window to scroll and change independently, as shown in Exhibit 6.12. However, the actual HTML implementation of frames is a bit shaky, and they are quite difficult to make work correctly. The most common criticism of frames, for instance, is that they make it difficult for users to accurately bookmark and return to a page with frames later. Relatively few online journalism sites use frames, and—for our purposes— frames allow few, if any, formatting effects that tables cannot provide. For that reason, this chapter does not address the use of frames for Web pages.

Frames allow individual portions of a browser window to be scrolled independently of one another.   **Exhibit 6.12**

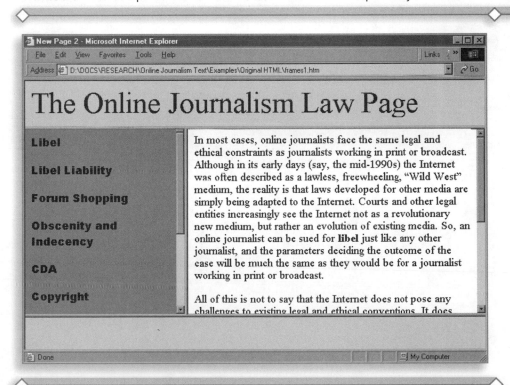

Creating Tables

A table has three basic characteristics: overall size, number of rows and number of columns. A table's size can be set either as an absolute value (for example, 600 pixels wide by 400 pixels high) or as a percentage (for example, 98 percent). A table set as an absolute value will always be the same size regardless of the size of the user's browser window. A table set as a percentage will change size to fit the user's browser window size. The effect of this difference is shown in Exhibit 6.13.

Exhibit 6.13 The effect of changing the browser size for tables set as a percentage (80 percent) and as an absolute value (600 pixels). In (a), the table set as a percentage is shown in two different browser sizes; in (b), the table set in pixels is shown in two different browser sizes.

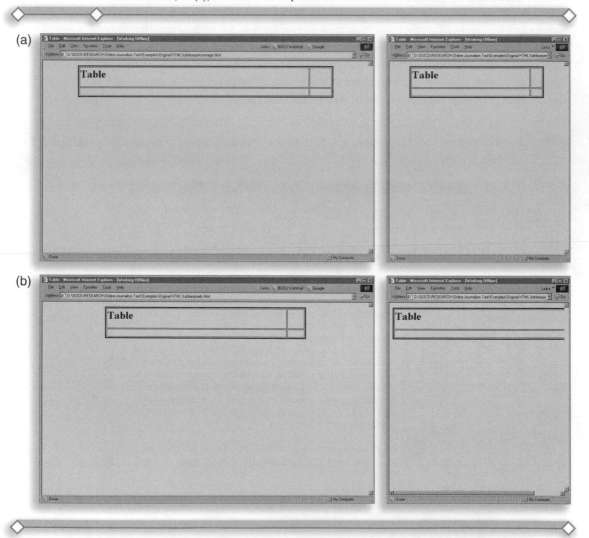

Generally, you are better off setting the table width as an absolute value; your page's design will be at the mercy of each individual user's browser window size if you don't. As long as you set your table for no wider than 750 pixels, as discussed previously in this chapter, you shouldn't have to worry about it fitting in the majority of users' browser windows.

A table is created in Dreamweaver by using the menu command Insert >Table. That brings up the main table **dialog box,** as shown in Exhibit 6.14. This box allows you to set the basic attributes of the table, including number of rows, number of columns and width (either in pixels or as a percentage). It also allows you

Dreamweaver's main table creation dialog box. **Exhibit 6.14**

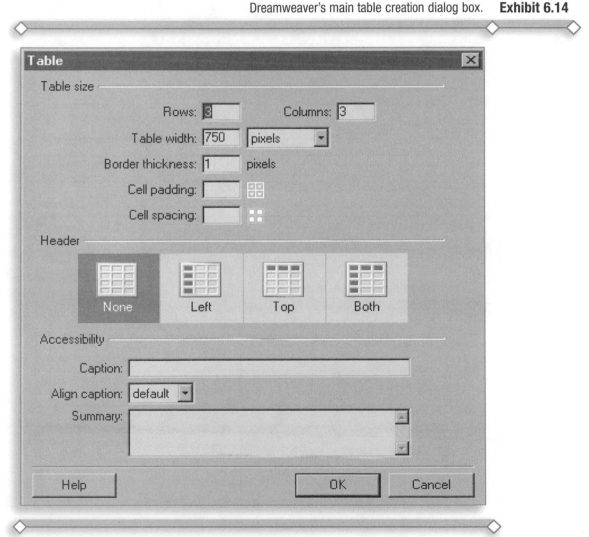

to set the **cell padding** (the space between the cell's content and the cell's border) and **cell spacing** (the space between individual cells). Exhibit 6.15 shows the effects of these two settings. The border setting allows us to set the width of the visual border that will appear between individual cells, as shown in Exhibit 6.16.

As discussed in Chapter 3, Dreamweaver's Properties window can be a valuable tool for using the program. This is true with tables as well. Exhibit 6.17(a) shows the parts of the Properties window with a table selected, while Exhibit 6.17(b) shows the Properties window with an individual cell selected.

Exhibit 6.15 Examples of changing cell padding and cell spacing values. In (a), the cell padding is set to 10 and the cell spacing is set to 0. In (b), the cell padding is set to 0 and the cell spacing is set to 10.

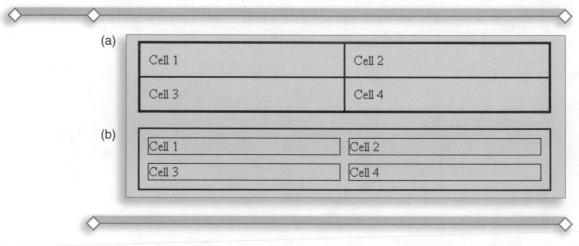

Exhibit 6.16 Different border sizes in HTML tables.

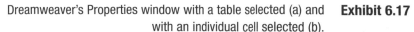

Dreamweaver's Properties window with a table selected (a) and **Exhibit 6.17**
with an individual cell selected (b).

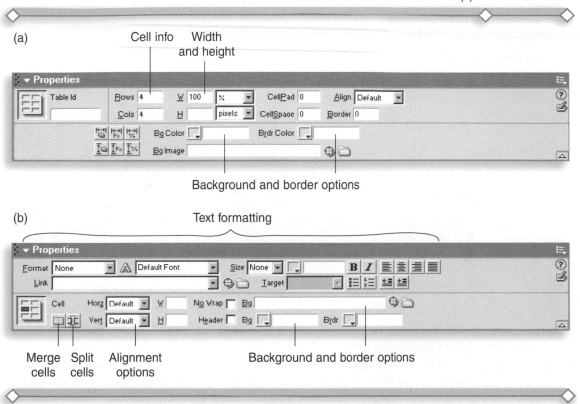

Copyright © 1995–2004 Macromedia Inc. Reprinted with permission.

Creating a Page Layout Grid

Tables can be an extremely valuable design element. They allow you to set up an online page design that can mimic pretty closely any kind of design you could do in print. However, if you're used to working with print layout programs, such as QuarkXPress or Adobe InDesign, you need to change your thinking a bit. Those print-based programs usually allow you to position items in different areas by simply placing them where you want them on the page. When using tables in HTML, you have to think more in terms of design "boxes," or containers where you will put different content items. Designing a page with tables is a lot like setting up a grid or scaffolding system—you create the outlines of the content areas, then place the content itself within those areas.

Let's say that we wanted to create a relatively simple page layout design like that shown in Exhibit 6.18. As you can see, the page will have a nameplate across the top, a navigation bar on the left side, a main content window next to it and a

Exhibit 6.18 A simple page layout design to be created using a table.

NAMEPLATE		
NAVIGATION BAR	MAIN CONTENT AREA	SIDEBAR

sidebar column to the right. You'll recognize this basic page design as typical of online journalism pages discussed earlier in this chapter.

We are going to create a table with two rows and three columns as our starting point for the page design. We want to make our page 750 pixels wide with no spacing between the cells. Also, we want the table's border to be invisible, thus making the table itself invisible. This is the normal procedure when using tables for page layout: We don't want the structure of the table to be visible to the user. The border lines would merely be distracting and sloppy looking. To create the initial table, we enter information in the Table dialog box as shown in Exhibit 6.19.

When we press "OK," Dreamweaver creates the table on the page as shown in Exhibit 6.20. By default, Dreamweaver creates all tables with equally sized cells. So, right now it doesn't look much like our finished design, but it's a start.

Next, we will make the columns the proper widths. Looking at our page design, let's say we want the left column (with the navigation information) to be 150 pixels wide and the middle (main content) column to be 350 pixels wide. That will leave somewhere around 250 pixels for the sidebar. To create this layout, we hold the **mouse** button and drag over the two leftmost cells to select them, as shown in Exhibit 6.21(a). Then, in Dreamweaver's Properties window (Exhibit 6.21(b)), we type in 150 for width. The table will then redraw, as shown in Exhibit 6.21(c). Then, we hold our mouse button and drag over the middle column's cells to highlight them and set their width to 350. That will

Information entered in the Table dialog box to create the basic table for Exhibit 6.20. **Exhibit 6.19**

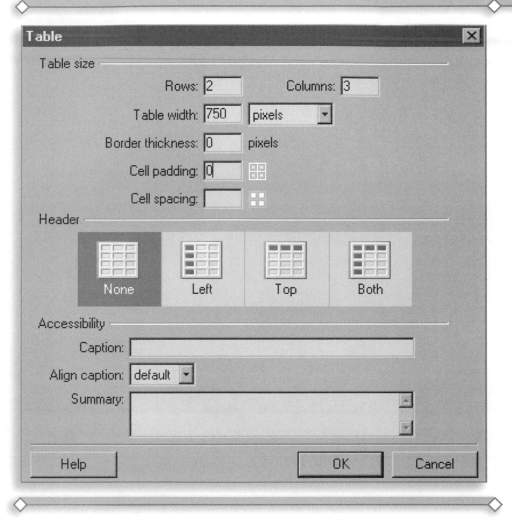

Copyright © 1995–2004 Macromedia Inc. Reprinted with permission.

create a table like the one in Exhibit 6.21(d). Now it's looking much closer to what we want.

We next need to make the nameplate across the top into a single cell that spans the entire width of the table. To do this, we hold the mouse button and drag over the two top cells to select them, as shown in Exhibit 6.22(a), and then click the "Merge Cells" icon in the Properties window, as shown in Exhibit 6.22(b). This will create the table shown in Exhibit 6.22(c). Now, we want to set the height of this nameplate to 100 pixels. We drag our mouse over the top cell to highlight

Exhibit 6.20   The basic table created by Dreamweaver.

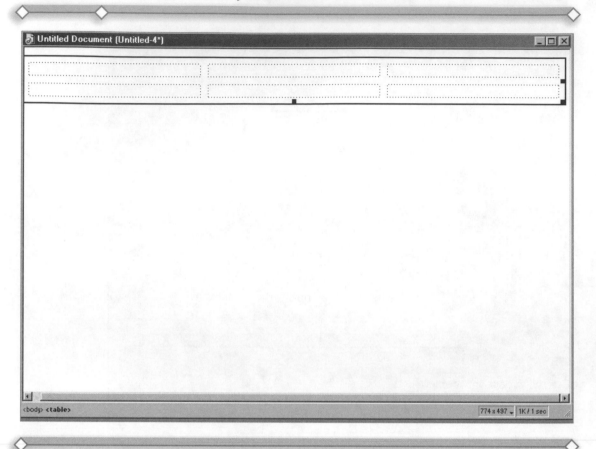

it and then type 100 for height in the properties window. That gives us the "finished" table shown in Exhibit 6.22(d).

This table could then become the basis for an online journalism story page, as shown in Exhibit 6.23. We have added content to each cell and given the left navigation cell a background color using the Properties window. It is also important when putting content in tables to set the vertical alignment to "Top" (see Exhibit 6.17b). Otherwise, the default is for the content to appear in the middle of the cell.

Be aware that once you have a table on the page, Dreamweaver still works the same way as it does without tables. The difference is that, in this case, each piece of content is contained within one of the table's cells. You can click the mouse inside one of the cells and insert a graphic, type text or paste something from

With the two leftmost cells highlighted (a), a new width can be entered in the Properties **Exhibit 6.21**
window (b) to change the width of the cells (c). The same process is used to change the
width of the middle column (d).

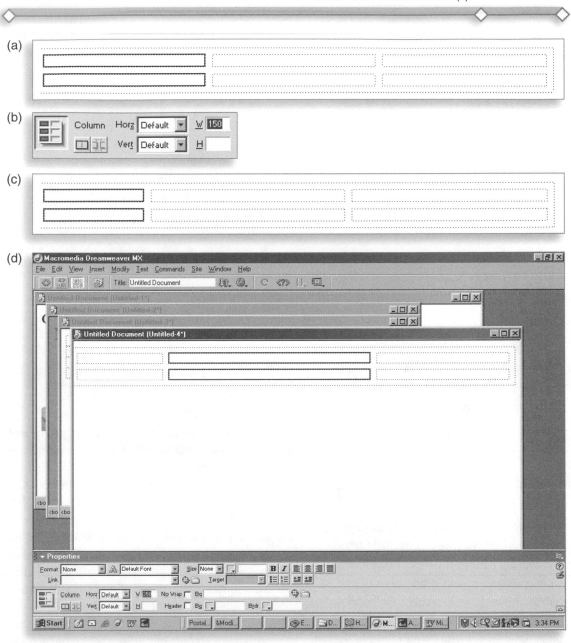

Exhibit 6.22 After highlighting the top two cells (a), the "Merge Cells" icon (b) is clicked, creating a single cell (c). The height of the cell is then set (d).

(a)

(b) merge cells icon

(c)

(d)

somewhere else. Note that when text is placed inside a table cell, its alignment properties now apply in regard to the cell, not to the overall page. For example, if you type text in a cell as shown in Exhibit 6.24(a) and then center it, it will appear as in Exhibit 6.24(b). The text is centered within the cell, not on the page itself. Using a table is also a good way to set your line length to an optimal level: Text will be constrained within the width of the cell containing it. Exhibit 6.25 shows how a block of text's line length is constrained by various cell widths.

Tables can be used to do much more with page layout, but these are the basics. It's a good idea to experiment with tables on your own so you can achieve the layout

On the Web

More information on using tables for page design, using Dreamweaver to create tables and making sure your tables will work well in various browsers. Also, a tutorial on using CSS positioning features to create page designs. Plus, why people hate frames:
Under Chapter 6, select **Using Tables to Design Web Pages.**

The finished table with content added.   **Exhibit 6.23**

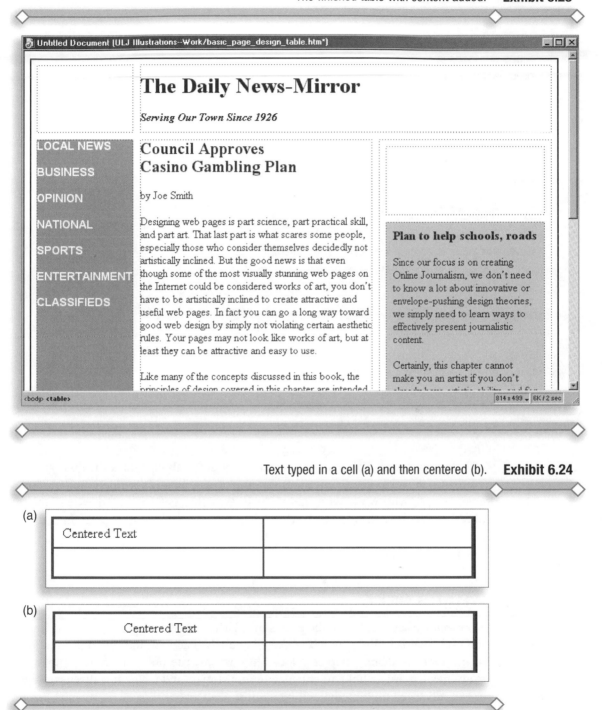

Text typed in a cell (a) and then centered (b).   **Exhibit 6.24**

(a)

Centered Text	

(b)

Centered Text	

Exhibit 6.25 Using various cell widths to constrain the line length of text.

(a)

Since our focus is on creating Online Journalism, we don't need to know a lot about innovative or envelope-pushing design theories.

(b)

Since our focus is on creating Online Journalism, we don't need to know a lot about innovative or envelope-pushing design theories.

(c)

Since our focus is on creating Online Journalism, we don't need to know a lot about innovative or envelope-pushing design theories.

effects you desire. You can find several resources about tables on this book's Web site. A word of warning, though: Tables can be a bit temperamental, and even people who work with them every day often get frustrated when tables don't act the way they should. Also, always test your layout designs in different browsers and on different computers (see "Many Browsers, One Page: The Dream of Web Design").

WHAT'S NEXT

Now that we have looked at the basics of HTML and design and the ways of finding information online, the next three chapters will address the actual production of online journalism. Chapter 7 looks at how to write online stories, Chapter 8 examines the use of links to enhance online stories, and Chapter 9 discusses the use of advanced multimedia and interactive elements.

Many Browsers, One Page

The Dream of Web Design

In a perfect world, we could design our Web page as we wanted it and then be confident that it would look exactly the same no matter what type of browser or computer our users had. Of course, we don't live in a perfect world, and nagging browser differences remain a fact of life for Web designers.

Things *have* gotten a little better, however, and the latest versions of Microsoft Internet Explorer and Apple Safari are more comparable in terms of page display than they've ever been. Still, because you can't assume that every user has the latest version, you have to consider the previous versions of these browsers as well. Netscape Navigator, for example, is rapidly fading as a front-line browser, yet it is still installed on many machines.

The main problems among browsers tend to involve text sizing and tables. Text sizing conventions vary widely among browsers and between PCs and Macs. Tables that appear perfect on Internet Explorer might be a mess in Netscape Navigator. Most of these problems come about not because browser makers don't follow the HTML standards, but because they implement them differently or have different default settings. That said, however, early versions of Navigator were pretty bad at displaying tables.

One way to improve browser compatibility is to specify settings whenever possible. For example, rather than leaving cell padding and cell spacing settings blank, set them to 0 if that's what you want. If you leave the settings blank, one browser might assume you want 0 but another one might think you want 10. When it comes to fonts, specifying specific sizes in pixels is the most certain way to make your text the same size in as many browsers as possible.

CSS formatting and the continuing separation of content and presentation will help matters. It will also make it easier to design a single Web page that will look good not only in all the standard browsers but also on handheld devices such as cell phones and on television screens. Through the use of **browser sniffing** (as discussed in Chapter 3), you can detect what kind of browser the user has and reformat your content accordingly.

For now, the best thing to do is make sure you test your Web pages on various browsers and types of computers. You can also keep abreast of the latest steps forward (and backward) in browser compatibility by checking the resources on this chapter's Web page.

Activities

6.1 Take a look at 10 online journalism sites of your choosing. How many of them use the basic design structure discussed at the beginning of this chapter? How do they modify the basic structure to create their own "personality"?

6.2 Analyze one of your favorite online journalism sites in terms of unity, contrast, hierarchy and consistency. How (and how well) does it follow these principles?

6.3 Try to re-create the page design of one of your favorite online journalism sites using tables. Don't worry about the content; just see if you can re-create the grid used in the site.

ENDNOTE

1. Andrew DeVigal, "Putting the Eyetrack Study to Good Use," July 12, 2000, http://poynter.org/content/content_view.asp?id=38357 (accessed November 4, 2003).

CHAPTER 7

GOALS

- To provide an overview of writing for online media

- To show how elements of journalism and story forms for other media can apply to online journalism

- To introduce the concept of "scanning" online material and discuss how to write and present stories to facilitate scanning

- To discuss online story forms that take advantage of the medium's unique characteristics

- To show how online stories can be updated with new information

WRITING AND EDITING ONLINE

Despite all of the bells, whistles and media forms available to the online journalist, the written word is still the heart of online journalism. When you consider the graphics, video and other media available on the Web, it is easy to lose sight of the fact that text is still what brings these various media together and makes them meaningful. "Surprise!" *Editor and Publisher* magazine announced after a study of how people use online journalism sites. "Words rule the Web."[1]

And words are likely to continue to rule the Web in the future. Despite the predictions that "newspapers are dead" and "books are irrelevant," people grow up reading from both print and electronic sources, and when they come to an Internet site, they expect to find words along with other media. Although, as the old saying goes, a picture is sometimes worth a thousand words, it usually takes more than just visual information to tell a story. The online journalist, like the print journalist and broadcast journalist before her, must still be a master of the word.

And just as in previous media, writing online is part science and part art. Online journalists must still know the rules of grammar and know how to spell; a mistake in either is just as embarrassing and damaging to a journalist's credibility online as it is in print. Online journalists also must understand the aesthetic principles that underlie online writing, even though those principles are still somewhat in flux. Finally, the "old" rules of journalism—including **fairness, attribution, accuracy, relevance** and **newness**—are still pertinent (see Chapter 1). While the medium may have changed, the online journalist still has much in common with his print and broadcast brethren.

But there are some considerations unique to online writing. First, technical aspects of the medium itself affect how we write for it, most importantly the fact that the **resolution** of a computer screen is much lower than that of a printed page. Online writing must also conform to, and at best take advantage of, the fact that the user can control information online. Finally, online's ability to be constantly and quickly updated means that stories often are not "finished" when they are posted online; instead, they must be written so that they can be updated with new information as events warrant.

This chapter offers an introduction to writing journalistic stories online. Just as this book in general is designed to take what you already know about journalism and apply it to a new medium, this chapter is designed to build on what you already know about writing for print or broadcast. Indeed, in many ways, online writing is a hybrid form of print and broadcast styles.

As you already know, many forms of online journalism exist, and the medium can be used in countless ways to tell journalistic stories. The forms of online writing are continually evolving as journalists experiment with new story forms and new ways of writing, but this chapter will examine the basic form used in the vast majority of current online stories as well as some ways to enhance it. That form is based around a primary textual story, often called the **main story.** The main story can either stand on its own or be supplemented with other types of media and other stories. This chapter will use principles and examples to show how these stories are written.

The following two chapters, which address using links and other media online, will then build on these writing principles. The use of links and other media can either supplement a main story or create an entirely new form of online story.

WRITING FOR THE ONLINE READER

Web **usability** expert Jakob Nielsen began his 1997 article "How Users Read on the Web" by saying simply, "They don't."[2] Instead of reading, Nielsen says, most online users **scan** pages, picking out individual words and other points of interest. Users scan instead of reading largely because of the computer screen's low resolution as compared to paper. Reading something from a computer screen takes longer and is more tiring to the eyes than reading the same information from a well-printed piece of paper. Studies by Nielsen and others have shown that reading from a computer screen is about 25 percent slower than reading from paper. You may experience this yourself when doing online research: You probably find yourself printing a lot of the on-screen information so you can read it more easily.

The resolution issues become even more pronounced as we consider other methods of consuming online information. The television screen has even lower resolution than the computer screen, so people who use their televisions to consume online media will have an even harder time reading. And handheld devices such as **PDAs (portable digital assistants)** and cellular phones are *much* lower in resolution than even television screens. These kinds of devices can display only a little information at a time and even that—at least compared to a printed page or even a full-size computer screen—not very well.

The news is not all bad, however. People *will* read online information if it is written well and takes into account the limitations of the medium. Although people may never read online text at the same level of detail that they read printed material, a need still exists for thoughtful, structured and elegant online writing (see "Story Structures" on p. 148). You can do a number of things in writing and presenting your online material to encourage thoughtful scanning and reading by the user.

Short Sentences and Paragraphs

Concise writing, a trait of good journalism in general, is particularly important online. Sentences should be kept simple and straightforward, and paragraph breaks should be used liberally. Short sentences aid scanning, as do short paragraphs with spacing between them.

Sentences online should be relatively short on average and ideally should be in the form SUBJECT > VERB > OBJECT. This encourages the use of active verbs, in which the subject performs the action: "The mayor vetoed the proposal." Sentences written like this are easier to read and understand than passive sentences: "The proposal was vetoed by the mayor." Complex sentences, with too many words and clauses, are much harder to comprehend, especially when scanned. If you find yourself using a lot of commas, semicolons and other punctuation (other than the period) in your online writing, you probably need to edit. Break complex sentences down into several simpler sentences, for example.

Exhibit 7.1(a) shows the lead of a hypothetical story. It is written in a style typical of that often used in print or in wire copy. For use on the Web, however, the lead crams in too much information. Instead of providing a single main point, this lead attempts to deliver three separate pieces of information: (1) that authorities are on heightened alert for terrorist attacks; (2) that police arrested a man with an assault rifle in his luggage; and (3) that the incident led to the closing of one of the airport's terminals. It also contains too many details: the fact that the

Exhibit 7.1   Lead written for a print or wire story (a) and rewritten for the Web (b).

(a)

With authorities on high alert for potential terrorist attacks, police today arrested a German man with an assault rifle in his luggage soon after he arrived at London's Heathrow Airport, prompting the evacuation of one of the airport's terminals.

(b)

Police have arrested a man with an assault rifle in his luggage at London's Heathrow Airport.

The arrest led to the evacuation of one of the airport's terminals, as authorities are on heightened alert for terrorist attacks.

man was German and that he was arrested soon after he arrived. These bits of information can easily be given later in the story.

Instead, the lead can be broken into two sentences, as shown in Exhibit 7.1(b). Now, the lead itself gives the main point of the story, and the following sentence fills in some of the less important information. The rest of the story would continue to fill in information. This improves readability by making each sentence (and paragraph) shorter, eliminating unnecessary information and providing space between paragraphs.

Subheads and Bolding

Brief, descriptive subheads can also aid scanning. Subheads can be used to signal a new topic, or a new portion of the online story, just as they do in print. Exhibit 7.2 shows an example from MSNBC.com that uses subheads to break up a relatively long story. The story is about treating spring allergies, and the subheads help signal the main topics that make up the story. They also are displayed in a bold font to make them stand out even more.

Ideally, subheads should be simple and descriptive, avoiding "cute" language or wordplay that requires deciphering on the part of the reader. In a few words—say, three to seven—the subhead should simply and explicitly tell the reader what the next part of the story is. The example in Exhibit 7.2 has four main parts (although only the first two are visible in the screen shot), and the subheads help signal to the reader what's coming next: "Pinpointing the Trigger" (figuring out exactly what causes your allergy symptoms), "Finding the Proper Combination" (deciding what medications work best for your allergies), "Inhaled Steroids" (advantages and disadvantages of these common prescription treatments, and "Alternative Treatments" (natural, non-prescription allergy remedies).

This story from MSNBC.com uses subheads to divide its main parts.   **Exhibit 7.2**

Story Structures

A good story must be well-organized. What is happening in the story must be clear to the reader/listener/user at all times. In fact, if a story is clearly organized, the person who reads it should never have to think about its organization—it should just flow naturally.

Story organization should begin before you write the first word. Before you can write a story, you have to have it clearly organized in your mind, knowing what you are going to include in the story and when. Although it may seem obvious, you have to ask and answer the question "What is this story *about?*" before you can begin to write it. Most stories have one or two main points, with the remainder of the story consisting of supporting information and background.

Several basic ways to structure journalistic stories have emerged over time, some of which also work well online. These structures are **inverted pyramid, chronological, narrative** and **thematic.**

After reading his obituary in a newspaper, early-20th-century humorist Mark Twain remarked that "reports of my demise are premature." The same might be said for the inverted pyramid story structure.

An inverted pyramid story is organized so that the most important information appears at the beginning of the story in the lead. As the story proceeds, the information becomes pro-gressively less important. The basic who, what, where, when, why and how information usually comes first, with supporting and background information later. Although many people see the inverted pyramid as something of a dinosaur, the fact is that it still works pretty well, especially online. Having the most important information at the very beginning of a story helps draw scanning users in, encouraging them to slow down and actually *read.*

If the important points of a story take place over a span of time, a chronological structure might be appropriate. A chronological story tells what happened in the order it happened. In practice, however, most chronological stories *begin* by giving the outcome of the story and then back up to tell the story from the beginning. For example, in telling the story of a daylong hostage situation, you would begin the story by saying that all of the hostages were rescued and that the hostage taker was in custody, *then* back up to the beginning and tell what happened chronologically. Once again, this structure achieves the effect of having a strong lead with important information likely to draw in scanning eyes.

The narrative structure uses vivid descriptions of people and places to "set scenes" and involve the reader the way a novel or short story might. For example, an award-winning story on salon.com that told of the more than 300

Story Structures, *continued*

women who had been murdered in a small Mexican town begins:

> The body of another murdered woman was found late last month in the Mexican industrial hub of Ciudad Juarez, dumped behind some shrubs in the squalor of the Anapra neighborhood, a ramshackle hodgepodge of corrugated tin and cardboard shacks on the sludge-washed banks of the Rio Grande. Her hands had been tied, and the evidence suggested she had been raped. The body was so badly decomposed that investigators calculated that she'd been dead for seven months.

Throughout the story, the writer uses such vivid descriptions, interspersed with factual data, to help involve the reader.

The narrative structure must be used cautiously online. Since users tend to scan rather than read, it can be difficult to draw them into a story using the narrative's indirect-lead approach. In order to work, online narrative structures must be compelling and must not become *too* literary. Narrative forms, such as the one above, can work, but only if skillfully executed.

The thematic story addresses various aspects of a complex story one by one. For example, a story of several local government figures involved in an organized crime scandal might address the main participants one by one. Thematic stories are particularly well-suited to **chunking,** as discussed later in this chapter, because the various parts of the story can be divided up and (usually) read in any order.

On the Web

More about online story structures, including the history (and future) of the inverted pyramid:
Under Chapter 7, select **Story Structures.**

Words displayed in bold text can be used in the body of a story as well. Just as in print, such bold words tend to attract the reader's attention, especially when he is scanning. However, this type of bolding is not often used in online stories because it can get distracting very easily. Exhibit 7.3 shows some text in which "information-heavy" words have been bolded in an attempt to aid scanning. As you can see, the scanning benefits are probably outweighed by the overall distraction of all of the bolded words scattered throughout the text. However, some sites often bold the opening paragraph of a story, which can aid scanning by drawing the eye immediately to the most important part of the story.

Exhibit 7.3   Too many bolded words can distract users.

> Yet **journalism** that does **not** pursue such lofty goals can still be **valuable** and **effective.** For a **democracy** to **function properly,** citizens **need** to be **informed** about the **day-to-day** and **continuing issues** that **influence** them. **People** want to **know** about the things that affect—or will affect—their lives **financially, socially** and **in other ways.** Thus, **journalism** that addresses **school vouchers, real estate tax hearings** or **city council meetings** serves an important purpose. To a **lesser** degree, **entertainment** or **sports journalism** also has value, although, unfortunately, **some** of what is practiced in **these areas** more closely resembles **promotion** than **traditional journalism.**

Bullet Points and Lists

When a story involves several important points, or when it lists a group of items, bulleted lists can make the information more scannable. In addition, bulleted lists create spacing and breaks that help readers quickly digest the main points.

Bulleted lists can be particularly effective at the beginning of a story by giving an overview of its main parts. In fact, portions of the bulleted text could be made into links that would take the user directly to each portion of the story. For example, a story about the mayor's announced plans to ease the city's deficit might begin with an explanatory sentence and then include the following bullet points:

- Property taxes to increase
- Curbside recycling eliminated
- 50 city workers to lose jobs

The rest of the story would go on to describe these changes in the order listed. The user could scan the main points of the story to decide whether she wanted to read the entire story.

Ordered lists (those that use numbers instead of bullets) also can be used, although only in cases where the order of items is important. The list of the top 10 finishers in a spelling bee would be one example, or a list of the five most livable cities as ranked by a national magazine. However, in the majority of cases, a bulleted list is preferable to a numbered list.

Voice

The Web offers great potential for creativity, despite the suggestions to shorten, simplify and structure your writing.

For years, critics have said that the basic journalistic form has become too formal and too impersonal. They say that traditional journalism has no human "voice" but is instead mostly cold and clinical. Despite the fact that journalists (especially broadcast journalists) are taught to "write more like people really talk," the average newspaper article reads very little like typical conversation.

Now, online journalism is emerging in forms that do give voice to journalists, allowing them to express personality and write more informally. Perhaps the most extreme example of this is the rise of **blogs,** which (as discussed in Chapter 4) allow the writer to express himself more informally. However, many other online sites are finding that it's

> ### On the Web
>
> More from usability guru Jakob Nielsen and others, resources for online writing and the debate over whether "voice" is a good thing for journalism:
>
> Under Chapter 7, select **Writing for the Online Reader**

sometimes OK to be "edgy." For example, consider this lead from slate.com's Dan Crane in a story about so-called "healthy" fast food: "Be it hangover cure, road-trip fuel, or lunchtime guilty pleasure, I have always been a sucker for salty, greasy, finger-lickin'-good, run-for-the-border-to-have-it-my-way fast food."

The Web's ability to serve niche audiences also provides an opportunity for putting voice in stories. **Dayparting** and other targeted content can allow journalists to be a bit less formal in their writing. For example, if your Web site is less hard-news oriented in the evening or on weekends, you can probably write in a less formal tone. Despite users' preference for scanning content, edgy writing—when done well—also can succeed online.

TEXT-BASED ONLINE STORY FORMS

Despite the Web's tremendous potential for offering highly interactive, immersive, multimedia content, the majority of online journalism takes more conservative forms. As Christopher Harper, formerly of *Newsweek* and ABC's *20/20* notes, storytelling on the Internet will eventually look very different from its print and broadcast ancestors, but as yet "we really haven't figured out what form it should take."[3] In the meantime, most media sites are using a basic form that looks quite like a print-based story.

That is not to say that this basic story form is merely print **shovelware**—although in some cases it is. However, it is possible to take advantage of some of the Internet's potential in terms of interactivity and easy access to additional information to enhance the basic story form in ways simply not possible in any other media. We will begin by discussing the most basic type of story form, which Jonathan Dube of CyberJournalist.net has dubbed **print plus.**[4] A print plus online story is basically a shovelware story that has been placed online, often supplemented with additional information or media types. We will then discuss two different ways of **layering,** or dividing text-based stories into parts. (Chapters 8 and 9 will look at ways of building on basic (and other) story forms using links and other media types, in effect adding the "plus" or **Web extras** portions.)

Print Plus

You can find at least a few—and probably many—examples of the print plus form on just about any online journalism Web site. The advantages of the form are that it can be produced from scratch relatively quickly and also can be converted from other forms—print, broadcast or wire copy—with minimal effort.

Exhibit 7.4 shows an example from washingtonpost.com. This story about an approaching winter storm is written in inverted pyramid style. The lead gives the most important information: the fact that even though the National Weather Service has canceled its winter storm warning, morning driving conditions are likely to be hazardous. The remaining paragraphs then fill in the details of the story.

The text portion of the story looks very much like a story that would appear in a print newspaper or as wire service copy. Thus, we have the "print" portion of print plus. The "plus" portion of this particular story includes a photograph of a resident shoveling snow, links to school and business closing information, winter driving tips, an audio segment of the next morning's weather forecast and other information. Thus, the story is essentially a print story with some Web-exclusive features added.

In general, however, print plus stories take little advantage of the Web's potential for user control. The user does make a decision to load the story page by clicking the headline on the main page but beyond that has no control over the story. Much like turning a page in a magazine and coming to a particular story, the user has little choice other than whether to read it or not.

By layering, we can offer the user greater choice and control over the presentation of the story. There are two main ways to layer a story: by level of detail or by topic.

Layered Stories: By Detail

When we layer a story according to level of detail, we start by providing a small amount of information and then progressively allow the user to choose whether to retrieve more information. Researcher Eric Fredin referred to this principle as "first a little, then a lot."[5] At each step in the process, the writer encourages the user to continue with the story, but ultimately the user chooses how much she wants to read about the story.

A story from the washingtonpost.com Web site in print plus format. **Exhibit 7.4**

A typical way to layer a story would be to present the information in four steps: (1) headline, (2) summary deck (also called summary blurb), (3) main story, and (4) advanced elements.

Headline. The headline is the initial line a user sees about the story. Exhibit 7.5 shows the CNN.com Web page with several headlines for various stories; to see one of the stories, the user clicks the appropriate link. For online stories, the headline should give a brief, direct overview of what the story is about. One difference

Exhibit 7.5   The CNN.com home page shows headlines for various stories.

From CNN.com. Reprinted with permission.

from print is that "cute" or indirect headlines do not work well online. This is because online headlines exist in isolation from the rest of the story—initially, the headline will be the only story element the user sees. Thus, the headline must directly tell the user what the story is about, piquing the user's interest in the story. For example, in Exhibit 7.5, the story about the death of the cloned sheep Dolly is headlined "Cloned Sheep Dolly Dead"—it is simple and direct. Online, a "cute" print headline such as "Goodbye Dolly" wouldn't give the reader enough information to decide whether to read the story. Other aspects of writing linked text will be discussed in Chapter 8.

Summary deck. If the user clicks the headline for the story, she then receives a brief summary of the story. For example, on the MSNBC.com main page, clicking the headline "More mall-weary shoppers go online" takes the user to the summary shown in Exhibit 7.6. Notice that the summary repeats the headline

A summary deck for a story from MSNBC.com.   **Exhibit 7.6**

From MSNBC.com. Used by permission of MSNBC.

exactly as it was written on the home page—this is important in confirming that the user has been taken to the correct page. Changes in the headline wording, even subtle ones, can confuse users and make them wonder—at least momentarily—whether they been taken to the correct page.

Beyond the initial headline, the summary adds a subhead, a summary lead of the story and a link to a video segment. For many users, this may be all the information they want or need, and so they could choose to leave the story. However, users who still want to know more can click the "Complete Story" link at the bottom of the page. The advantage of this form is that users who want only a cursory overview of the story can get it without having to load the entire story. Of course, the user might choose to view the video portion of the story as well.

Main story. At this level, the story looks very much like the print plus form. The user is given the complete text of the story, as shown in Exhibit 7.7. The main story fills in the details and background of the summary deck.

Advanced elements. After viewing the entire main story, users may still want to know more. At this level, an online site can offer additional information through links and multimedia elements (as will be discussed in Chapters 8 and 9).

Stories layered by level of detail do not have to include all four of these steps. Many Web sites, for example, combine the headline and a short summary on one page. The user then clicks the headline (or, in some cases, the summary) to go to the main story.

Layered Storles: By Topic

An online story also can be layered according to the different main topics of the story. The user is then presented the story in parts, with each part corresponding to one of the story's main points. Dividing a story in this manner is often called chunking—literally, breaking the story into chunks. One main advantage of chunking is that it can present complex stories in small, easily understandable sections. If skillfully written, chunked stories encourage users to continue to each successive section. Alternately, chunked stories can be designed so that the different layers can be read in *any* order independent of one another, thus truly taking advantage of the Internet's nonlinear capabilities.

An example of a chunked story is "The Inspections Maze: How UN Inspectors Uncovered Iraq's Biggest Bioweapons Facility" from *The Christian Science Monitor*'s Web site. This story tells how United Nations inspectors in 1995 were able to expose and eventually destroy an Iraqi bioweapons facility. Exhibit 7.8 shows the story's first page, which presents an introductory overview of the story. The story consists of this initial page and six additional pages, each presenting an important chronological step in the process of uncovering the facility.

A main story from MSNBC.com.   **Exhibit 7.7**

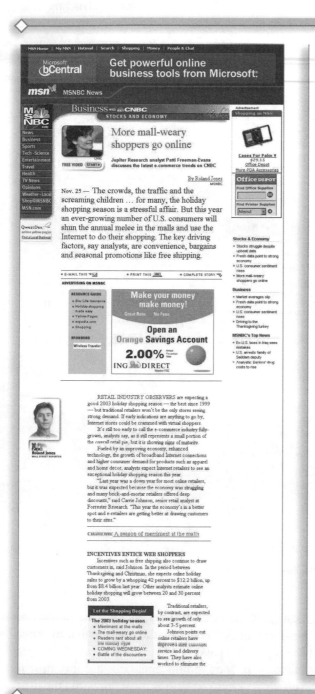

Exhibit 7.8   The first page of a story from csmonitor.com layered by topic. Links under the headline allow the user to jump to any of the story's other six sections.

THE CHRISTIAN SCIENCE MONITOR   csmonitor.com   back to csmonitor.com

THE INSPECTIONS MAZE
How UN inspectors uncovered Iraq's biggest bioweapons facility

| Intro | The suspicions | Cat & mouse | Dissension in the ranks | Cracking the cover | The confirmation | Destruction & exit |

Destination: Al Hakam
posted November 6, 2002

By Ben Arnoldy and Dave Hauck | *Staff writers of The Christian Science Monitor*

In February 1995, a team of United Nations Special Commission (UNSCOM) inspectors left Baghdad on a bus headed for Al Hakam, an hour southwest of the Iraqi capital.

For years, UNSCOM suspected that the remote, 10-square-mile facility was producing more than just pesticide and chicken-feed supplement, as the Iraqi government claimed. Some inspectors were certain it was a biological-weapons factory.

But this visit, like those before, failed to resolve the question.

"The Iraqis became very skilled over the years at deception and denial techniques," says Jonathan Tucker, a member of a UN inspection team that visited Al Hakam in 1995. "At the time of our visit, there was still some uncertainty about whether Al Hakam was, in fact, a bioweapons production facility."

It took a several teams of weapons inspectors – from the US, France, Sweden, Britain, Russia, and other nations – a year of digging before Iraq admitted that Al Hakam was producing biological weapons.

With a new UN resolution expected to pass this week, inspectors will be back in Iraq later this month armed with new technology and the lessons learned at Al Hakam. The UN estimates there are some 700 sites to examine. But if Al Hakam is any indication, the Iraqi inspection games are just beginning.

Map of Iraq with location of Al Hakam

Inspectors head to Al Hakam. UN

Play video: QuickTime | RealVideo

next: The suspicions >

The user can either move through the story linearly by clicking the link at the bottom of each page ("next: The suspicions >") or view the sections out of order by clicking one of the links at the top of the page.

Writing a chunked story takes more than simply breaking a conventional story into smaller pieces. To be effective, chunked stories must "reward" the user at each page and—if designed to be read linearly—encourage him to continue to the next page. The structure used in chunked stories is often called the *cham-*

pagne glass or *hourglass* structure because it begins broadly and then narrows to a point of interest or excitement. Ideally, these points of excitement should occur about every 21 lines of text, which is about how many lines fit on a typical computer screen. At the end of each page, the story should pique the reader's interest in what's coming next. In much the same way that a "tease" in television news encourages viewers to stay tuned for an interesting upcoming story, individual pages in chunked stories should end with a "tease" for the next part. "Writing has to be good to keep you going," notes online newspaper designer Mario Garcia.[6] However, the story chunks should also be written so that each can stand on its own, in case the user decides not to continue or decides to read the sections out of order.

In the Iraq inspections story, the first page ends with an effective tease for both the overall story and the next page. The final paragraph ties the 1995 inspections to the new set of inspections that was just beginning as the story was published in late 2002. It attempts to build readers' interest by noting that the 1995 inspection story illustrates what later inspectors were likely to face: "The UN estimates there are some 700 sites to examine. But if Al Hakam is any indication, the Iraqi inspection games are just beginning."

The parts of the Iraq inspections story *can* be read in any order (by using the links at the top of the page), but the story flows much more naturally if read linearly. Other stories, such as one about the Western exploration by Lewis and Clark on *National Geographic*'s Web site, lend themselves more to nonlinear reading. As shown in Exhibit 7.9, the *National Geographic* story is divided into 22 sections. When the user moves her mouse over a section number, a brief description of that section appears under the chapter list ("The Journey Begins May 21–July 31, 1804"). These descriptions encourage readers who are particularly interested in a specific portion of Lewis and Clark's journeys to proceed directly to that part. Alternately, the user can simply move linearly through the sections.

On the Web

More resources on online story forms and layering, including links to examples. Plus, innovative ways to chunk stories:
Under Chapter 7, select **Text-Based Online Story Forms.**

UPDATING ONLINE STORIES

Since the Internet is a nearly instantaneous news medium, users expect updated information, especially in breaking stories. The writing style used in such stories, therefore, has to easily allow for adding and modifying information as events unfold.

The inverted pyramid style is most often used in such stories because it can be modified easily. A straightforward, inverted pyramid story can be initially

Exhibit 7.9   This story from nationalgeographic.com is designed to be read in either a linear or a nonlinear fashion.

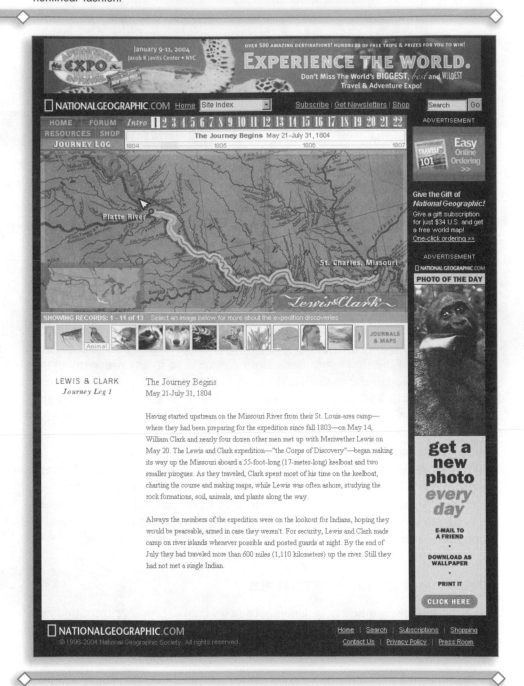

posted on a Web site and then modified with additional information or restructured over time.

An example from CNN.com illustrates this process. On a day that the U.S. government was expected to raise the terror alert level from yellow to orange for only the second time ever, CNN's main page carried a link to the story, as shown in Exhibit 7.10. The "Developing Story" link was an indication to readers that the story was "breaking" in nature. The text of the initial story, posted at 11:49 a.m., and subsequent updates at 12:38 p.m. and 1:23 p.m. are shown in Exhibit 7.11.

The CNN.com home page contains a link to the "Developing Story" about the increased terror alert level.   **Exhibit 7.10**

Exhibit 7.11   Three versions of the terror alert story from CNN.com. The first was posted at 11:49 a.m., the second at 12:38 p.m. and the third at 1:23 p.m. Changes to each story are highlighted.

Bush to raise terrorism threat level

From Kelli Arena
CNN
Friday, February 7, 2003 Posted: 11:49 AM EST (1649 GMT)

WASHINGTON (CNN) — President Bush will raise the national terrorism threat level Friday from an elevated risk of terrorist attacks to a high risk, sources have told CNN.

The national threat levels, developed after the September 11 attacks, are part of a color-coded system. Currently the level stands at elevated risk — or yellow. High risk would be orange.

The threat level change is expected to be announced at a 1 p.m. ET news conference, government officials said. Both Attorney General John Ashcroft and Homeland Security Secretary Tom Ridge will be on hand.

Earlier sources told CNN that U.S. government officials had recommended to the president that he raise the threat level, following several days of debate within the government about whether to take such an action.

Counterterrorism officials have said they are more worried about a possible terrorist attack due to several factors, including an increase in the so-called "chatter" level.

Worldwide chatter prompted the State Department on Wednesday to issue a new worldwide warning that cautions Americans to be vigilant and aware of their surroundings.

The stepped-up chatter indicates a greater amount of intelligence coming in about a possible attack, especially by al Qaeda, the culmination beginning this weekend of the Hajj pilgrimage to Mecca, Saudi Arabia, and the continuing confrontation with Iraq, according to officials.

On Wednesday, sources told CNN that the FBI is closely watching a "handful" of people believed to be Iraqi intelligence officers in the United States. There is also surveillance of at least several hundred Iraqi nationals living in the United States who are thought to be supporters of Iraqi President Saddam Hussein.

Also worrisome to U.S. officials is increased intelligence from a variety of sources in recent weeks suggesting a possible future attack in the United States that could include chemical or biological weapons.

The information does not single out any specific chemical agent or target, but officials said they are mostly concerned about the vulnerability of so-called "soft targets," such as apartment buildings, sports arenas and amusement parks.

Since the inception of the color-coded threat level system — officially called the Homeland Security Advisory System — in March 2002, the status has been yellow the whole time except for a short period around July 4 when it was raised to orange.

Bush to raise terrorism threat level

From Kelli Arena
CNN
Friday, February 7, 2003 Posted: 12:38 PM EST (1738 GMT)

WASHINGTON (CNN) — President Bush will raise the national terrorism threat level Friday from an elevated risk of terrorist attacks to a high risk, sources have told CNN.

In addition, the heads of the nation's military branches on Friday were considering raising security levels at bases across the country.

"There is a large spike in threat reporting that shows al Qaeda cells are possibly close to attacks," a senior military official told CNN.

Also, state security officials said security will be increased at major bridges and tunnels. The officials said they would be calling authorities in the private sector and asking them to heighten security at key pieces of infrastructure such as nuclear power plants, railroad lines, and ports.

State Department officials told CNN that arrests of suspected terrorists in Britain with the chemical agent ricin, in France with cyanide compounds and in Spain with other chemicals prompted the caution.

The national threat levels, developed after the September 11 attacks, are part of a color-coded system. Currently the level stands at elevated risk — or yellow. High risk would be orange.

The threat level change is expected to be announced at a 12:30 p.m. EST news conference, government officials said. Both Attorney General John Ashcroft and Homeland Security Secretary Tom Ridge will be on hand.

Decision follows days of debate

Earlier sources told CNN that U.S. government officials had recommended to the president that he raise the threat level, following several days of debate within the government about whether to take such an action.

Counterterrorism officials have said they are more worried about a possible terrorist attack due to several factors, including an increase in the so-called "chatter" level.

Worldwide chatter prompted the State Department on Wednesday to issue a new worldwide warning that cautions Americans to be vigilant and aware of their surroundings. The chatter concerned possible a chemical or bioweapons terror attack against the United States.

Exhibit 7.11   Continued.

The stepped-up chatter indicates a greater amount of intelligence coming in about a possible attack, especially by al Qaeda, the culmination beginning this weekend of the Hajj pilgrimage to Mecca, Saudi Arabia, and the continuing confrontation with Iraq, according to officials.

Ridge called governors

Sources said that Ridge had been calling state governors and emergency preparedness officials to brief them on the threat, telling them that the level of chatter was at its highest level since the terrorist attacks of September 11, 2001.

Ridge has also contacted officials in 13 sectors of private industry which control 85 percent of the critical infrastructure in the nation, including the energy, finance and transportation sectors. The officials said they were particularly concerned about chemical, biological and radiological threats.

On Wednesday, sources told CNN that the FBI is closely watching a "handful" of people believed to be Iraqi intelligence officers in the United States. There is also surveillance of at least several hundred Iraqi nationals living in the United States who are thought to be supporters of Iraqi President Saddam Hussein.

Also worrisome to U.S. officials is increased intelligence from a variety of sources in recent weeks suggesting a possible future attack in the United States that could include chemical or biological weapons.

The information does not single out any specific chemical agent or target, but officials said they are mostly concerned about the vulnerability of so-called "soft targets," such as apartment buildings, sports arenas and amusement parks.

Since the inception of the color-coded threat level system — officially called the Homeland Security Advisory System — in March 2002, the status has been yellow the whole time except for a short period around July 4 when it was raised to orange.

U.S. raises terrorism threat level

Friday, February 7, 2003 Posted: 1:23 PM EST (1823 GMT)

'Soft targets' focus of threat

WASHINGTON (CNN) — The federal government on Friday raised the national terrorism threat level to "orange," indicating a "high risk of terrorist attacks."

The move is only the second time since the September 11 terror attacks that the level has risen above "yellow," or elevated risk.

Attorney General John Ashcroft, Homeland Security Secretary Tom Ridge and FBI Director Robert Mueller made the announcement at a Washington news conference.

Ridge outlined how the public might be affected by the heightened security level.

"...increased security personnel at points of entry," Ridge said. "In fact, limited points of entry and exit, enhanced identification checks, restrictions to travel around federal facilities and airports ... will be implemented."

Ashcroft described the threat. "Recent intelligence reports suggests that al Qaeda leaders have emphasized planning for attacks on apartment buildings, hotels and other soft or lightly secured targets in the United States," he said.

In addition, the heads of the nation's military branches on Friday were considering raising security levels at bases across the country.

"There is a large spike in threat reporting that shows al Qaeda cells are possibly close to attacks," a senior military official told CNN.

Also, state security officials said security will be increased at major bridges and tunnels. The officials said they would be calling authorities in the private sector and asking them to heighten security at key pieces of infrastructure such as nuclear power plants, railroad lines, and ports.

State Department officials told CNN that arrests of suspected terrorists in Britain with the chemical agent ricin, in France with cyanide compounds and in Spain with other chemicals prompted the caution.

The national threat levels, developed after the September 11 attacks, are part of a color-coded system. Currently the level stands at elevated risk — or yellow. High risk would be orange.

Decision follows days of debate

Earlier sources told CNN that U.S. government officials had recommended to the president that he raise the threat level, following several days of debate within the government about whether to take such an action.

Exhibit 7.11   Continued.

Counterterrorism officials have said they are more worried about a possible terrorist attack due to several factors, including an increase in the so-called "chatter" level.

Worldwide chatter prompted the State Department on Wednesday to issue a new worldwide warning that cautions Americans to be vigilant and aware of their surroundings. The chatter concerned possible a chemical or bioweapons terror attack against the United States.

The stepped-up chatter indicates a greater amount of intelligence coming in about a possible attack, especially by al Qaeda, the culmination beginning this weekend of the Hajj pilgrimage to Mecca, Saudi Arabia, and the continuing confrontation with Iraq, according to officials.

"Recent reporting indicates an increased likelihood that al Qaeda may attempt to attack Americans in the United States and/or abroad in or around the end of the Hajj, a Muslim religious period ending mid-February 2003," Ashcroft said.

Ridge called governors

Sources said that Ridge had been calling state governors and emergency preparedness officials to brief them on the threat, telling them that the level of chatter was at its highest level since the terrorist attacks of September 11, 2001.

Ridge has also contacted officials in 13 sectors of private industry which control 85 percent of the critical infrastructure in the nation, including the energy, finance and transportation sectors. The officials said they were particularly concerned about chemical, biological and radiological threats.

On Wednesday, sources told CNN that the FBI is closely watching a "handful" of people believed to be Iraqi intelligence officers in the United States. There is also surveillance of at least several hundred Iraqi nationals living in the United States who are thought to be supporters of Iraqi President Saddam Hussein.

Also worrisome to U.S. officials is increased intelligence from a variety of sources in recent weeks suggesting a possible future attack in the United States that could include chemical or biological weapons.

The information does not single out any specific chemical agent or target, but officials said they are mostly concerned about the vulnerability of so-called "soft targets," such as apartment buildings, sports arenas and amusement parks.

Since the inception of the color-coded threat level system — officially called the Homeland Security Advisory System — in March 2002, the status has been yellow the whole time except for a short period around July 4 when it was raised to orange.

CNN's Kelli Arena and Jeanne Meserve contributed to this report.

The text added to the second and third story versions is highlighted. As you can see, the second story, posted less than an hour after the first, retains the basic structure but adds and updates information. The lead remains the same, but information about security at military bases and at the state level is added just below it. Doing this helps keep the most timely information near the top of the story. The time of the scheduled news conference is also corrected. Additional information about possible terrorist "chatter" and Homeland Security Secretary Tom Ridge's calls to state governors is placed in the body of the story. The final four paragraphs of the story remain the same. The addition of subheads makes the text easier to scan by delineating the main sections of the newly expanded story.

The third story was posted less than an hour after the second. This story included information from a news conference with Ridge, Attorney General John Ashcroft and FBI Director Robert Mueller. The new lead reflects the "official" elevation of the security alert, and five additional paragraphs present information from the news conference. More information from the news conference appears in the middle of the story.

In this manner, online stories can be updated to emphasize the latest or most important information. Much like the rings of bark on a tree grow outward over time, an online story also can develop using an initial story as its basis. The key to successful updating is to integrate the new information smoothly into the existing story, maintaining the inverted pyramid style of keeping the most important information near the beginning.

> ## On the Web
>
> Potentials and pitfalls of online updating, including the never-ending deadline: Under Chapter 7, select **Updating Online Stories.**

WHAT'S NEXT

Chapter 8 discusses how links to additional information can be used to enhance online stories. Since links are usually presented in textual form, the chapter will emphasize not only how to select links but how to present link text effectively. In many ways, it will build on the principles of good writing presented in this chapter.

Activities

7.1 Practice writing effective online headlines for different types of news stories. Use stories from a newspaper, wire service or other media.

7.2 Look at some of the leads for stories in a newspaper. How well would these leads work online? How could you improve them?

7.3 Practice rewriting some newspaper, wire service or broadcast stories for use online. What are the main things you're doing to them to make them more effective for use online?

ENDNOTES

1. Joel Davis, "The Good Word: Eye-Opening Study Discovers Web Newsreaders Are Text-Driven," *Editor & Publisher,* May 22, 2000, p. i7.

2. Jakob Nielsen, "How Users Read on the Web," http://www.useit.com/alertbox/9710a.html (accessed February 10, 2003).

3. Paul Eisenberg, "Online Storytelling: Seeking New Forms, Presentation," http://www.freedomforum.org/templates/document.asp?documentID=8009 &printerfriendly=1 (accessed January 29, 2003).

4. Jonathan Dube, "Online Storytelling Forms," http://www.cyberjournalist.net/storyforms.htm (accessed January 29, 2003).

5. Eric S. Fredin, "Rethinking the News Story for the Internet: Hyperstory Prototypes and a Model of the User," *Journalism and Mass Communication Monographs,* September 1997, p. 17.

6. Poynter Institute, "A New Media Renaissance," http://209.241.184.51/centerpiece/onlineseminar/mgarcia.htm (accessed February 19, 2003).

USING LINKS IN ONLINE STORIES

- To show the basic techniques of creating links in HTML
- To introduce issues involved in linking, including legal and ethical concerns and link maintenance
- To discuss the process of selecting links to use in online stories
- To show basic techniques of presenting links in online stories, including main story links and sidebar links
- To introduce the concepts of using links in shells

At several points in this book, we have discussed the use of links in online journalism. However, you may not yet have thought about just *how important* links are to an effective online presentation. In fact, links are second only to text in their ability to convey information and meaning to the **user.** Links allow the user not only to move among different parts of your story but also to access related information available on other Web sites. In this way, links not only can provide a seamless and logical means of letting the user experience your story but also can encourage the user to explore further on his own.

Consider, for example, a story you might write about a local group that rescues racing greyhound dogs and makes them available for adoption. Like a good work of journalism in any medium, your **main story** should provide contextual relevance to the topic. Thus, it is likely you will touch upon such issues as how many other groups in the country do this kind of work, how racing greyhounds are treated and how many of them are destroyed each year. For the majority of users, that would probably be enough. But some users might want more—maybe your story really strikes a chord with some people who want to know much more about the issues involving racing greyhounds, their treatment and their adoption. Links allow you to satisfy these users without requiring casual readers to wade through a lot of information that doesn't interest them.

Although almost anyone can create a Web page with hundreds of links on it, this chapter approaches linking as a *journalistic* function. That is, our goal is not to overwhelm the user with the sheer number of links we've found but rather to carefully select and present the best links that help tell the story and encourage further exploration. As online journalists, we may look at hundreds of links in the course of putting together our story but end up providing only a few in our finished presentation. However, those few should be the *best* few: the most relevant, the most reliable, the most compelling.

As you read this chapter, you will discover how time-consuming it can be to select and present links, but at the same time you may develop an appreciation for how they can enhance online stories. I begin with a discussion of how links are created using HTML code, building on concepts discussed in Chapter 3. I then address some of the issues involved in linking and some of the ways links can be used to enhance online stories. Next, I discuss how links can be most effectively presented. Finally, I look at how links can be incorporated into **shells** to create and enhance online stories.

CREATING LINKS USING HTML

Using the Anchor Tag

As you may remember from Chapter 3, the main tool for creating links in HTML is the <a>, or anchor, **tag.** Basically, the anchor tag tells the browser to display a new page when the link is activated. So, when a user clicks the link, she is taken to a new page designated by the link (see also "Creating Named Anchors").

Thus, the HTML code:

Visit my <a href="personal.bgsu.edu/~jfoust"> web page </a>.

designates the text "Web page" as a link to the address shown. A graphic can be designated as a link in a similar manner:

<a href="http://personal.bgsu.edu/~jfoust"><img src="tree.jpg"></a>

You will notice that the graphic, inserted by the <img> tag, is enclosed by the start and end anchor tags. Thus, when the graphic is clicked, it will take the user to the designated page.

Creating Named Anchors

The anchor tag can be used to designate a particular portion of a page to link to. By default, when you link to a new page, the top portion of the page displays; if the information you want is actually located further down the page, the user won't be able to see it without scrolling.

For example, suppose we have written a story that is divided into three main parts: "History of Greyhound Racing," "How Racing Dogs Are Treated" and "Adoption." We have placed the entire story on a single page called "greyhound_racing.html," as shown in Exhibit 8.1, but we want to be able to separately link to any of the three parts from a second page.

Our first step is to create three named anchors on the story page. These anchors will be placed at the beginning of each of the three sections. To create a named anchor, we simply insert the code

```
<a name="history"> </a>
```

in the appropriate place on the page. In this case, it would be just before the "History of Greyhound Racing" heading shown in Exhibit 8.1. Similarly, we would create named anchors for "How Racing Dogs Are Treated" (a name = "treated") and "Adoption" (a name = "adoption"). It doesn't matter what we name the anchors; we just need to remember exactly what they are.

Creating named anchors in authoring programs is easy as well. In Dreamweaver, for example, you simply select Insert > Named Anchor and then type in a name.

Now, we can create the links on the second page. To designate the named anchors, we simply add the name to the end of the href attribute, preceded by the pound sign (#). Thus, we could create the following three links:

```
<a href="greyhound_racing.html#
history> History of Greyhound
Racing </a>
<a href="greyhound_racing.html#
treated> How Racing Dogs are
Treated </a>
<a href="greyhound_racing.html#
adoption> Adoption </a>
```

Now, each link will take us to the appropriate part of the greyhound_racing page designated by the named anchor. Each link still displays the same page, but a *different part* of the page is displayed based on the named anchor, as shown in Exhibit 8.2. The user can still scroll up or down the page, but what she will see initially is determined by the named anchor. As you may notice, the anchor named "history" is redundant, since if we left it off like this:

```
<a href="greyhound_racing.html>
History of Greyhound Racing </a>
```

the top portion of the page would still display. However, when using named anchors, it is a good practice to be consistent and use a designated top anchor name to display the top of the page.

Exhibit 8.1   A single story page divided into three parts using named anchor links.

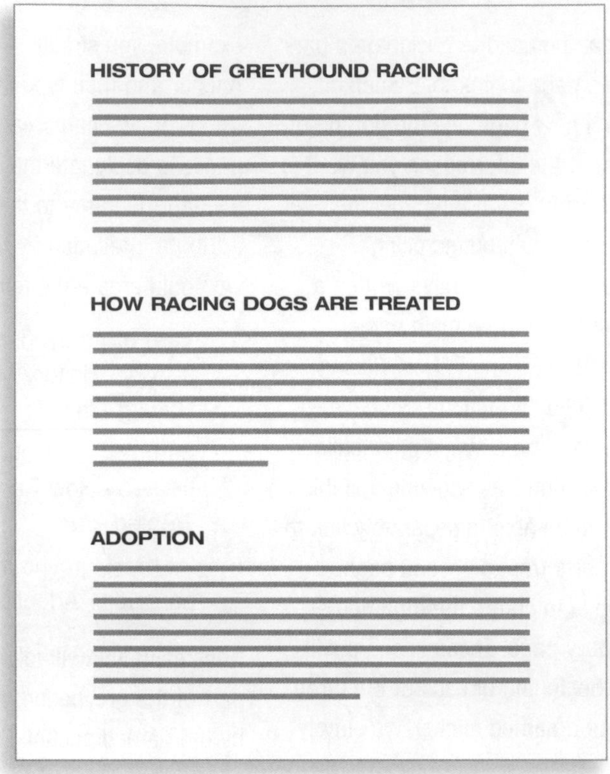

HISTORY OF GREYHOUND RACING

HOW RACING DOGS ARE TREATED

ADOPTION

Setting the Link Target

Normally, a new page indicated by the link will open in the same browser window, replacing the page from which it was called. However, you can tell the browser to open a new window by using the target **attribute.** For example:

View my <a href="resume.html" target="_blank"> resume </a>.

will open the new page in a separate browser window when the user clicks the link. The page the link appeared on will remain displayed in its own browser window, which will now be underneath the new window.

Whether links should open in new windows or in the existing windows is a topic of debate among Web designers. Some designers like to open pages—especially those outside the current site—in new windows. That way, the initial page remains on the user's screen, even though it will at least temporarily be covered

Three different portions of the page shown in Exhibit 8.1 will be shown based on which   **Exhibit 8.2**
named anchor link has been activated.

HISTORY OF GREYHOUND RACING

#history

HOW RACING DOGS ARE TREATED

#treated

ADOPTION

#adoption

by the new window. However, other designers prefer to use the default target, which opens the new page in the existing window. Proponents of this method argue that users can just as easily return to the previous page by clicking the browser's "back" button and that users often get annoyed when new windows open on their screens. There is no right answer in this debate, but you should understand that the more common method is for the new page to replace the existing page in the same window.

On the Web

More information on creating links in HTML and with authoring programs:
Under Chapter 8, select **Creating Links Using HTML.**

LINKING ISSUES

Before selecting online sources to include as links in a story, you should consider some general issues. These include whether you need permission to link to Web pages, how the links will be maintained and how great the risk of taking users away from your story is.

Permission to Link

Although legal and ethical issues relating to the use of links will be discussed in greater detail in Chapter 10, for now we should briefly address the issue of legal permission to link to a given Web page.

In nearly all cases, you can freely link to another person's or organization's Web site. Some specific considerations will be discussed in Chapter 10, but generally it is fine to link to anyone else's content as long as you don't imply that you produced the content.

It is, however, likely that the organization you work for will place some restrictions on links you can include. For example, unless your organization is involved in a partnership with the local television station, you probably won't be able to link to information on that station's Web site or the Web sites of other competitors.

Link Maintenance

When you include a link to external information in your story, you create an obligation to ensure that the link is accurate and that it *remains* accurate over time. Users become very frustrated when links don't work, and it hurts your site's credibility, even if the problem is at the other end of the link. After all, you're the one who put the link on your site.

Consequently, you need to confirm that your links work when the story is published. Make sure that the link is operational and that it actually takes the user to the promised information. Be aware that some sites require registration or a subscription to access their pages. Perhaps the link works properly on your computer (since you've registered or subscribed to the site), but it may give other users an annoying error message. So, make sure that the links work on other computers, not just your own.

Since information is constantly changing and moving around on the Internet, you also need to check links from time to time to make sure they are still working. If your story is still up on the Web six months from now, it's likely that users will still be accessing it, so you need to make sure the links still work. If they don't, they should be removed, replaced or repaired by entering the new address.

In other cases, you may need to update your links so that they point to the most timely information on a topic. The link that was cutting-edge two months ago may now have been updated by something newer and more relevant.

Finally, you should warn users if they will need extra software to access a site. If a site you're linking to requires Flash or some other **plug-in,** make sure you warn users in your link, as in the following example:

Interactive map of the new playground.

(Requires Flash plug-in)

Sometimes users don't mind the delay of downloading additional software to use a site, but they need to be told about it ahead of time.

Taking Users Away from Your Story

Another issue to consider about external links is the potential downside of taking users away from your story. In theory, you include links in your story with the hope that the user will explore the linked information then come back to your site. However, it's quite possible, given the Internet's seamlessly interconnected structure, that the user might begin an exploration that *doesn't* lead back to your site. For this reason, many news organizations' sites don't have a lot of external links. However, it can be argued that if your content is compelling enough, and if users find your external links valuable enough, they *will* come back to see what else you have to offer.

SELECTING LINKS

Chapter 5 discussed in detail the process of locating relevant information for stories on the Internet. As we know, these online sources can be put to two main uses: (1) providing information that helps you investigate and write your story and (2) providing, through linking, additional information users can explore on their own.

Although the two uses may overlap, our main focus here is the latter. We will assume that your journalistic training and the tips on finding online information addressed in Chapter 5 will allow you to find the basic sources you need to complete your main textual story. Here, we are concerned with selecting the sources you will actually make available to the user through links.

Link Functions

The links that you include as part of your story may serve several functions. They can be used to provide background information, to back up or cite assertions made in the story, to provide alternate points of view or to encourage further exploration of the topic. The number of each kind you use—or whether you even use some kinds at all—will depend on the type of story you're writing.

Background. Background is information that provides a basis for some part of your story. In the greyhound example earlier, background information might include data on the number of dog racing tracks in the country, where they are located and a state-by-state estimate of the number of dogs involved in racing. The user may be able to follow and understand the story without this information but may still wish to see it. For example, as the user reads your story, she may wonder, "How many racing dogs are there in my state?"

Backing up information. You can also use links to back up information in the story. This is normally done when making assertions that are surprising or controversial. In these cases, you can actually *show* the user the source of the information—be it a press release, a quote from a political figure or a report by a government agency. It is roughly equivalent to how you might use footnotes in a term paper to indicate the source of your information. Here, the user may choose to merely accept the assertion or may click the link to see the actual source if she is skeptical.

Alternate points of view. In the same vein, you might provide access to alternate points of view. Our greyhound story may present a fairly unfavorable view of the dog racing industry, but we could provide links to dog racing enthusiasts and organizations that would give a different perspective. For example, the Greyhound Racing Association of America's Web site (http://www.gra-america.org) has a page titled "Is Racing as Bad as They Say?" which disputes claims made by animal activists. Of course, this organization is biased in favor of greyhound racing, but providing the link can allow the user to access different points of view. To play on the slogan of a certain cable news network, we might say, "We link, you decide."

Further exploration. Finally, links can encourage users to explore any or all aspects of the story in more detail or to learn about related issues. In our greyhound story, we might provide links about the physical makeup of greyhounds ("Why are they so fast?"), laws pertaining to dog racing and betting ("Why can't I bet on greyhound racing in my town?"), ways to get involved ("How can I help find homes for these dogs?") or links comparing dog racing with horse racing. The goal of these kinds of links is to encourage the user not to just stop when he finishes reading the story but to continue to be interested. Naturally, not everyone (or even a large percentage) of users will take advantage of these opportunities, but for those who do, it creates a greatly increased level of involvement with the story (and with the news organization).

Paring Links

As noted at the beginning of this chapter, our goal is not to try to impress the user with the number of links we've found. Since we are journalists, we should instead strive to provide the *best* links, the ones that are the most relevant, worthy and compelling. A good journalist does not include every fact in a print or broadcast story—just the most important ones. Even though links can provide ways to expand on topics not directly addressed in the main story, you still want to pare your list of links down to the essentials.

Choosing links to include in your story gets to the very essence of what it means to be a journalist. You are searching out information, assessing and contextualizing it and then presenting it to the user in an understandable, compelling way. Recall the sidebar in Chapter 1 that discussed Vannevar Bush's Memex machine and his prediction of "trailblazers" who would help the common person make sense of the glut of available information. Journalists, through the skillful searching, assessing, contextualizing and presenting of linked information, can be modern-day trailblazers, contributing in small, individual ways to making sense of the mass of information available online.

Providing a link to information in essence provides your tacit endorsement of the information. In some cases, you might not actually be saying you *agree* with the information, but you are saying it's relevant and worthy of consideration. If you are skeptical of information but want to include it anyway, you should alert the user of that fact in the link text, as will be discussed in the next section. In no case should you include links to information that you think is weak, irrelevant or uninteresting.

There is no "right" number of links to include in a story. Ideally, the content should drive the number. Remember, you can't provide links to *every* related piece of information; rather, you want to pare down the available links to the *best* ones.

> ## On the Web
>
> Resources and ideas on selecting links, including more on Vannevar Bush and journalists as Internet "trailblazers":
> Under Chapter 8, select **Selecting Links.**

PRESENTING LINKS

Selecting the links is half the battle. The other half is presenting the links in a way that will inform users and encourage them to click on them. The general rule of presenting a link is that it should be clear to users *what they are going to get* when they click it. Under no circumstances should the user have to wonder, "What's this link for?" By the presentation, users should *know* what's on the other end of the link.

Ideally, your presentation of the link should provide an overview of what the link is about and *who* the linked information comes from. Either by the link's location on the page or by the use of text, the link should also be clearly connected to the part of the story it relates to. So, for example, a link to greyhound adoption centers nationwide should be located near the part of the story that discusses adopting greyhounds. Links should be integrated to the main story; they should not appear "tacked on" as an afterthought but, rather, should be seen by the user as an integral part of the complete story. On occasion, background or overview links may relate to the story as a whole, not to any particular part. These links can be located anywhere in the story; often, they are placed at the end.

There are two basic ways to present links: (1) by **hyperlinking** text in the main story itself, or (2) by creating separate links, called sidebar links, in addition to the main story.

Main Story Links

Main story links are created from words in the text of the story itself. These will show up as underlined blue text, so users will know they are links. The link shown in Exhibit 8.3, for example, would take the user to the full text of the report mentioned in the story.

In selecting which words to make into links, consider what will make the link's intent clearest to the user. Linking just the word *report* in Exhibit 8.3 does this most effectively. If, on the other hand, "Animal Welfare Association" had been made the link, this would have implied that the link was to that organization's **home page.** A link generally should encompass no more than three to five words of text. Ideally, linked words should be information-heavy (usually nouns), indicating what the link is. Linking entire sentences makes the main story awkward to read and often obscures what the link actually is. For example, if we had linked the entire sentence in Exhibit 8.3, as shown in Exhibit 8.4, the user wouldn't have much idea what the link is. Is it the report? A link to the Animal Welfare Association? A link to a page about greyhound abuse?

Exhibit 8.3   A main story link.

A recent <u>report</u> by the Animal Welfare Association estimated that more than 300 racing greyhounds are seriously injured each year.

Linking entire sentences creates text that is awkward to read and that obscures what **Exhibit 8.4**
the link actually is.

A recent report by the Animal Welfare Association estimated that more than 300 racing greyhounds are seriously injured each year.

The advantage of main story links is that, by definition, they achieve integration with the main story. When you link words in the main story, you are not creating any separation between the links and the story itself—and you locate the link near the part of the story it relates to.

The disadvantage, however, is that it is difficult to provide overview and source information about links, even when you choose information-heavy words. The example in Exhibit 8.3 does provide this context because of how the story text is written. It's pretty clear that clicking the link will take the user to the report mentioned, and we have cited the report's source and given an overview in the story. But it is not always possible to write your main story so that link information will be clear without disrupting the flow of the main story. For example, Exhibit 8.5 shows a link to a national list of greyhound adoption agencies. However, it is not immediately clear to the user what the link is, and certainly there is no source for the link. Rewriting the story to include this type of information would make the main text cumbersome and hard to read.

Main story links can be effective for very general links, such as those to the main page of a person, company or other organization mentioned in a story. For example, Exhibit 8.6 shows a link to the organization mentioned in the main story. Even here, however, it may not always be clear to the user what such a general link leads to. For example, if we link a person's name, will that take the user to that person's home page, take him to a page with information about that per-

An unclear main story link.   **Exhibit 8.5**

The Anytown adoption agency is one of more than 100 in the United States.

Exhibit 8.6   A main story link to an organization's home page.

The Greyhound Racing Association of America says racing dogs are not abused in any way.

son, or send e-mail to the person? The key is always clarity—it should be obvious to the user what lies on the other end of the link.

Also, these kinds of links—to general home pages—do not usually encourage exploration on the part of the user. The kinds of links that do—targeted links to specific pages containing information that can propel the story forward—are much more difficult to present as part of the main story. Nor can you provide additional text that *encourages* the user to explore the topic further. To do these things, it is usually most effective to use sidebar links.

Sidebar Links

Sidebar links are separate from—but located in proximity to—the main story. Since the link text is separate from the main story, you don't have to worry about link descriptions disrupting the flow of the main story. This allows you to more easily and completely describe linked information.

Sidebar links can be located anywhere on the page, although placing them in a separate **cell** of a **table** to the right of the main story is a common technique. You can separate the sidebar links, placing them in groups near the portions of the story they relate to, or position all of the links at the end of the story. The former technique encourages user exploration in **chunks**—the user may read part of the main story, explore some of the related information and then return to reading the main story. The latter technique encourages the user to read the entire story, then look at the links and decide whether to explore the topic further. Most sites tend to put links at or near the end of stories, in part because it is easier to group all the links together in one place rather than separate them out.

The link text should summarize what is at the other end of the link. In effect, you should write links that users don't have to click on to find out where they lead—they should already know by your description. You should also avoid describing the linking process or the apparatus of linking. For example, don't use phrases like "click here" or "point your browser to this link," "surf to this location" or "follow this link." Users have become sophisticated enough to know generally how links work and to recognize links on the page. There is no need to describe the process to them. As Web inventor Tim Berners-Lee says, "Use links, don't talk about them."

Let's say that we have three links for our greyhound adoption story: (1) to the "Is Greyhound Racing as Bad as They Say?" page at the Greyhound Racing Association of America, (2) to a page about why greyhounds make great pets from the National Greyhound Adoption Program, and (3) to an interactive directory of greyhound adoption centers from adopt-a-greyhound.org. Exhibit 8.7(a) shows examples of poorly presented links. None of these link presentations tells us the source of the information, and they don't provide enough information in general about what the link is. Who says greyhounds make great pets, and who is asking if greyhound racing is as bad as they say? The third link gives a better indication of what the link is, although it, too, needs to be more specific. It also contains needless process information ("Click Here"). Exhibit 8.7(b) shows much better link text. In each case, we provide a source for the information and a description of what is at the other end of the link. We have also carefully selected the words that actually make up the link.

Exhibit 8.8 shows another example of sidebar links in a story from *The Topeka Capital-Journal Online*. The story involves a controversy about whether wind farms should be built in a particular county. The "What's Next" box at the end of the story contains several links to more information. It begins, however, by telling

Poorly written link text (a) and improved link text (b). **Exhibit 8.7**

(a)

Is <u>Greyhound Racing</u> as Bad as They Say?

<u>Greyhounds</u> make great pets.

<u>Click here</u> for a Greyhound Adoption Directory.

(b)

The Greyhound Racing Association of America <u>disputes criticisms</u> of greyhound racing.

The National Greyhound Adoption Program says greyhounds have many traits that make them <u>great pets.</u>

An <u>interactive directory</u> from adopt-a-greyhound.org can help you find greyhound adoption centers near you.

Exhibit 8.8   A story from *The Topeka Capital-Journal* showing pull-out links.

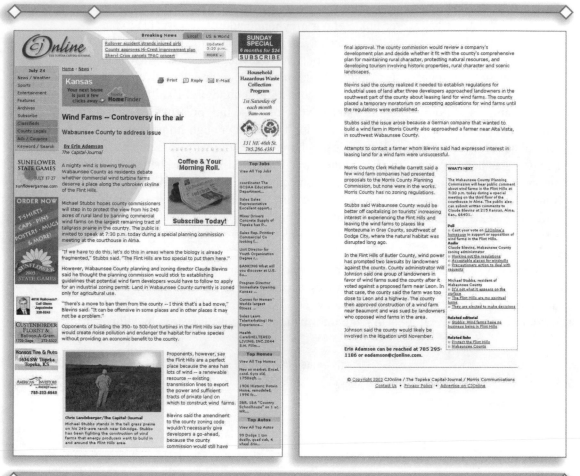

From CJOnline.com. Reprinted with permission.

readers what the next step in the story is—in this case, a meeting where the county's planning commission will hear public comment on the wind farms. There are links to an online poll, audio **clips** from participants in the story, a previous *Capitol-Journal* editorial on the topic and links to two Web sites. Most of the links indicate fairly clearly to the user what will happen when he clicks them. The lone exception is the "Protect the Flint Hills" link, which takes the user to a Web site of a group opposing the wind farms. This fact is not expressly apparent from the link text.

Another approach is shown in an example from Slate.com presented in Exhibit 8.9(a). The main story contrasts the on-air personalities of conservative radio talk show hosts Rush Limbaugh and Dr. Laura Schlessinger. At the end of

Sidebar links at the end of a story from Slate.com.   **Exhibit 8.9**

Related in Slate

If you missed the link on Dr. Laura's hypocrisy, click <u>here</u>. Last year, David Plotz chronicled how Dr. Laura ginned up a specious GOP crusade against pedophilia in <u>"Thank Heaven for Little Boys."</u> Jodi Kantor's <u>"Explainer"</u> described how Rush Limbaugh and other conservatives hawked a video accusing President Clinton of murder. In 1998, Plotz assessed another broadcast moralizer, <u>Jerry Springer.</u>

Related on the Web

Dr. Laura's snazzy <u>site</u> urges you to subscribe to her magazine and buy her books and <u>gear,</u> including her trademark, "I'm my kid's mom" T-shirts. You can also read her column and listen to the last five days of her <u>show.</u> <u>Stopdrlaura</u> is headquarters for the anti-Schlessinger crusade. This bustling site has tons of articles about advertiser withdrawals, numerous unflattering clips and photos of Dr. Laura, and a collection of her <u>quotes</u> about gays. The Family Research Council, a Christian conservative group, vigorously <u>defends</u> Dr. Laura against the campaign. You can buy Vickie Bane's unauthorized bio of Schlessinger <u>here</u>. Rush's spare <u>home page</u> lets you listen to today's show and subscribe to his newsletter. This <u>site</u> gathers pro and con articles and reports about Limbaugh. The official *Monday Night Football* <u>page</u> stays mum about whether Rush will be hired.

From *Slate Magazine*. Reprinted with permission from United Media.

the story, there is a sort of "annotated bibliography" describing additional information available from *Slate* and other online sources. As shown in Exhibit 8.9(b), this text provides a lot of contextual information about the available links, giving the user a very good idea of the kinds of information they contain. These rather vivid descriptions might encourage users to look at the additional sites, because overall they make the links sound quite interesting.

Exhibit 8.10 shows another example of how sidebar links could be grouped and presented in a way that would encourage user interaction. The hypothetical main story is about how U.S. presidential candidates and their supporters are making a lot of campaign stops in Michigan. The links help to provide background and other related information about this main story. For example, one of the first questions a reader might have is *why* so much campaigning is going on in Michigan. The first three links—grouped under the heading "Why Is Michigan So Important?"—can provide this answer. The first link is to an analysis of just why the state is so important, the second shows how the state fits into various electoral scenarios and the third provides a historical perspective of how important the state has been in past presidential elections. Notice that each link

Exhibit 8.10   A page with a main story and pull-out links grouped and written to encourage user interaction.

Michigan is a battleground, and the candidates are here

BY JOHN LIVINGSTON

What do Dick Cheney, George W. Bush, Al Gore, Michael Moore and Ralph Reed all agree on?

That Michigan is a really big deal right now. All the candidates and their pals are here this week, with 4 weeks left until election day.

"Michigan is a big battleground. You can't win the White House without winning Michigan," Fred Walters, GOP spokesman, said Tuesday.

"The winner of this contest will be determined by states in the midwest--states like Michigan," said Sam Stevenson, the Democratic caucus chair. "Naturally, you'll see a lot of Republicans, Democrats, and their supporters there over the next few weeks.

Democratic nominee Gore is to campaign in Oakland County tonight; Texas Gov. Bush will visit a school in inner-city Detroit tomorrow. This week's visits will be the seventh to the state for each candidate since August, with more expected by election day.

[Complete listing of previous Gore and Bush visits to Michigan.]

After last night's final presidential debate, held in St. Louis, the candidates now begin the final stretch run to election day. The debate, which many thought was a draw, was voters' last chance to see the candidates debate directly on the issues.

[View the complete transcript of the debate from voter.org.]

Michigan played prominently in the second debate, held last week in North Carolina, as both candidates made an effort to mention the state by name several times [see examples].

Michigan ranks as a top-tier campaign battleground, and its 18 electoral votes are a must-win factor in either candidate's calculations. Polls taken last week in Michigan showed the presidential race a virtual dead heat.

Spending time in a key state gives candidates and their supporters a chance to directly influence a vote with a handshake or a word -- and, more important, a shot at free air time and space on television, radio and in newspapers to deliver their message.

Why is Michigan so important?

Michigan is one of several midwest "Swing States" that will determine the outcome of the election. Voter.com has an analysis of Michigan's importance to the election.

Electoral scenarios at CNN.com show ways that Bush or Gore could win the White House.

Michigan's electoral history: see how the state has voted in past presidential elections.

Who's here and when?

A complete listing of current Bush and Gore scheduled visits to Michigan.

Other scheduled Republican and Democrat campaign visits to Michigan.

Ralph Nader and Pat Buchanan campaign stops in Michigan.

Electoral maps at ABC News and CNN show how the fifty states are currently leaning.

What is the electoral college and how does it work? Allpolitics.com offers a history and explanation.

provides a context, a basic description of the link and a source for the information. The user thus has a very good idea of what is on the other side of the links.

The next set of links contains more detailed listings of when and where various candidates and representatives will be in the state. This supplements the main focus of the story. Next to a part of the story that discusses how Michigan is currently leaning is a link to current polling information for all 50 states. And, in case the user wonders how the electoral college works (especially after the 2000 election), there is a link to a site explaining it. Finally, in a portion of the story not shown in Exhibit 8.10, the story discusses commercials being run by the candidates, with links to video examples and analyses of the claims made.

All of these examples begin to show how the process of presenting links as a sidebar can also help "sell" the link. Working like a tease before the commercial in a television newscast, good link text encourages the user to click the link. Remember, your process of choosing links has been a time-consuming one, and you've chosen what you believe are some of the best available links—thus, you should let the user know that you think they're good. You shouldn't oversell the link or promise something the link doesn't deliver, but you *do* need to make sure that the link's description emphasizes why you chose to include the link. Of course, a potential downside of this technique (as well as of including links within the text of the story itself) is that if the user does click the link as she's reading, it will tend to disrupt the flow of your story. In addition, as discussed earlier in this chapter, there is the concern that the user might not come back.

This technique is similar to the way online journalism sites promote individual stories on their home pages. As discussed in Chapter 7, stories are often layered from headline to summary to main story. At the first layer, the headline (and its accompanying subhead) is usually designed to give an overview of the

> ### On the Web
>
> More about presenting links, plus examples of different linking options:
> Under Chapter 8, select **Presenting Links.**

story's topic and make it sound interesting. The examples from *The Christian Science Monitor* in Exhibit 8.11 show this technique.

SHELLS

A shell is a collection of related links and information organized onto a Web page. Often, this information surrounds a main story or stories like a clamshell—hence the name. Other names for shells include evergreen packages, contextual navigation, verticals and orbiting content. Shells, if done right, can give the user access to a wealth of information related to a particular topic.

Jane Ellen Stevens of *Online Journalism Review* has identified four basic types of shells: beat shells, issue shells, story shells and user shells.[1]

Exhibit 8.11   Story headlines from the home page of *The Christian Science Monitor* are written to describe the stories and make them sound interesting.

Beat Shells

Beat shells gather information relating to traditional newsbeats, such as education, politics, business and health. One of the most comprehensive shells is *The Topeka Capital-Journal*'s Kansas Legislature shell, shown in Exhibit 8.12. The *Capital-Journal* uses this shell to surround stories relating to the Kansas Legislature. As you can see, the main story includes a box with related links, much like the wind farm story discussed previously. However, surrounding the story are many other links

The Topeka Capital-Journal's Kansas Legislature beat shell.   **Exhibit 8.12**

providing information about the Kansas Legislature. Along the left-hand side are links to the roster of legislators, including members of committees in the Kansas House and Senate. There is also general information about the Capitol area, including history, a virtual tour, maps and information about how a bill becomes law in Kansas. Archival information from previous stories is available, as is the full text of bills passed and under consideration. The right-hand column includes other special features, including an update on the main issues the legislature is addressing.

As you can see, beat shells can be an excellent potential resource for many different audiences. In the legislature example, high school students in a government class might click the link to learn how a bill becomes law, lobbyists might use the site to track the progress of a bill or a parent might click the link to find out what the legislature is doing about school budgets. No doubt many journalists in Kansas include the Kansas Legislature shell as part of their regular beat checks.

Issue Shells

An issue shell is similar to a beat shell but usually involves a more specific topic. Many news organizations, for example, produced shells for their post-September 11 "War on Terror" stories, bringing together background information, historical timelines and information about fighting terrorism overseas and domestically. Some news organizations produce issue shells of particular interest to their target or local audience. The (U.K.) *Guardian Unlimited,* for example, has an issue shell on the ethics of genetics, as shown in Exhibit 8.13. There is really no fundamental difference between a beat shell and an issue shell, except that issue shells normally cover a narrower topic.

Story Shells

A story shell usually involves an even narrower topic that is covered for a finite period of time. Many news organizations create story shells around multipart series, usually triggered by the print or broadcast stories the organization is running. The Web site of *The Detroit Free Press,* for example, contained a shell format for its three-part print series on the dangers of lead.

Since such multipart stories usually involve topics that will remain of interest over time, they are particularly well suited to shells. Such series often generate significant word-of-mouth interest, and making them available "permanently" on the Web site allows more people to access them over time.

User Shells

A user shell presents information of interest to the user based on her particular interests. For example, a user may fill out a survey noting her interests, and then the Web site (through automation) will tailor its coverage to these preferences. This type of shell is sometimes referred to as "The Daily Me," as it allows a user, in essence, to create a news site based on her own specific interests. The same concept is used by online commerce sites such as amazon.com, which will show you other merchandise based on what you've already purchased—"If you like Eminem . . . you may want to look at this new album by 50 Cent."

The Ethics of Genetics issue shell from the (U.K.) *Guardian Unlimited.*   **Exhibit 8.13**

"The Guardian Review - exemplary coverage of ideas, books and arts that matter; unfashionably intelligent; a pleasure to read."
Susan Sontag
Click here to subscribe and get your first THREE months FREE

Guardian Unlimited
Fresh Pages

Sign in | Register

Go to: Guardian Unlimited home   Go

GuardianUnlimited   **Special reports**

| Home | UK | Business | Online | World dispatch | The Wrap | Weblog | Talk | Search |
| The Guardian | World | News guide | Arts | | Special reports | Columnists | Audio | Help | Quiz |

**Special report
The ethics
of genetics**

Interactive guide
Sequencing the human genome

Search this site

Go

Are you a force to be reckoned with in business?

Online
For the latest internet news click here

Wheels
For the latest news and views on cars click here

Go to ...

Ethics of genetics: archived articles

Sex selection

November 2003: Full text of the HFEA report on sex selection (pdf)

Monitoring and campaign groups

GeneWatch UK

Latest

Attempt at human cloning has failed, says fertility doctor
February 5: Panos Zavos, the fertility doctor who said two weeks ago that he had transferred a cloned human embryo into the womb of a 35-year-old woman, announced yesterday that, as widely expected, his client had failed to become pregnant.

Donor anonymity

Sperms of endearment
January 25: As donors lose the right to anonymity, two middle-aged men paid in the past for their semen reveal their hopes and regrets for the children they'll never know. By **Mary Braid**.

Cryonic preservation

House of the temporarily dead
January 23: Construction work on Stephen Valentine's creation, a fantastic edifice housing thousands of cryonically preserved bodies awaiting reanimation, starts in two years. He talks to **Steve Rose** about the battle to conquer death.

Cancer

Care for lung patients at risk
January 22: Medical care for patients with the fatal lung disorder cystic fibrosis will be slashed this year because funding is being diverted to find lucrative cures for diseases such as cancer, a leading charity has warned.

Human cloning

Scientist attacks hype over clone research
January 19: A leading fertility researcher has warned that the media storm surrounding an American doctor's claims to have produced a cloned embryo will only serve to paint a heavily distorted picture of work in this field.

On the Web

More information about shells as well as links to examples:

Under Chapter 8, select **Shells.**

Traditional news organizations have been slow to adopt such user-driven formatting, but others are beginning to tailor news coverage to the user's wants and wishes. Sites like Yahoo! allow you to set preferences for the types of news, sports or entertainment you're interested in and then will show you the appropriate stories. For example, you might specify that you're interested in business news or technology news. User shells such as this are likely to increase in importance over time, because they allow the user to exploit the user control and dynamic content capabilities of the online medium.

WHAT'S NEXT

Chapter 9 will discuss the use of **multimedia** elements, such as video and audio, for online journalism stories. Following Chapters 6, 7 and 8, it completes the section of the book examining the basic principles of online journalism production.

Activities

8.1 Try to find 5 to 10 good links that could be used in a story about how the North American Free Trade Agreement (NAFTA) has affected your area. Look for links that serve a variety of functions (background, elaboration and so forth).

8.2 Practice writing link text for stories you may be working on. How might you present these links as part of main story text or as pull-outs?

8.3 How might you make a shell using one or more of the story ideas in Activity 8.2 as a starting point? What kinds of links would you include in the shell, and how would you present them?

ENDNOTE

1. Jane Ellen Stevens, "What's in a Shell?" http://www.ojr.org/ojr/business/ 1030664973.php (accessed November 18, 2003).

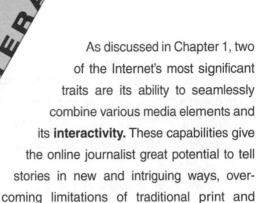

MULTIMEDIA AND INTERACTIVITY

As discussed in Chapter 1, two of the Internet's most significant traits are its ability to seamlessly combine various media elements and its **interactivity.** These capabilities give the online journalist great potential to tell stories in new and intriguing ways, overcoming limitations of traditional print and broadcast media.

Never before has a medium been able to bring together the media types available to the online journalist. Journalists can take advantage of the Internet's multimedia capabilities, combining text, links, graphics, video, audio and rich content to tell their stories. For example, an online story can provide video or audio clips of the sources quoted in the text portion of the story, photographs and maps, or sophisticated graphic-based animations to illustrate complex concepts.

Interactivity allows the user to actually manipulate the information in a story or construct his or her own story out of individual media elements. For example, you might provide an online calculator that allows users to type in salary and other information and see how proposed new tax laws would affect them. Or, you could divide the story into small **chunks** of individual information in various media forms and allow users to control how they want to experience the information. The key is that the user is actually *involved* in the information and thus is not only more interested but more *informed.* "The Web is a marvelous tool for self-directed learning," says Amanda Hirsch of PBS.org. "Users don't just consume it; they get it." Or, in the words of a Chinese proverb: "I hear and I forget; I see and I remember; I *do* and I understand."

At its most advanced, interactivity allows users to actually *contribute* to the story, adding their points of view to the existing information. Thus, an interactive online journalism story can be an amalgam of contributions from journalists, experts and individual readers. When a user visits the online story, he will see not only what the journalist originally posted but also what other users have added. For example, the PBS *Frontline* program broadcast "The Farmer's Wife," chronicling the economic and personal struggles of the Buschkoetters, a farm family facing foreclosure. In the companion Web site, *Frontline* offered users the chance to contribute their thoughts about the family and the plight of struggling farmers in general (see Exhibit 9.1). These comments, in many cases accompanied by responses from the Buschkoetter family, were compiled on the Web site for others to experience.

Producing highly interactive or multimedia stories requires not only a lot of time and effort but also specialized skills and tools. For that reason, this chapter will concentrate on the basic concepts of interactivity and multimedia rather than providing specific "how-to" examples as the previous two chapters have done. It is beyond the scope of this chapter, for example, to teach you how to edit and prepare video clips for use on the Internet or to tell you step by step how to set up a chat room to accompany a story. Instead, I will concentrate on the types of media elements available to the online journalist, the basic concepts of interactivity and the kinds of tools needed to produce highly interactive or multimedia presentations.

I begin by providing an overview of the basic types of media elements, including how they are produced and used. Next, I look at some of the ways advanced interactivity can enhance journalistic storytelling, and some of the issues that should go into making decisions about the types of media and interactivity journalists should use. Finally, I look at some examples of how media organizations are using interactive or multimedia elements in innovative ways to enhance online storytelling. Perhaps more than anything else, this chapter's purpose is to get you to *think* about interactivity and multimedia and how they can be used—together or separately—to enhance journalistic stories. Like words and links, all of these elements are merely tools; the key for journalists is putting them to use skillfully.

"The Farmer's Wife" Web site accompanying the PBS *Frontline* program.   **Exhibit 9.1**

TYPES OF MEDIA ELEMENTS

The basic types of media elements—text, graphics, sound, video, rich content and links—were first discussed in Chapter 2. Since this section will build on some of the concepts discussed there, you may find it useful to review the "Types of Digital Media" section of that chapter before continuing. Chapters 7 and 8 have discussed text and links in detail, so this section concentrates on the remaining elements: graphics, sound, video and rich content. For each element, we will look at the basic ways it can be used in online journalism stories, and at the basic process of preparing it, including software and hardware tools.

Graphics

Graphic elements can be used many ways on Web pages. For example, Chapter 6 discussed how graphic elements can be used to add interest to a page's visual design. More substantively, graphics can be powerful tools for journalistic story-telling. As an online journalist, you have to be continually aware that graphics can be part of your storytelling arsenal and that some stories can be best understood only with a *combination* of words and graphic elements.

A graphic can be a photograph, an original creation such as a map or chart, or a combination of the two. Using computer design tools such as Adobe Photoshop, there is almost no limit to the types of graphic elements that can be created. Producing quality graphics, however, usually takes some artistic talent, be it the trained eye of a photographer or the skilled hand of a graphic artist using a digital drawing pen. As discussed in Chapter 2, graphic elements aren't actually part of a Web page's HTML (hypertext markup language) coding—instead, they are separate files that are inserted onto the Web page by a browser program. As discussed in Chapter 6, you should take care to make sure your graphic file sizes are as small as practical so you don't slow page-load times too much.

Uses of graphics. Graphics can be used in a number of ways in online journalism. A photo or series of photos can accompany a text-based story, or produced graphics—such as maps, technical illustrations or information graphics—can help tell the story.

Photographs. Photographs can help us see things about a story that words cannot convey. Think of some powerful journalistic photographs you have seen and how vividly they helped convey the emotion or essence of a story. Remember the photograph of the firefighter carrying the injured child from the rubble of the Oklahoma City bombing in 1995, or the photographs of smoke billowing from the World Trade Center towers on September 11, 2001? These photographs gave the stories an emotional and visceral aspect that no other media could provide. The old saying "a picture is worth a thousand words" is often true when it comes to journalism. Of course, photographs can also add to text-based stories in less emotional ways—such as showing a face shot of a city council member or the president of a corporation or a shot of the cornfield where a new warehouse is going to be built.

Produced graphics. Produced graphics can take a number of forms. Maps can help specify the location of a news story in relation to a larger area. Where is Qatar? A map of the Middle East could show the nation highlighted in relation to other countries with which most people are more familiar. A map could also be used to show the location of the new downtown sports stadium, showing which existing buildings would have to be removed.

Technical illustrations. Technical illustrations can help show how a complex system or structure works. For example, you could create a graphic that compares how a traditional piston engine works to how an innovative new design achieves more power and better fuel economy. Or, you could create an illustration that shows how computer **viruses** spread over the Internet and bog down the network. Such technical illustrations work best when they give just enough information to make the concepts understandable; illustrations that have too much detail or information tend to confuse people. The key is to make sure the illustration focuses on the important points you're trying to convey.

Information graphics. Information graphics can be used to show the relationships between numbers or concepts. Perhaps the best-known information graphic type is the pie chart, which shows how different percentages add up to 100. Other types of information graphics, such as bar charts and line charts, also can show data trends or comparisons. For example, you might use a bar chart to show how many cars each of the major American, European and Asian manufacturers sold during a particular model year. Again, a key to well-designed information graphics is that they are clean, uncluttered and easy to understand. It should be easy for someone to figure out immediately what the graphic is saying.

When used in these ways, graphics online are not unlike graphics that accompany newspaper or magazine articles. However, the Web allows you to do things you can't do in print. For example, the Web does not have the spatial limitations of a print publication. A magazine or newspaper has only a limited amount of space for photographs and artwork, but on the Web, you are limited only by the amount of space on your computer. Thus, you can provide much more graphic information online than in print. Many newspapers, for example, make their staff photojournalists' work available in online photo galleries. Photojournalists love this because while they may get only one of their shots into the printed newspaper, they can have many more published on the Web site. The Web also allows you to add movement and interactivity to graphic elements, as will be discussed in "Rich Content" later in this chapter.

Sound

Sound can enhance online journalism stories in a number of ways. Specific sound bites from sources—or even entire interviews—can be made available online. In some cases, you might provide other types of sound—the recording of a 9-1-1 call, an intense conversation on the police radio or a snippet of music, for example. Individual segments of digital sound such as these are normally referred to as **clips.**

Deciding when to use sound. You should make decisions about using sounds in online stories based on journalistic principles. The most basic question should be whether using the sound helps tell the story. Also, does it contribute enough to the story to justify the process of producing the clip and the user's downloading of the clip?

These are questions that have to be decided on a case-by-case basis, but there are some general issues you can consider. First, sometimes actually *hearing* a human voice say something carries much more emotion and power than simply seeing the words in print. The voice of a person talking about a loved one lost to gang violence or a drunk driver, for example, is likely to carry much more emotion than can come across with mere words on a screen. A fiery speech by the mayor or an impassioned plea by a citizen at a city council meeting for more police in dangerous neighborhoods is likely to be much more compelling to users if they can *hear* it rather than just read the words.

In other cases, the actual sounds of a particular environment, often called "natural sound" or "nat sound," can convey to users a sense of being there or help drive home the story in a way that words can't—for example, the sound of a train whistle recorded from someone's living room in the middle of the night, showing the effect of the new train route through a residential area, or the sounds of parents reacting angrily at a school board meeting after the board decided to cut back on sports programs. These are the types of stories that can potentially benefit from sound; the question must be, however, "Does the addition of sound actually help tell the story?"

Integrating with the story. When using only HTML, it is difficult to tightly integrate sound clips into stories. Sound clips basically exist as separate entities from the main part of the story, as shown in the example from *The Topeka Capital-Journal* in Exhibit 9.2. When a user clicks a sound link, a **plug-in** in her browser is activated, which then plays the clip. It normally takes a few sec-

Audio
Claude Blevins, Wabaunsee County
zoning administrator
:: Working out the regulations
:: Acceptable places for windmills
:: Precautionary action to deal with
requests

Michael Stubbs, resident of
Wabaunsee County
:: It's not what it appears on the
surface
:: The Flint Hills are my spiritual
home
:: They are elected to make decisions

From CJOnline.com. Reprinted with permission.

onds for the sound player plug-in program to load and activate, and there is an additional waiting period as the sound downloads. For this reason, sound clips in basic HTML can cause something of a standstill in the storytelling experience: The user in effect has to say, "OK, I'm going to stop now and listen to the sound clip."

A more immersive effect can be achieved with sound by supplementing HTML with rich content programs such as Java or Flash, as will be discussed later in this chapter. When used with these programs, sound playback can be more tightly controlled and integrated with the rest of the story. A song or music clip might play automatically in the background when a user reaches a certain point in the story, for example, or the user can listen to a conversation between police as she views an animated map of a car chase route.

Digitizing. Before sound can be used on the Internet, it must be **digitized,** or converted into digital form. This usually involves plugging a playback device, such as a tape recorder, record player (if you can find one), radio or minidisc player, into a computer's sound card input and then using an audio editing program to digitize the sound. This will create a digital file of the sound. Simple audio editing programs come with versions of the Windows and Macintosh operating systems, and other, more advanced programs are also available.

As part of the digitizing process, you will be able to select the quality level of the finished product. Higher quality sound digitizing provides more clarity and less distortion but requires larger file sizes and greater **bandwidth.** In other words, higher quality sound clips will take longer for the user to download. Here you have to ask yourself how important sound quality is: It makes more sense to digitize a music clip or interview at a higher quality than a recording from a police radio or telephone conversation, for example. This has nothing to do with the journalistic value of these clips, merely the fact that sound from telephones and police radios is low-quality to begin with, so you need not use the highest-quality digitizing options.

Selection of digitizing quality includes three parameters: **sampling rate, bit depth** and channels. The sampling rate measures how often the original sound is analyzed as it is converted to digital. The higher the sampling rate, measured in kilohertz (kHz), the better the quality. Bit depth refers to the range of high frequencies (treble) to low frequencies (bass) that will be included in the digitized sound; the higher the bit depth, the greater the range and the higher the quality. The common bit depth choices are 8-bit and 16-bit. Finally, the number of channels indicates whether the sound is to be digitally recorded in mono (one channel) or stereo (two channels). Mono is fine for voice or other sounds, but music is usually recorded in stereo. You will need to experiment with your particular application to find a suitable compromise between quality and file size.

Most digital sound formats allow you to choose from among several quality levels. The format you use to save your digitized sound will be largely a matter of personal or organizational choice. If you plan to stream the audio, for example, you will need to use a **streaming** format, such as **RealAudio.** If you want to achieve the best compromise between quality and file size for music, the MP3 format might be best.

Editing. Once you have digitized your sound, you will likely then edit it into one or more shorter clips. You may digitize an entire interview, for example, then create one clip of the full interview and several shorter clips of highlighted portions. Editing can be performed with one of several popular programs, including Sony's Sound Forge and DigiDesign's Pro Tools. These programs allow you to choose the beginning and end points of clips precisely and also modify the sounds. For example, you might adjust the sound so that the person's voice is more clearly audible over the background noise or you may create an echo or reverb effect.

Once your clips are finished, you will then link to them from an HTML file or integrate them into a multimedia presentation.

Video

Video can be used in many of the same basic ways as sound. Of course, the addition of visual information to the sound information can make it an even more valuable asset to an online journalism story. You can use video to show interviews or sound bites or to show actual events—press conferences, sports plays, emergency landings or drug raids, for example. Video segments on the Internet, like sound segments, are usually referred to as clips.

Deciding when to use video. The same decision-making process that applies to sound clips should also be used for video clips. Basically, does the addition of video help tell the story enough to make it worthwhile to produce the clip and for the user to download and play the clip? In most cases, you have to think in terms of *compelling* video—images that move the audience in ways that words (or sounds or still images) can't. If the video clip can help users understand the story or lend an additional emotional impact to the story, it's probably worth using. If the video is merely going to be seen as decoration, it probably shouldn't be used. If the video is unique or something users haven't seen before, it's more likely to be effective online. If the video is of something most users *have* seen before (such as the president walking from the White House to his waiting helicopter or the shot of the closing stock bell at the New York Stock Exchange), it's probably not worth using.

Integrating with the story. Video in HTML is also subject to the same integration problems as sound. In fact, in most cases, video clips disrupt the flow of storytelling even more than sound clips do. This is largely because of video's even greater resource demands. Beyond the delays of starting the video plug-in program, the video clip itself will be much larger in size than a comparable audio clip. Unless the user has a high-speed Internet connection, he may become frustrated with the time it takes to download the clip, with the quality of the playback, or with both.

Video can be integrated into rich content programs too, but at least some of the file size and bandwidth problems remain. The bottom line is that video on the Internet works well if the user has a high-speed connection, but not if he doesn't. This situation is likely to improve as technology advances and as more users gain affordable access to high-speed connections. But, as noted in Chapter 2, video remains something of a Holy Grail among Internet-based digital media.

All of this is not to say that video should not be used in online journalism— far from it. However, it should be used judiciously, and it should be presented in a way that allows users to choose whether they want it. An online story based solely on video, for example, is likely to be useless to users with dial-up connections. Video-only stories also offer little advantage over stories that can be seen on television. There is no denying the power of video's moving images and sound, but it simply shouldn't be overused in online stories.

Digitizing. Like audio, video must be in digital form before it can be put on the Internet. This means getting the video information from the camera or other source onto a computer. Increasingly, video cameras output digital signals and record onto digital tape, so in many cases the camera can simply be connected to a computer using a **Firewire** (also called IEEE-1394) or other digital connection. If the camera is not digital, you will have to connect its audio and video outputs to inputs on the computer. Unlike audio, which can be digitized using most any standard sound card, video can only be digitized using a specialized **video capture** card.

As you digitize video, you will make choices about the quality of the finished product. Again, the higher the quality, the larger the file size and the greater the bandwidth requirements. As discussed in Chapter 2, several parameters can be manipulated to affect the quality of digitized video. You also can choose from a variety of **compression** methods, which are mathematical codings that make video files smaller. MPEG-1 or MPEG-4 compression is commonly used for Internet applications, and the streaming **RealVideo, Windows Media** and **QuickTime** formats use their own compression schemes. Within these individual compression methods, you can usually choose other parameters, such as whether you want to emphasize smooth motion or frame detail. Again, experiment with a number of settings to see which one works best for your desired application.

Editing. You also will need specialized video editing software to combine and edit individual clips. Programs such as Adobe Premiere (see Exhibit 9.3) or Apple Final Cut Pro allow you to edit individual clips together, change the beginning and end points of clips and manipulate audio tracks. They also allow you to perform special effects, such as dissolves (where one video shot "fades" into another) and slow motion. Most editing programs then allow you to save the finished product in a variety of formats and with a wide range of quality parameters.

Once saved in an appropriate format, video files are handled very much like audio files on the Internet. A simple line of HTML code creates a link to the video clip. When the user clicks the link, her browser starts the appropriate plug-in (provided it has already been installed) and plays the video clip in a new window. Most players allow the user to perform simple control operations on video clips, such as pause, fast-forward and rewind.

Rich Content

We have seen in earlier chapters that HTML has several limitations when it comes to laying out text and designing pages. It also is rather limiting when it comes to interactivity. HTML, as we know, works on a "page" metaphor—a link usually takes

Adobe Premiere video editing software.   **Exhibit 9.3**

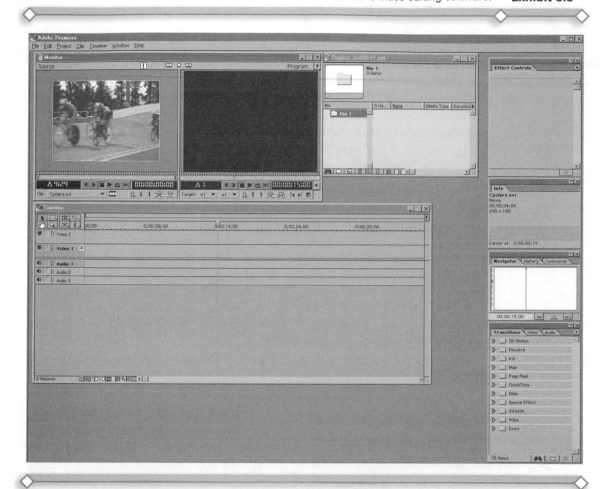

Adobe product screen shot reprinted with permission from Adobe Systems Incorporated.

a user to an entirely new page. There is no way in HTML, for example, to merely change part of an existing page or to precisely synchronize the playback of video or audio clips. For these reasons, developers have created additions to HTML that allow much greater interactivity and control of individual media elements, creating what is often called rich content. The most common of these are Java and Flash.

Java. Java is a programming language introduced by Sun Microsystems in 1995. Sun designed Java to integrate with HTML but overcome some of its limitations. In essence, Java allows you to create individual programs that are run through HTML. After some wrangling with Microsoft, Sun's Java was adopted as a standard in the industry, and now all browsers support Java programs. In other words, users don't need to download additional plug-ins to experience Java-based content. Java applications—often called "applets"—can be created using programs available from Sun and others. Many Web sites use Java to create small animations or interactive features, such as quizzes or polls. These types of features are particularly popular with Web users, and they help engage users in the content. For example, people might be more interested in a story about whether to build a new sports stadium if they can cast a vote for or against it and then see how other users have voted. One or more Java applications can run on a single Web page, or Java applications can open their own browser windows.

Flash. Macromedia's Flash operates on the same basic principle as Java—its applications, like Java's, run through HTML while providing increased interactivity and control. Flash, however, uses vector-based graphics, which download more quickly than traditional bitmap images, such as GIFs or JPEGs. To create Flash applications, you need Macromedia's Flash program; to play them back, you need to have Macromedia's Flash Player plug-in installed. Flash has rapidly become a standard in the industry, and many browser installations automatically add the Flash Player plug-in. Macromedia also makes it relatively easy for users to install the plug-in if they visit a site that contains Flash content. However, Flash support is still not quite as ubiquitous as Java's.

Nonetheless, Flash is very popular among Web developers because of its support for multimedia and streaming content, its slick authoring program and its close integration with the Dreamweaver HTML authoring products. A high level of interactivity can be programmed into Flash applications, which also can integrate video, audio, graphic and text elements.

In fact, a Web site can be composed almost entirely of Flash content. A user could visit the initial page, which would call a Flash application that would then contain all of the content. However, in practice, this is not well-suited to journalistic sites. Most journalistic sites use Flash only for advertisements or special features, if they use it at all. Again, the issue is one of bandwidth—highly interactive Flash applications with lots of video, sounds and graphics take a while to download, especially for users with slow connections. Users who are promised something compelling that they want are likely to wait for a Flash application to download and start, but users who are just visiting a site's home page are unlikely to wait. Still, Flash can be a valuable tool for online journalism, especially for special feature stories (see "Examples of Interactive and Multimedia Content" later in this chapter).

On the Web

Examples of journalistic uses of graphic elements, sound, video and rich content. Plus, more about Java and Flash programming tools: Under Chapter 9, select **Types of Media Elements.**

ADVANCED INTERACTIVITY

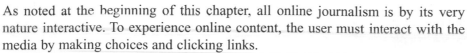

As noted at the beginning of this chapter, all online journalism is by its very nature interactive. To experience online content, the user must interact with the media by making choices and clicking links.

But it is also possible for interactivity to extend beyond mere user control of existing information. The Internet creates a two-way information flow between the journalist and the user, allowing users to become active participants in the storytelling process. Individual users can contribute information to a story that is then available to future readers of the story, thus building a continuing, "living" flow of information.

Such interactivity can be both exciting and frightening for journalists. At the same time that it provides many potential new sources and points of view for stories, it raises significant legal and ethical questions. For example, how does a news organization that provides for user interaction with stories screen users' contributions for accuracy? And, is the news organization responsible for things users say? These and other questions are discussed in more detail in Chapter 10.

Truly interactive journalism also forces journalists to think about stories in new ways. Traditionally, stories are "finished" when they air on a newscast or when they appear in a printed newspaper, but interactive online stories continue to develop. A user may point out something that the initial story missed or got wrong, to which the journalist should respond. "On any given story, there's someone in the audience who knows more about it than we do," says Michael Skoler of Minnesota Public Radio. "The goal should be to tap into that expertise."

Forums and Blogs

The main methods of facilitating user contribution to stories are **e-mail, chat** and **discussion boards.** E-mail allows users to send messages that can then be posted to a part of the story page or on a separate page. Chat allows users to interact with one another—and perhaps the journalist who worked on a story—by typing in questions and answers. It is likely that the journalist would be made available only during a limited time period (say, an hour or two), but the transcript of the chat could then be made available for later users. Discussion boards facilitate continuing conversation about story topics—users can contribute information whenever they want. These messages are then compiled and made available to future users. **Blogs,** as discussed in Chapter 4, also can allow users to participate in discussions of particular topics.

All of these methods can be automated, meaning that computers can be programmed to automatically add user comments to the story package. However, in practice, most news organizations moderate the process in some way. You have no doubt had experiences in chat rooms or discussion boards where others posted irrelevant or derogatory information, and unmoderated discussion forums on the Internet can quickly degenerate into useless and annoying free-for-alls. The challenge, of course, is one of resources: Screening a mass of user contributions to weed out the valuable from the trash takes time, and many online organizations simply don't have the personnel to dedicate to such work. Washingtonpost.com (as discussed in Chapter 4) has designated employees to screen and moderate chat sessions with news makers, but moderators are more the exception than the rule. CJOnline, for example, uses community volunteers to moderate its discussion boards.

On the Web

Examples of forums, blogs, databases and other interactive features:
Under Chapter 9, select **Advanced Interactivity.**

These challenges aside, in cases where online journalism organizations have given users the chance to contribute to the dialog, it has been a worthwhile experience for users and even the community at large. *The Seattle Times* Web site, for example, offered users the chance to contribute their ideas about how the Seattle metropolitan area should raise and spend money for transportation projects. The newspaper later compiled and published many of the ideas from the "You Build It" Web page, some of which actually had an impact on policy makers' opinions. "The Farmer's Wife" Web site mentioned earlier in this chapter created a virtual community of support for the Buschkoetter family and other struggling farmers.

Databases

Another method of facilitating interactivity is by providing searchable **databases** for users. More and more journalistic organizations are compiling data on crime statistics, population trends or school test scores and making it available through their Web sites. Then, users can search the data according to different criteria. For example, a user could find crime statistics for a particular area of the city or see how his school's test scores compared to others in the area.

MAKING MEDIA DECISIONS

The various types of media available to the online journalist should be considered for their potential as storytelling tools. Like choosing links, deciding what media to use—and how to use them—should be a journalistic function. In making these decisions, the journalist has to consider the nature of the story, the target audience and the available resources.

Nature of the Story

The nature of the story largely determines the appropriate types of media. A highly visual story, such as a tornado touchdown or the implosion of a downtown building, would benefit more from video than, say, a story about city council tabling a motion to raise sewer taxes. The same kind of thought should go into decisions about sound and other elements, as discussed previously in this chapter. Remember, also, that the written word is still the primary unit of information on the Internet and that other media will have to be given context by words on the screen. Like presenting links, you should present media in a way that makes it clear to the user just *what* it is she is looking at. What is this video clip? When was it shot? What does it mean? This is still done primarily with the written word.

Although the nature of the story should drive the media used and not vice versa, the online journalist should keep in mind that these media might allow the story to be told differently. For example, the aforementioned sewer story might not scream out for a video clip, but perhaps a graphic or animation could be created that would show *why* this heated discussion about sewer rates is occurring. Say, for instance, that the city needs to raise sewer rates because the present sewer system must be updated to deal with the rapid growth of certain "trendy" neighborhoods on the outskirts of town. A graphic could show how the sewer system is supposed to work and why it is not working properly now; perhaps an animation produced with Flash or Java could show *why* the current system is inadequate. These media types might help users understand the issues more clearly so that they can make more informed decisions.

It is also important to *edit* the media used in online stories. As journalists, our goal is not necessarily to give the user *everything* but to give him the *most relevant and compelling* information. So, is it really valuable to give the user a 5-minute clip of a councilperson speaking about technicalities of the sewer system? Probably not. By the same token, there probably isn't much value in providing a videographer's unedited raw tape of tornado footage. These media should be *edited* so that they give the user only what's really relevant.

Target Audience

The online journalist also has to consider the target audience in making media decisions. This includes the "What does the audience want and need to know?" question that should be asked by all journalists, but also should include a consideration of the audience's equipment. How fast is the average user's computer? Does the typical user have a Flash player installed? How fast is the typical user's connection? The answers to these questions need to factor strongly in deciding what media to use. If most of a site's users connect with dial-up **modems**, that site probably shouldn't use a lot of bandwidth-intensive video or rich content. Unfortunately, figuring out what resources users have takes guesswork in many cases, although it is relatively easy to find out how fast users' connection speeds are. For example, MSNBC.com has determined that more than 50 percent of the users of its Web site have **broadband** connections, and that number is rapidly growing. In response, the site has started offering features that rely more on digital sound, video and rich content to tell stories.

Available Resources

The journalist also needs to consider the resources available at his end of the story. If the resources to properly produce and present certain kinds of media are not available, they should not be offered. If the site's **server** computer, for example, is likely to crash if more than two people try to stream a video clip at the same time, then it's not a good idea to offer video clips. Doing so will only aggravate users—not only the ones who couldn't stream the video clips but all of the other ones who tried to connect to your site after the computer crashed.

EXAMPLES OF INTERACTIVE AND MULTIMEDIA CONTENT

Like many aspects of online journalism, the use of multimedia and advanced interactivity is not being exploited to its fullest potential. Whether it ever will be depends largely on how successful those organizations who try such innovative ideas are and on how skillful journalists are in working with multiple media elements. This section provides a brief sampling of some ways such elements can be used in storytelling. These examples are certainly not the only ones you can find, nor are they necessarily "the best," most innovative or flashiest (no pun intended). They are, however, representative of different ways of combining multimedia and interactivity in online journalism.

Agence France-Presse has created a number of Flash-based features on sports. Its Formula One auto racing feature, for example, includes text, pictures and animations (see Exhibit 9.4). It also includes qualifying and race results, building an accumulative database as the racing season progresses. For example, you can see how a particular driver has qualified and finished each race and also get background information on cars, drivers and teams. During the Formula One season, Agence France-Presse updates the feature with the latest qualifying and race results, stories, pictures and animations. The feature is a treasure trove for Formula One enthusiasts, providing an almost limitless amount of information in a highly interactive, engaging package. Agence France-Presse senior editor Marlowe Hood says designers set out to "create environments that people want to stay in."

MSNBC's "Spam Wars" (see Exhibit 9.5) is similar in concept. Using the "cat and mouse" metaphor, the feature shows a step-by-step chronicle of how e-mail spammers evade detection and continue to fill people's e-mail boxes with unwanted messages. The user controls the flow by clicking navigation buttons

Agence France-Presse's Formula One Flash feature. **Exhibit 9.4**

From Agence France-Presse. Copyright 2004 by Agence France-Presse. Reprinted with permission.

and receives nearly instantaneous results—once the full program has loaded, there is no waiting for new parts to download.

Sometimes, various elements can be gathered on a single "main" page of a story, similar to the way **shells** are constructed (see Chapter 8). This main page gives the user an overview of what is available and allows him or her to select the elements he or she desires. "The Farmer's Wife" page discussed earlier is set up this way, with links to the various media elements available from the opening page (see Exhibit 9.1). Another example is *The Los Angeles Times'* feature of the Cathedral of Our Lady of the Angels, a new Catholic church in downtown LA. The opening page assembles links to various text-based stories about the cathedral, each with a descriptive paragraph (see Exhibit 9.6). Also provided are audio and video clips, including a video clip showing the church's organ being fine-tuned using voices in the church's choir. Links to various still photos and a Flash-based virtual tour of the cathedral showing its various floors and features are also available.

Exhibit 9.5   A screen from MSNBC's "Spam Wars" interactive presentation.

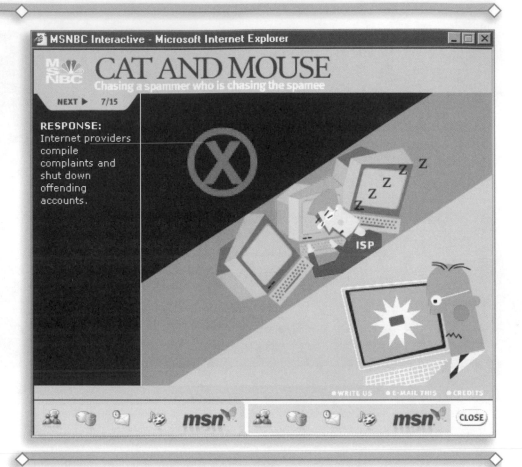

From MSNBC.com. Used by permission of MSNBC.

The *Times'* "Mortal Wounds" feature on black-on-black homicide is set up in the same basic way, as shown in Exhibit 9.7. A main page contains text-based stories, and other features—including a Flash photo gallery—are linked from it. A message board allows users to add comments to the story or talk about their own experiences.

The Center for Public Integrity's "Well Connected" story chronicles the frequent travels of Federal Communications Commission officials (FCC) and the fact that many of the trips are paid for by the industries the FCC is supposed to regulate. As part of the story, the Center provides a searchable database that allows users to view these trips by commissioner, sponsor and event (see Exhibit 9.8). The Online News Association, which awarded the site first place in its Enterprise Reporting category, called the story "a classic investigative reporting project."

The Los Angeles Times Web page for the Cathedral of Our Lady of the Angels. **Exhibit 9.6**

Exhibit 9.7 The "Mortal Wounds" Web page from *The Los Angeles Times*.

The Center for Public Integrity's "Well Connected" feature's searchable database. **Exhibit 9.8**

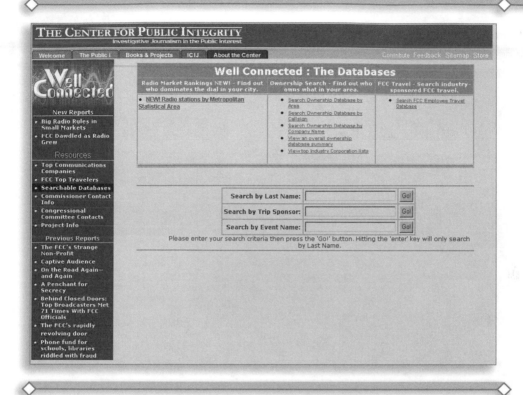

In some cases, multimedia and interactivity can be combined into features that resemble virtual reality or games. The goal of these features is to engage users, encouraging them to interact with the information so that they can better understand it.

Slate.com's "Enron Blame Game" is a Flash-based feature that allows the user to explore various aspects of the Enron corporate scandal. The game (shown in Exhibit 9.9) presents various players in the scandal much like the letters in a *Wheel of Fortune* puzzle, complete with a virtual Vanna White. The subheading of the screen is "Where It's Always Someone Else's Fault." When the user clicks on one of the squares, the bottom of the screen shows who that person or group blames for Enron and other corporate scandals.

Minnesota Public Radio's "Budget Balancer" page allows users to try their hands at balancing the state's budget (see Exhibit 9.10). Users can choose to make "broad swipe" changes, such as raising taxes or cutting various departments across the board, or can select targeted changes. Pie charts show what programs

Exhibit 9.9   Slate.com's "The Enron Blame Game."

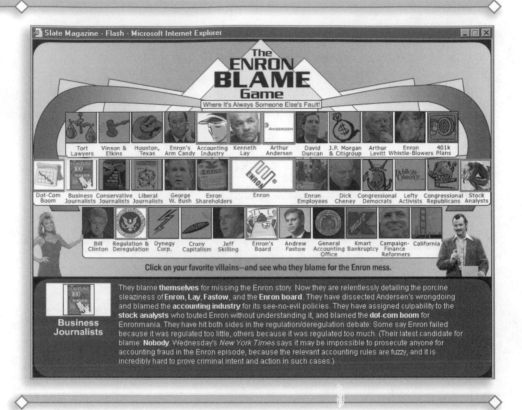

From Slate Magazine. Reprinted with permission from United Media.

the state spends money on as well as the sources of income. As users work, a deficit clock in the upper right corner shows the current surplus (or, more likely, deficit). When certain changes are selected, the program displays a "Look Out" message that warns of possible pitfalls. When completed, the program compares the user's plan to what the governor actually proposed. Much like *The Seattle Times* transportation projects page mentioned earlier, "Budget Balancer" gives users a real-life taste of what it's like to balance needs with available money.

MSNBC's "Soft Target" piece is even more interactive, representing a small-scale virtual reality simulator (see Exhibit 9.11). This feature, included as part of MSNBC's coverage of domestic terrorism, allows the user to pretend she is an airport baggage screener. The program opens with graphics and a voice-over that explains how it works. Then, for 2 minutes, x-ray views of bags scroll by as if on a conveyor belt, and the user must identify bags with suspicious-looking items. While doing this, the user can "zoom in" on a particular part of a bag or select a special color screener that can identify organic material used to make bombs. All the while,

A screen from Minnesota Public Radio's "Budget Balancer" feature.   **Exhibit 9.10**

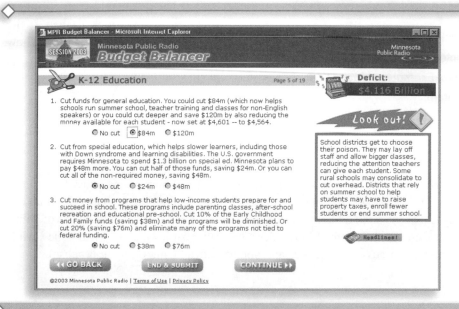

MSNBC's "Soft Target" feature allows users to pretend they're airport baggage screeners.   **Exhibit 9.11**

From MSNBC.com. Used by permission of MSNBC.

On the Web

Check out these examples and other examples of multimedia and interactive content:
Under Chapter 9, select **Examples of Interactive and Multimedia Content.**

the user can hear the voices of passengers, and they get agitated very quickly if the screener slows down to take a closer look at a bag. At the end of the 2 minutes, the user is graded on how well she did. The program not only allows a user to "play" with baggage x-ray machines, it also helps drive home the pressures and challenges real-life screeners face.

WHAT'S NEXT

This chapter completes the four-chapter discussion of how online journalism stories are produced using text, links, multimedia elements and interactivity. The final two chapters of the book address issues facing online journalists and the future of online journalism itself. Chapter 10 provides an overview of legal and ethical issues, while Chapter 11 discusses challenges and opportunities facing online journalism.

Activities

9.1 Go to the area of Macromedia's Web site that shows examples of Flash presentations (you can find the link in the "Types of Media Elements" section of this chapter's Web site). Most of the examples aren't journalistic in nature, but find a few that demonstrate techniques that *could* be used to tell journalistic stories. How could you adapt these techniques to journalism?

9.2 Try out some of the "game" interactive elements discussed at the end of this chapter. Does interacting with information help you gain a better understanding of it?

9.3 Consider a story you might be working on now or have worked on in a previous course. How might you have used video, audio, rich content or advanced interactivity? How would these features help advance the story in ways that using only text could not?

CHAPTER 10

- To discuss issues of responsibility for libelous material, especially how they affect internet service providers and journalistic Web sites
- To examine aspects of copyright on the Internet, including the concept of fair use and digital copying
- To introduce the issues involved in online journalism sites' user agreement contracts
- To address the legal and ethical issues of linking, including deep links, inline links, framing links, associative links and links to illegal or infringing content
- To introduce ethical questions raised by blogging and how they can affect journalists

All journalists face legal and ethical issues on a daily basis. In fact, legal and ethical guidelines play such an important role in distinguishing journalism from other types of writing that many legal and ethical decisions become second nature to working journalists. No competent journalist, for example, would copy a story from a rival news organization (a violation of **copyright** law) or fail to disclose a financial relationship with a company she was writing about (a violation of an ethical tenet). The fact that these types of decisions are made without much conscious thought says a lot about how legal and ethical guidelines are ingrained in the journalistic profession.

Of course, not all legal and ethical decisions are so cut-and-dried. Sometimes, in fact, legal and ethical guidelines may lead a journalist in two different directions. It may be legal to identify the name of an alleged rape victim, for example, but most journalistic organizations refuse to do so for ethical reasons. The point is that working journalists need to understand the legal and ethical issues they will face in their daily work and know how to make the right decisions—or at least decisions based on the right criteria.

In most cases, online journalists face the same legal and ethical constraints as journalists working in print or broadcast. Although in its early days (say, the mid-

1990s) the Internet was often described as a lawless, freewheeling, "Wild West" medium, the reality is that laws developed for other media are simply being adapted to the Internet. Courts and other legal entities increasingly see the Internet not as a revolutionary new medium but rather as an evolution of existing media. So, an online journalist can be sued for **libel** just as any other journalist can, and the parameters deciding the outcome of the case would be much the same as they would be for a journalist working in print or broadcast.

All of this is not to say that the Internet does not pose any challenges to existing legal and ethical conventions. It does. The Internet's seamless nature, its ease of access and its ability to allow information to appear and disappear almost instantly all create new legal and ethical issues. In some cases, these legal issues are still in limbo, as courts have either not yet decided them or have reached conflicting decisions.

This chapter does not attempt to provide a complete overview of the legal and ethical issues of journalism. Instead, it concentrates on the legal and ethical issues that raise concerns specifically to online journalism. These issues include libel, obscenity and indecency, copyright, the laws and ethics of linking and the ethics of writing **blogs.**

LIBEL

Libel is defined as the publication of false information that is defamatory, or likely to harm someone's reputation. It is closely related to slander, which involves spoken words or gestures, but carries stiffer penalties because published information is considered more permanent. In general, statements contained in Web pages, public chat rooms or discussion boards are considered published—and thus subject to libel suits. So, a journalist who makes a libelous statement in a Web-based story is just as responsible as one who does so in a print-based story. However, two aspects of libel law do have special relevance for online journalists: the question of libel liability, or who *else* might be responsible for a libelous statement; and forum shopping, the practice of filing a lawsuit in a court more likely to find that a libel has been committed.

Libel Liability

Journalists—and the organizations they work for—can be held responsible for libelous statements they make. But can an Internet service provider (ISP) be held responsible for statements made in its discussion forums or on Web pages it provides access to? Can a news Web site be liable for statements made by readers in its discussion forums?

Two early court cases in the United States offered somewhat conflicting guidance on whether ISPs could be held liable. In 1991's *Cubby v. CompuServe,* a federal district court in New York held that the CompuServe ISP was not liable for defamatory statements made by a subscriber in one of its online forums. The court said that since CompuServe had not exercised any editorial control over the information in its forums, it was playing a role similar to a news vendor, bookstore or library, none of which are liable for libelous statements made in materials they sell.[1] Four years later, however, a state court ruled that a different ISP *was* responsible for statements made on one of its bulletin boards. In *Stratton Oakmont, Inc. v. Prodigy Services Co.,* the court said that the Prodigy ISP was responsible for libelous statements because it had actively engaged in screening and editing the content of its bulletin boards.[2] Prodigy had marketed itself as a family-friendly ISP and thus had made efforts to control the content of its bulletin boards. This fact, the court said, made Prodigy liable for statements contained in the bulletin boards.

Uncertainty over the liability of ISPs led U.S. lawmakers to address the issue in the Communications Decency Act (CDA), which was passed as part of the landmark Telecommunications Act of 1996.[3] Section 230 of the CDA says: "No provider or user of an interactive computer service shall be treated as the publisher or speaker of any information provided by another information content provider."[4] Although the U.S. Supreme Court eventually struck down the portions of the CDA dealing with indecency on the Internet (as discussed later in this chapter), Section 230 still stands and is now the defining law for the liability of ISPs. In two notable cases, 1997's *Zeran v. America Online* and 1998's *Blumenthal v. Drudge and America Online,* courts held that Section 230 protected ISPs from liability for statements made by others.[5] The latter case arose when Sidney Blumenthal, a White House aide in the Clinton administration, was accused of spousal abuse by the Drudge Report Web site. Blumenthal sued both Matt Drudge and America Online, which included the *Drudge Report* as part of its service. The federal district court allowed the portion of the suit against Drudge to go forward but noted that AOL was protected by the CDA. In the *Zeran* case, the federal appeals court said that the CDA "plainly immunizes computer service providers like AOL for liability for information that originates with third parties."[6]

It is less clear, however, whether a journalistic Web site would be protected from liability for statements made by users on its discussion forums or in its **chat** rooms. Although print-based newspapers have traditionally been protected against liability for reader statements in letters to the editor because they are judged to be opinions (which are protected from libel suits), letters asserting statements of fact can still bring libel cases. Thus, a statement made in a discussion forum that is clearly an opinion could not be considered libelous, but a statement asserting factual information could be. The question would be, "Who is liable for the statement: the writer, the journalistic organization or both?"

No significant court cases have provided guidance on this issue. A Web site, then, has three basic choices:

1. Screening and editing all content appearing on discussion boards and in chat rooms
2. Exercising no control over what users say
3. Choosing not to provide discussion boards, chat rooms or other user feedback features

The first choice, if done systematically and thoroughly, would likely screen out potentially libelous material but also would require significant human resources and expense. If a libelous statement did get through, a court would be more likely to hold the Web site liable because, as in the *Prodigy* case, it was exercising editorial control. The second choice makes it much more likely that potentially libelous statements would be made public, but the Web site could argue in court that it was merely providing a forum—not creating or editing the content. Because of this uncertainty, many online journalism sites choose the third option.

Forum Shopping

Most traditional media have a limited distribution range. A local print newspaper, for example, might be distributed only within a single county or state, and a local television station's range may be only 50 miles. Material on the Internet, however, can potentially reach nearly *everywhere,* crossing national and international borders.

This means that Internet information also crosses national and international legal jurisdictions. Thus, a news organization based in the United States that publishes a Web site could potentially be sued for libel in a court located in a country halfway around the globe. Forum shopping potentially gives plaintiffs the power to choose courts that are more likely to rule in their favor. This is not insignificant because many countries have libel laws that place a much greater burden on the publisher to prove something is *not* libelous than do U. S. courts, which generally place the burden of proof on the plaintiff.

For example, a reporter for *The Guardian,* a London-based newspaper, was put on trial in Zimbabwe for "publishing falsehoods." The paper argued that Zimbabwe did not have jurisdiction in the case because the paper (and Web site) was not published there. Although the reporter was ultimately found not liable,

On the Web

More about the cases and sites discussed, including updates. Plus, a look at how other countries' libel laws compare to those in the United States:

Under Chapter 10, select **Libel.**

the Zimbabwe court rejected *The Guardian*'s claims that it did not have jurisdiction. Similarly, Australian courts rejected the Dow Jones Company's efforts to have a libel case brought by an Australian businessman heard in New Jersey rather than Australia.

Thus, organizations that publish on the Internet need to be aware that they can potentially be held responsible for "libels" that would be quickly thrown out of courts in the United States.

OBSCENITY AND INDECENCY

Although they are often used interchangeably in causal conversation, the terms **obscenity** and **indecency** actually have distinct legal meanings. Unlike indecency, obscenity refers to a relatively narrow range of material that describes or displays sexual material in a manner designed to cause arousal and lacks artistic, literary or scientific value. Material that is judged to be obscene is not protected by the First Amendment, and thus federal, state and local governments can enact laws regulating or prohibiting it. Indecency encompasses a much broader range of sexual and nonsexual material, including certain words, nudity or other things that could offend manners or morals.

Traditionally, courts have applied the obscenity standard to print-based media and the indecency standard to broadcast media, such as television and radio. In other words, a wider range of prohibited material exists for broadcast media (and, to a lesser extent, cable and subscription networks) than for print media. Courts have justified the stricter indecency standard because of broadcast's scarcity (only a limited number of channels are available) and pervasive nature (a person easily can avoid a printed publication likely to contain indecent material but might happen accidentally upon an indecent broadcast program).

The Communications Decency Act of 1996 (discussed earlier in this chapter) sought to apply the stricter indecency standard to the Internet. The CDA prohibited, subject to a $250,000 fine and up to 5 years in prison, "any comment, request, suggestion, proposal, image, or other communication that, in context, depicts or describes, in terms patently offensive as measured by contemporary community standards, sexual or excretory activities or organs" on the Internet.

The legal challenge to the CDA was seen as a defining moment in the development of the Internet. For the first time, the U.S. Supreme Court would be called on to decide whether the Internet would be treated like a print medium or like the much more restricted broadcast medium. Many freedom of speech advocates feared that the Supreme Court justices—not exactly a young and hip group—would not understand the significance of the nascent Internet.

The Court, however, struck down the CDA, calling its ban on indecent material on the Internet "vague and overbroad." In doing so, the Court noted that the Internet shared neither broadcast's scarcity nor its pervasive nature and thus should

On the Web

More on the difference between obscenity and indecency, the debate about the Communications Decency Act, the cases discussed and updates: Under Chapter 10, select **Obscenity and Indecency.**

not be regulated as strictly. The Court still prohibited obscenity on the Internet, because obscenity was prohibited on all media.[7]

Similarly, the U.S. Supreme Court's 2002 decisions in *Ashcroft v. ACLU* and *Ashcroft v. Free Speech Coalition* ruled that further attempts to restrict indecent material on the Internet violated the First Amendment.[8] Clearly, when it comes to obscenity and indecency, the Internet is treated more like print than broadcast. Although this may be more significant to operators of online pornography sites than to the typical journalist, it is still important because it likely presages the general way the courts will view the Internet in future disputes. Clearly, most courts recognize that the Internet has unique attributes and that comparisons to existing media must be made logically and cautiously.

COPYRIGHT

Copyright law grants the creator of an artistic or literary work the exclusive rights to use (or not use) the work as she sees fit. In other words, the copyright holder has the exclusive power to print, disseminate, license, transform or add to the work. Copyright protects original works of authorship "fixed in a tangible medium," meaning that they are perceptible directly or with the aid of a machine. Book pages, videotapes, DVD discs and computer files are all examples of tangible media for the purposes of copyright. When someone illegally copies or otherwise uses a copyrighted work, he is said to have *infringed* on the owner's copyright.

A wide variety of works can be copyrighted (see Exhibit 10.1). Things that cannot be copyrighted include slogans, short phrases, extemporaneous speeches, facts or ideas, common information (such as calendars or phone books) and government works. Copyright protection lasts for a certain amount of time (normally, the life of the author plus 70 years), and after that it enters the **public domain,** meaning anyone is free to use it.

As applied to the Internet, copyright law protects, among other things, Web pages, e-mails and postings to discussion groups. So, such items are recognized by law as being the property of their authors and generally cannot be reproduced without permission from the authors. Copyright holders may indicate ownership of their work by including a copyright notice, but works are still protected under copyright law even if they don't. The general form of a copyright notice includes the word *Copyright,* the copyright symbol (©), the year of creation and the copyright holder's name.

List of works that can be copyrighted.   **Exhibit 10.1**

Literary works, including short stories, novels and poetry

Musical works, including lyrics, musical scores and recorded versions

Dramatic works

Periodicals

Maps

Works of art, including cartoons and product packaging (e.g., CD and book covers)

Sculptural works

Technical and architectural drawings

Photographs

Movies and other audiovisual works

Computer programs

Compilation of works

Derivative works

Although such a notice is not required, it is still a good idea to include one wherever possible to remind people that the work belongs to the copyright holder.

Fair Use

One exception to the exclusive right of copyright holders to control the dissemination of their work involves the concept of **fair use,** which allows others to use part of a copyrighted work in certain situations. Fair use doctrine is based on the notion that there is no such thing as a completely original thought or idea and that all artistic and literary works are to some degree derivative of previous works. Thus, to facilitate the creation of new works that build on the concepts of previous works, copyright law allows portions of copyrighted works to be reused without the permission of the copyright holder.

Fair use is designed to allow criticism, commentary, news reporting, teaching and research involving copyrighted works. In these endeavors, the law recognizes that it is often necessary to actually *use* part of the original work. For example, a book critic may want to cite several passages of a new novel as an example of how he thinks the author's prose is disjointed, or a reporter may wish to use excerpts of a book written by a presidential candidate. These types of uses are permitted under fair use, which was written into the U.S. Copyright Act of 1976 after developing in court cases over nearly a century.

In determining whether a particular situation constitutes fair use, courts look at four factors:

1. The purpose and character of the use

2. The nature of the copyrighted work

3. The amount and substantiality of the portion used

4. The effect of the use on the potential market for or value of the copyrighted work

Fair use is important to understand not only because it can be useful for journalists who want to excerpt copyrighted material, but because it leads to many copyright disputes. Although the four factors just mentioned can give a broad outline of whether a specific use is actually fair use, the guidelines are also somewhat vague. In most copyright infringement cases, in fact, the party accused of violating copyright will cite fair use as at least a partial defense.

Copyright on the Internet

Copyright is especially important on the Internet because no previous medium has made it so easy to copy its content. Nearly anything that appears on a Web page—text, a photograph, an animated graphic, a sound or video clip, even the HTML coding of the page itself—can generally be copied with a few mouse clicks. Once copied, the material can then be pasted onto a new page, saved to the copyright infringer's hard drive, e-mailed to others or manipulated in any number of ways. Unlike other digital media such as DVD discs, which are protected against copying by electronic safeguards, there is no way to protect most Internet content. Thus, being able to go after copyright infringers through the legal system is particularly important to Internet content creators.

One such case involved a Web site called FreeRepublic.com, which calls itself "The Premier Conservative News Forum." One of the features of FreeRepublic.com allowed users to post and comment on news articles, including ones that had appeared on the Web sites of *The Los Angeles Times* and *The Washington Post*. In 1999, the two papers sued the operators of the FreeRepublic Web site for copyright infringement, citing numerous instances where the entire text of Web-based articles had been republished without their permission. Users had simply used the cut-and-paste features of their software programs to post the articles, with the encouragement of the operators of FreeRepublic.com. A federal district court in California agreed that the site had violated the papers' copyright and ordered the Web site to remove the offending material.[9]

In another case, the operator of a **bulletin board system (BBS)** scanned more than 100 digital photographs from *Playboy* magazine and posted them online. When *Playboy* sued, the BBS operator cited fair use as a defense, but a court rejected that claim and ordered him to remove the offending images. The court further ruled that the operator had violated *Playboy*'s trademark rights by describing the images using the terms *Playboy* and *Playmate.*[10]

The most famous Internet copyright case involved the Napster Web site, which allowed users to exchange copyrighted music files in the MP3 format. Although copyrighted files were not actually posted on Napster's Web site, the company's software facilitated the exchange of files among individual users. The rock band Metallica, and later the Recording Industry Association of America (RIAA), sued Napster for copyright infringement, and courts eventually forced the music service to end its free file-sharing services. Napster's service, the courts ruled, clearly violated the rights of individual copyright holders. Meanwhile, similar sites, such as Gnutella and Kazaa, raise the same types of legal issues. The RIAA has also

> ### On the Web
>
> More information about copyright and fair use, including links to cases and updates. Also, the continuing debate over Napster and other online file-sharing sites. Plus, some public domain sites where you can download images and other material:
>
> Under Chapter 10, select **Copyright.**

gone after individual downloaders, forcing them to pay settlement monies to avoid court. One 12-year-old girl, for example, had to pay $2,000 for 1,000 songs she had downloaded.

The liability of ISPs in copyright infringement cases is not clear. The portions of the CDA absolving ISPs from liability for libelous content do not apply to copyright infringement; thus, there is a "gray area," much like what existed in the area of libel liability before Section 230 of the CDA was enacted. The key consideration seems to be whether the ISP knew or should have known that its users were violating copyright. Here again, ISPs that screen material downloaded by users are likely to be liable for copyright infringements, while those that do not aren't.

Copyright and the Online Journalist

As an online journalist, you should generally assume that anything you encounter on the Internet is copyrighted, unless it is expressly offered for public domain use. This includes e-mails, bulletin board postings, images, musical lyrics, cartoons, sound and video files and Web page content.

Seeing Through the Shrinkwrap of User Agreements

Did you know that every time you visit an online journalism site you are entering into a legal contract?

Nearly every online journalism site (as well as the vast majority of commercial sites of all types) have a set of rules on which they condition use of the site. These conditions are normally spelled out on a page called "User Agreement," "Terms of Use" or something similar. The agreements are usually structured in such a way that you as a user agree to them by the mere act of visiting the site—even if you have never seen the agreement itself. It is similar to the "shrinkwrap" agreements that accompany most software—you assent to the terms of the agreement by the act of purchasing, installing and using the software. It doesn't matter whether you read the contract.

What is remarkable about these agreements is that, in some cases, they attempt to expand the scope of copyright law while at the same time seeking to limit a site's liability for information contained on it. Researcher Victoria Smith Ekstrand examined the user agreements of the top 50-circulation newspaper Web sites and found that many prohibit the copying of *any* material on the site—including material that is considered public domain under copyright law.[1]

Some sites also claim copyright ownership of postings made by users in online forums while at the same time absolving themselves of responsibility for the postings. A number of sites even point out that there is no guarantee the information on the site is accurate or up-to-date. Imagine if your daily newspaper arrived on your doorstep with such restrictions!

As discussed in this chapter, copyright law has been designed both to protect authors *and* to facilitate information flow. Thus, it is unclear whether user agreements that seem to go beyond the scope of copyright law would stand up if challenged in court.

In the meantime, however, as more and more people get their news and information online, such restrictive user agreements could damage the free flow of information. This is particularly troubling for the practice of journalism. "The cumulative effect of promoting terms of access to news may create new risks for a healthy marketplace of ideas and a vibrant, free-flowing public domain from which new works, including news stories, are created," Ekstrand notes. "Restrictive terms of access shrink the availability of public domain information, the lifeblood of journalism and of all new creative and informational works."[2]

[1] Victoria Smith Ekstrand, "Online News: User Agreements and Implications for Readers," *Journalism and Mass Communication Quarterly 79,* no. 3 (Autumn 2002), pp. 602–618.

[2]   Ibid., p. 613.

Thus, even though it is in many cases very easy to include such content as part of your online stories, you are legally prohibited from doing so. For example, you can't simply cut and paste an image from a news site and include it in your story, or use a song from a CD as a soundtrack for your Flash site, without getting express permission from the copyright holder. You do not own material just because you can copy it to your Web page.

Fair use provisions do allow you to use *parts* of copyrighted material in some cases. For example, you could include a short section from a company's online quarterly report. In these cases, of course, you should **attribute** the information so users know where it came from, just as a journalist would attribute information from print or other sources.

Associated Press (AP) wire copy—as well as stories from other news agencies—is also copyrighted. AP copy is so ubiquitous on journalistic Web sites that many beginning journalists mistakenly believe that it is in the public domain. However, AP copy is definitely copyrighted, and Web sites that use it legally are paying the Associated Press for the right to do so. Unless you or your organization has an agreement with the AP, you can't copy their stories to your Web site. The same restrictions apply to the use of AP photos.

If you're at all in doubt about whether something is copyrighted or how much material fair use allows you to include, you should err on the safe side. If you don't *know* you can use something, don't use it.

LINKING LAW

Linking is the aspect of the Internet for which the norms of previous media offer the least guidance. Although it may seem like a harmless function—indeed, the linking of information seamlessly and easily is one of the main factors in the Internet's popularity—linking can raise difficult legal and ethical issues.

The legal issues revolve around copyright and unfair competition. Unfair competition includes such violations as trademark infringement (using another's trademark without permission), dilution (using a trademark improperly), passing off (giving the impression that another's work is your own) and false or deceptive advertising. When links are presented in certain ways, as you are about to see, they can give misleading impressions about the source of the linked content or the relationship between the linker and the linkee. In other cases, links might be seen as encouraging or aiding illegal activities. Courts in the United States have recognized that links are a form of speech and thus are protected by the First Amendment. However, as in all constitutional issues, these First Amendment rights must be balanced with other issues, including copyright, unfair competition and other laws.

Unfortunately, not a lot of case law exists to guide would-be linkers. Unlike other legal areas, there are few rules that can be easily followed. In fact, as one observer summed up the situation:

Unfortunately, many times the legal question "Can I do 'X'?" is not easily answered by following a simple rule. It is often answered by someone attempting to do "X," getting sued, and having the courts ultimately decide whether "X" is legal or not. It's clear that caution in linking is becoming a requirement.[11]

The legal issues surrounding linking can be broken into five main categories: deep linking, inline linking, framing, associative linking and linking to illegal or infringing material.

Deep Linking

Deep linking refers to the practice of bypassing a Web site's home page or other introductory material by linking to a page "deep" within the site's structure (see Exhibit 10.2). Many Web site operators object to the practice of deep linking because advertising revenue is often based on the total number of page views or on the number of views of the home page.

Exhibit 10.2 Deep linking.

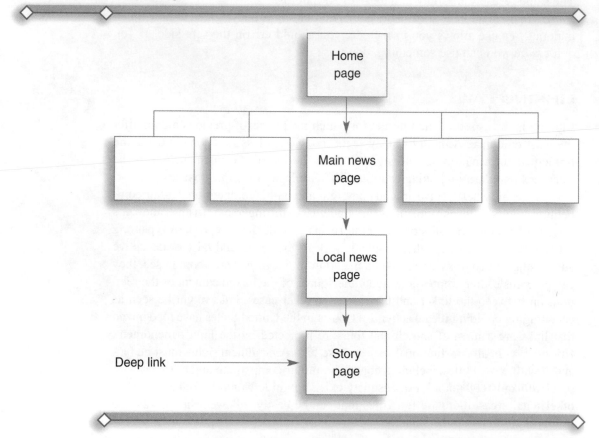

For example, if you visit the home page of a particular news site, it might take you three mouse clicks to get to the story about last week's pro football game. Thus, you start on the home page, click the "Sports" link to go to the main sports page, then click "Football" to go to the football page and, finally, click the link to the story you want. You have viewed a total of four pages, including the home page. A deep link directly to the story, on the other hand, bypasses the three preliminary pages and takes you directly to the story.

In two separate cases, Ticketmaster has sued the operators of Web sites that used deep links to pages within its site. In the first case, Ticketmaster sued Microsoft because its seattlesidewalk.com Web site contained several links to event pages within the Ticketmaster site. Ticketmaster argued that such linking implied a relationship between Microsoft and Ticketmaster, and that the practice deprived Ticketmaster of the ability to control its content. The two companies eventually settled the case out of court, with Microsoft agreeing to link only to Ticketmaster's home page.

In a second case, Ticketmaster sued tickets.com, a rival Web site that also contained deep links to Ticketmaster content. Although this case is still pending, a judge refused to issue an injunction forcing tickets.com to remove its links, at one point likening deep links to a library card catalog that allows a user to easily find information. A federal appeals court affirmed that decision, although it is still possible that Ticketmaster will win when the case goes to trial.[12]

Thus, the legality of deep linking is very much in limbo. Many observers believe that courts will ultimately refuse to restrict deep linking as long as the linking site makes it clear that it has not created the linked content. Another reason for this belief is that Web sites—if they choose to—can actually block deep linking through technological means. In other words, if a site does not want others to deep link to it, it can simply install technologies that will automatically send deep links to the home page. Still, an increasing number of sites are attempting to place legal restrictions on deep linking. For example, KPMG International, a business consulting firm, forbids links that bypass its home page, and many sites reserve the right to request the removal of links they object to. It is unclear whether these restrictions would stand up to legal challenges, however.

Inline Linking

Recall from Chapter 3 that you can place an image on a Web page using the <img> tag in HTML. The "src=" attribute of the <img> tag designates the source file for the image, and it can point to either a file on the local server or a file somewhere else on the Internet. So, in essence, you can place a copy of an image that belongs to someone else on your Web page without actually copying the file itself. The <img> tag simply follows the URL, retrieves the image file and places it on the page. This process is called **inline linking.**

Inline links are potentially problematic because they can be used to display copyrighted images in a new setting without permission of the copyright holder. In one case, a man wrote HTML code that displayed the daily "Dilbert" comic strip on his personal Web page. The "src=" attribute for the image tag simply pointed to the comic strip as posted on the United Media Web site, which had permission to publish the comic. United Media complained, and the man eventually removed the offending link.

The only significant court case on inline linking involved Ditto.com, a search engine that let users find graphic files on the Internet. Ditto.com displayed "thumbnail" (small) versions of the graphics on its page, allowing users to click the thumbnail to retrieve the actual image, which opened as an inline graphic in a new window. Photographer Lesley Kelly sued Ditto.com for indexing copyrighted images contained on his Web site, challenging both the fact that Ditto.com had created thumbnail versions of his work and the fact that the images were displayed full-size as inline links. Kelly argued that both practices violated his public display rights under copyright. The court eventually ruled that the thumbnail images amounted to fair use but remanded the case back to the lower courts for further discussion of the use of the full-size images.[13] Much like deep linking, then, the law on inline linking remains unclear.

As an online journalist, however, you should generally apply the same standards to inline linking that you would to actually copying something to your page, as discussed in the previous section. If something is copyrighted, you can't include an inline link to it without express permission.

Framing

Some similar issues arise in regard to **framing** external content. As discussed in Chapter 3, Web pages can be broken into different sections, called **frames,** and each section can have independent content. In framing a link, for example, you could have content from your Web page (a logo, navigation bar, advertisements and so forth) surrounding external content (as shown in Exhibit 10.3). In effect, you would be taking someone else's content and putting a frame around it to make it look as if you produced it. The frames could even be set so that only a portion of the external page would be visible, cutting out advertising or other information surrounding a story, for example.

Framing in such a manner to make it look as if you produced something you didn't is clearly an ethical violation. It is also legally problematic, although here again the courts have provided little guidance so far. In one case, CNN, *The Washington Post* and several other media organizations sued the operator of TotalNEWS.com, a Web site that framed content from other media sites. As is so often the case, however, the parties settled their differences out of court, with TotalNEWS agreeing to cease its practice of framing and to instead provide normal links to content produced by others.

Framing another site's content.   **Exhibit 10.3**

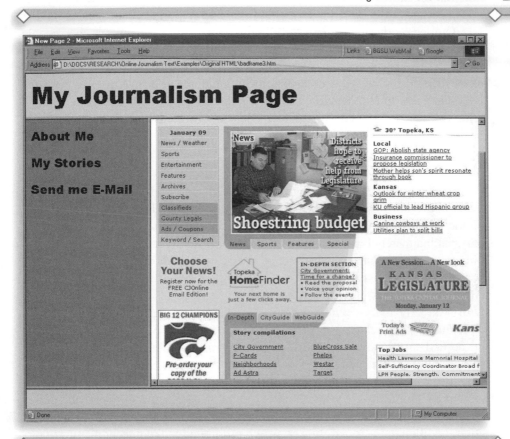

Portions from CJOnline.com. Reprinted with permission.

Associative Linking

Associative linking considers how a page's content can affect the reputation of sites it links to. For example, in 1999, the Archdiocese of St. Louis sued an Internet site after the site included a link to the archdiocese's trademarked "Papal Visit 1999" on the same page with links to sexually explicit Web sites. A U.S. district court ruled that the unauthorized use of the trademark had diluted and tarnished it.[14]

Similarly, the Council of Better Business Bureaus (BBB) has a policy that prohibits nonmember companies from linking to its Web site, http://www.bbb.org. The BBB oversees the practices of companies, endorsing and permitting as members those that conform to its standards. The idea behind the linking prohibition for nonmembers is that allowing a company to link to the BBB Web site implies an endorsement of the company by the Better Business Bureau. Here again, it is unclear whether the BBB's policy would stand up to a legal challenge.

The legal concept behind prohibiting such associative links is that people might hold a linked site in lower regard because of other links that appear on a page. Courts have noted, however, that for such links to be prohibited, a clear and close relationship must exist between the link and the offensive material. If a site contains a link to a trademarked site and a link to *another* site that then contains a link to, say, pornography, that likely would not be a close enough connection.

Linking to Illegal or Infringing Material

Perhaps the most controversial legal questions arise over links to illegal material or material that infringes on others' copyrights or trademarks. The controversy is based on the fact that the Web site operator does not possess or post illegal or infringing material but merely links to a site that does. Some observers have seen court prohibitions on such linking as a threat to the open flow of information on the Internet.

In two separate cases, however, United States courts have said that the First Amendment offers no protection for links to illegal or infringing content. *Universal City Studios v. Reimerdes* involved a computer program called DeCSS, which unlocks the copyright protection on commercial DVDs and allows them to be copied on a computer. The DeCSS program, which originated in Norway, spread quickly over the Internet as various sites made it available for download. One of those sites was www.2600.com, the Web site for the magazine *2600,* also known as *The Hacker Quarterly* (see Exhibit 10.4). A group of movie studios sought an injunction ordering the site to remove the program, citing 1998's Digital Millennium Copyright Act, which prohibited making technologies to circumvent digital copyright protection available. A court granted the injunction.

Consequently, the site removed the program from its Web site but substituted a series of links to other sites that provided the program. Again, the movie studios argued for—and got—injunctions requiring removal of the links.[15] *2600* magazine appealed the case, but a federal appeals court affirmed the lower court's ruling. In a related ruling, the California Supreme Court said that a man's First Amendment rights were not violated by an injunction ordering him to remove a link to DeCSS from his Web site.[16]

A second case involved Jerald and Sandra Tanner, who ran a Web site criticizing the Church of Jesus Christ of Latter-Day Saints. After the Tanners posted portions of the copyrighted *Church Handbook of Instructions* on their Web site, a branch of the church won a court injunction ordering them to remove the copyrighted material. Like *2600,* the Tanners

On the Web

More information, analysis and updates on linking issues, including links to sites and cases discussed:

Under Chapter 10, select **Linking Law.**

The Web site for *The Hacker Quarterly,* http://www.2600.com.   **Exhibit 10.4**

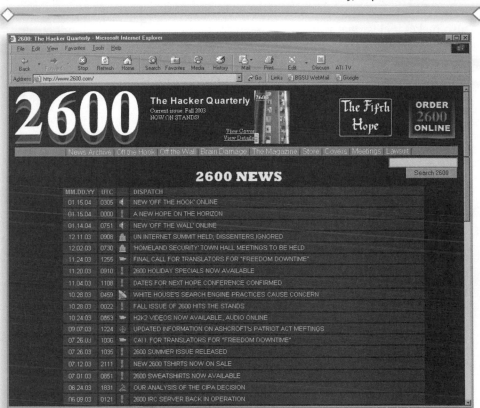

substituted links to other Web sites that contained the copyrighted work. Again, the church was able to get an injunction ordering them to remove the links.[17]

Legal Implications for Online Journalists

As discussed in Chapter 8, online journalists need to be thorough when searching out, selecting and presenting links in their stories. The legal issues discussed in this section offer some further guidance for preventing lawsuits and other legal problems. As always, it is best to do some further checking if you're unsure about the legal implications of including a particular link in your story.

The proper presentation of links also can prevent legal problems and other misunderstandings. As discussed in Chapter 8, link text should always tell the users what they are going to get when the link is activated—including the source of the information. So, if the link will take users to information not created by you or not on your Web site, you should tell them that in the link text. Such a disclaimer also makes it clear that you're not taking credit for something you didn't create.

ETHICAL ISSUES

Linking

Linking can also present difficult ethical issues for an online journalist. These issues generally center on whether presenting links promotes a noxious point of view or muddies the separation between journalistic and advertising functions.

There may be times when you will do stories about certain groups with unpleasant or controversial points of view. For example, you might be writing an exposé of local white supremacist groups. The ethical question becomes whether you should include links to Web sites operated by those groups. On one hand, it could be argued that you should, since if reasonable people go to these Web sites, they will be further repulsed by the ideas they contain, thus further weakening those groups' standing in the community. However, including a link could also be seen as promoting the site, giving it and its ideas further dissemination. There is no clear answer to questions like these; they are likely to be decided on a case-by-case basis, perhaps with a meeting of several members of the newsroom staff.

You should also strive to achieve **fairness** in the links you choose to include in your stories. As discussed in Chapter 1, the journalistic tenet of fairness mandates that we include as many different points of view as possible. Thus, you should include a variety of links that represent different points of view.

The issues involved in keeping editorial and advertising content separate are no less important. In print and other traditional media, a clear distinction usually exists between advertising content and editorial content. The Internet, however, allows both types of content to intermingle as if they were one and the same. Thus, online journalists potentially face difficult ethical questions when the lines between advertising and journalism are blurred.

For example, should a book review on your site include a link to an online retailer offering the book for sale? The answer should be "no," unless the link is clearly separated from the editorial content and labeled as advertising. Similarly, many sites use targeted advertising that includes specific ads based on the user or the content of the page (see Chapter 11). Much of this targeting is automated, as computers look for certain keywords or attributes of the user and then include an ad based on this information. For example, next to a story about a snowstorm, an ad for a snow removal company might appear. In a way, this is no different than a sporting goods company placing an ad on a paper's sports page, but on a Web page users might not realize the separation. Again, the critical issue is making it clear to users that the link is not an editorial endorsement but rather an advertisement.

Blogging

The practice of blogging, as discussed in Chapter 5, raises particular ethical questions. As a more free-form and unfiltered form of communication, blogging is normally not subject to the same checks, balances and structures of traditional journalism. Thus, it raises the question, "Can bloggers be journalists?" Or, perhaps the better question is, "Can journalists be bloggers?"

A growing number of media organizations embrace blogging, with some, such as MSNBC.com, running blogs through traditional editing processes to ensure journalistic integrity. Others see blogging as decidedly *not* a legitimate form of journalism, preferring the more structured format of traditional stories.

More specific ethical questions can arise when a working journalist also blogs. As discussed in Chapter 4, more and more journalists are also maintaining blog sites, usually addressing their specific "beat" or area of expertise. The issue then becomes whether the journalist is being a journalist when she is blogging, and whether the journalist's media organization is responsible for what the journalist writes in her blog. What if the journalist covers issues in her blog that the parent media organization doesn't cover? Does that make the media organization appear weak? What if the journalist criticizes her parent media organization in a blog?

During the Iraq war in 2003, CNN correspondent Kevin Sites started posting stories, pictures and commentary to a blog. At first, CNN asked him to insert a disclaimer saying that the blog was the work of Sites, not CNN. However, CNN then told Sites to stop contributing material to the blog, an order he complied with. In a statement to the press, CNN did not address the ethical questions of blogging, instead noting that it felt that Sites should be devoting his writing time to his CNN stories. "Covering a war for CNN and its 35 international networks is a full-time job," said a CNN spokesperson. "We've asked Kevin to concentrate on that for the time being."[18]

> ### On the Web
>
> More analysis on the ethical debates over blogging and linking:
> Under Chapter 10, select **Ethical Issues.**

Aaron Barnhart's TVBarn.com Web site, in contrast, is fully endorsed by *The Kansas City Star,* the paper for which he works as a television critic (see Exhibit 10.5). TVBarn.com contains links to Barnhart's articles that appear in the *Star,* and the *Star* has a link to the TVBarn.com Web site.

The ethical questions surrounding blogging are likely to grow as the practice becomes more common. The questions about blogging, in fact, mirror many of the larger questions that face journalism—specifically, online journalism—in the coming decades.

Exhibit 10.5   Aaron Barnhart's TVBarn.com Web site.

E-mail Aaron • Search • TV Barn Ticker • Talkin' TV at tvbarn2

**All the TV Barn links
in your mailbox
every week!**

Enter your e-mail to get TV Barn's Monday newsletter (**more info**):

[Join!]

Monk's back. So's Maher.

A&E's got "Between the Lines," HBO is bringing back Bill Maher for 23 weeks and the "agin' Cajuns," aka the Hackberry Ramblers, are playing in many towns courtesy of PBS. Don't miss any of them.

The existential "Monk"

TV Barn contributor Coeli Carr's examination of dualism in the popular USA cable series will appeal particularly to the Jung at heart.

Reality show filler: Why it's not going away
TV Barn Radio/Paul Harris...
On NBC, greed trumps all

For the millions of us who fail to be fascinated by the wealth, business acumen and hairpiece of celebrated New York tycoon Donald Trump, last Thursday left us feeling about as cheated as a Parmalat creditor.

ABC needs to issue an APB for 'NYPD'

Yes, "NYPD Blue" is coming back. But why do I have to tell you that? Isn't that the network's job?

What's new at CES? Bullishness

With very few exceptions, this winter's edition of the Consumer Electronics Show was a repeat of the last two years' exhibitions, writes TV Barn contributor **Gary Dretzka**. But this year, exhibitors actually expect to *sell* their wares to the masses.

Sensationalism mars "Frontline"

There's little new to report in tonight's "Frontline/World" documentary, "Forbidden Iran," which promises more than it delivers.

DVDs may resurrect "Family Guy"

That's right -- Seth MacFarlane's frenetic comedy about the bizarre Griffin clan may go back into production. Why? Reruns of "Family Guy" topped the DVD bestseller list for 2003.

DVD makers blind to access problems

Scores of blockbuster movie titles are released on DVD every year that are missing accessibility features for people who need help watching movies. But the studios have already *paid* for those features. So why are they being left off the disc?

"My Big Fat Obnoxious Fiance" -- too good to be true?
TV Barn Radio/Paul Harris...
TV's midseason: Uh, curb your enthusiasm

The new year begins with retreads, spinoffs and reality sequels galore. Be still, my heart! It's a snarky start to 2004 for TV Barn.

2003 proved TV a mixed medium

Did a lot of television in 2003 suck? Sure -- but a lot of TV didn't suck this year, too, proving once again that a 500-channel universe has greatly improved the quality of the medium, even if it's raised the confusion level at the same time.

Tom Heald's
**Remote Patrol
Quiz of the Day:**

Which alien invader(s) were on the earth for the most episodes (not including cartoon counterparts or reunions)?

X) "Alien Nation"
F) "ALF"
I) "Mork & Mindy"
L) "My Favorite Martian"
E) "V"

Click for the answer and today's Remote Patrol

Topics du jour at tvbarn2:

OK, I'll Bite...
Dougie Zucker Trying to Save Banfield's Job?
Green cheese making a comeback
ABC Accuses CBS of checkbook Journalism (No, Not on Jacko)
The belated death of Channel4000.com
Dennis Miller
Ashleigh Banfield
Carol Mosely-Braun

New to TV Barn?

FAQ: About this site and Aaron Barnhart
Feedback: Click here to send Aaron e-mail
We're talking TV on the **tvbarn2 message board**
LIVE! **TV Barn Radio** with Paul Harris every Tuesday at 12:35 p.m. CT on "The Big 550" (**latest chat**)
Publicists: **Please read!**

Friends of TV Barn

Paul Harris
Andy Ihnatko
Heath Row
Mark Evanier
Jim Romenesko
Harvey Pekar
Phil Rosenthal
Mark Pender
Robert Feder
Charlie Meyerson
Brian Unger

Support TV Barn

The Critics

It Oughta Be a Crime - **TeeVee.org**
Other TV critics

Misc.

The **TV critic's toolbox**
TV ratings **explained**
Top 25-rated shows for each season

WHAT'S NEXT

From financial questions about how online journalism will be supported to social questions about who will have access to online journalism, the final chapter introduces the challenges—and opportunities—that face online journalism in the coming years.

Activities

10.1 Examine the user agreements of some of the journalistic sites you visit often. What do they say about copyright, linking and responsibility for postings made by users? Do you think these user agreements would stand up to court challenges?

10.2 Consider the legal questions presented by the various types of links described in this chapter. What are the competing interests in each? In other words, what types of rights need to be balanced with the prospective linker's free speech rights?

10.3 Look at some of the stories, photos and other media elements from third parties on a journalistic Web site such as CNN.com or MSNBC.com. Obviously, the sites have agreements with these third parties to use their copyrighted works. Look for photo credits and other text that acknowledges the copyright owner. How many different copyright owners can you find?

ENDNOTES

1. *Cubby v. CompuServe,* 776 F. Supp. 135 (S.D.N.Y. 1991).

2. *Stratton Oakmont, Inc. v. Prodigy Services Co.,* 23 Med. L. Rptr. 1794 (N.Y. Sup. Ct. 1995).

3. 104 Pub. L. 104, title 5, 110 Stat. 56 (1996).

4. Sec. 230, http://www4.law.cornell.edu/uscode/47/230.html (accessed November 10, 2003).

5. See *Zeran v. America Online, Inc.,* 129 F.3d 327 (4th Cir. 1997); and *Blumenthal v. Drudge and America Online,* 992 F. Supp. 44 (D.D.C. 1998).

6. *Zeran v. America Online, Inc.,* 328.

7. *Reno v. ACLU,* 521 U.S. 844 (1997).

8. See *Ashcroft v. ACLU,* 122 S.Ct. 1700 (2002); and *Ashcroft v. Free Speech Coalition,* 122 S.Ct. 1389 (2002).

9. *Los Angeles Times v. Free Republic,* 200 U.S. Dist. LEXIS 5669, No. 98-7840 (C.D. Cal. 1999).

10. *Playboy Enterprises v. Frena,* 839 F. Supp. 1552 (M.D. Fla. 1993).

11. George H. Pike, "To Link or Not to Link," *Information Today,* June 2002, p. 20.

12. See Carl S. Kaplan, "Legality of 'Deep Linking' Remains Deeply Complicated," http://www.nytimes.com/library/tech/00/04/cyber/cyberlaw/07law.html (accessed August 21, 2003); and 2001 U.S. App. LEXIS 1454.

13. *Kelly v. Arriba Soft Corp.,* July 7, 2003, http://www.linksandlaw.com/decisions-55.htm (accessed February 10, 2004).

14. *Archdiocese of St. Louis v. Internet Entertainment Group,* 34 F. Supp. 2d 1145 (E.D. Mo. 1999).

15. *Universal City Studios v. Reimerdes,* 111 F. Supp. 2d 346 (S.D.N.Y. 2000).

16. *DVD Copy Control Association v. Andrew Bunner,* 2003 Cal. LEXIS 6295.

17. *Intellectual Reserve v. Utah Lighthouse Ministry,* 75 F. Supp. 2d 1290 (D. Utah 1999).

18. Susan Mernit, "Kevin Sites and the Blogging Controversy," *Online Journalism Review,* April 3, 2003, http://www.ojr.org/ojr/workplace/1049381758.php (accessed September 10, 2003).

CHAPTER 11

GOALS

- To discuss the economic structure of online journalism, including models for funding online sites
- To address issues pertaining to online journalism's current role in society and the opportunities and challenges it faces in the future
- To show how convergence may affect online journalism in both positive and negative ways
- To discuss how online journalism can provide services to underrepresented communities

OPPORTUNITIES AND CHALLENGES

Throughout this book, we have seen how online journalism as a field is only in its infancy. It is impossible to know what online journalism ultimately will look like—either as a journalistic form or as an industry. Just as the pioneers of television journalism could not have envisioned television news as it exists today, today's online journalists are writing only the first chapter in the medium's development. It is an important chapter to be sure, but it is only the beginning.

As such, this book has not sought to be a primer for what is today the cutting edge of online production nor necessarily to teach you in depth the particular tools used today. Instead, its purpose has been to provide the basic knowledge and skills that will prepare you to work in a field that is changing constantly. I have tried to emphasize the basics: the tenets of journalism, the characteristics of online media and the skills required for online work. The idea is that no matter how online journalism develops in the coming years, you'll be prepared to "go with the flow," adapting to the changes as they come.

But while it is impossible to predict with certainty what online journalism will resemble in the future, it is possible to examine the overarching issues likely to determine its development. As these issues develop or are resolved, they will contribute significantly to shaping online journalism. Broadly speaking, I can discuss these issues in terms of *opportunities* and *challenges.* Some issues present opportunities for online journalism to expand—in scope, style or influence—while other issues might challenge online journalism, potentially thwarting its development and expansion or steering it in potentially undesirable directions. Some issues, in fact, present *both* opportunities and challenges.

This chapter examines some of these broad issues, including the economic structure of online journalism, the role of online journalism in society, **convergence** and service to underrepresented communities.

THE ECONOMIC STRUCTURE OF ONLINE JOURNALISM

Perhaps the most important issue facing online journalism is determining how it will pay for itself. At present, no clear business model for online journalism has emerged. During the early days of the Internet (say, a decade ago), many journalistic and other organizations were more than willing to pump resources into online ventures because it seemed the Internet held the potential to make everyone rich. But reality soon set in, and the burst of the "dot.com bubble" caused investors to take a more skeptical approach to the Internet. Today, as one observer notes, online journalism "is still a big experiment," and journalistic organizations "are trying just about anything" to find a profitable business model.[1]

Some evidence suggests that at least some online journalism sites are turning the corner to profitability. Several newspaper chains, including Tribune Publishing Company and Knight Ridder, have reported that their Web operations are now making money. A 2002 survey by an industry group showed that between half and two-thirds of newspaper Web sites were profitable. While newspaper sites earned an estimated $655 million in revenue in 2002, sites run by television stations were less successful, bringing in only $55 million. The Online Publishers Association, a trade group representing magazines and newspapers, also has reported increased profitability for its members. A large chunk of newspapers' revenue, experts note, comes from selling online classified advertising (see Exhibit 11.1).[2]

Classified advertising notwithstanding, there are three main ways to pay for an online journalism site: (1) selling advertising on the site, (2) charging users subscription fees and (3) charging for "value-added" services.

Selling Advertising

The traditional model that has funded most journalism in the United States for more than a century is selling advertising. Just as a newspaper can sell space on its pages or a television station can sell time on its air, a Web site can sell parts of

Classified advertising can be a significant source of revenue for both print and online newspapers. **Exhibit 11.1**

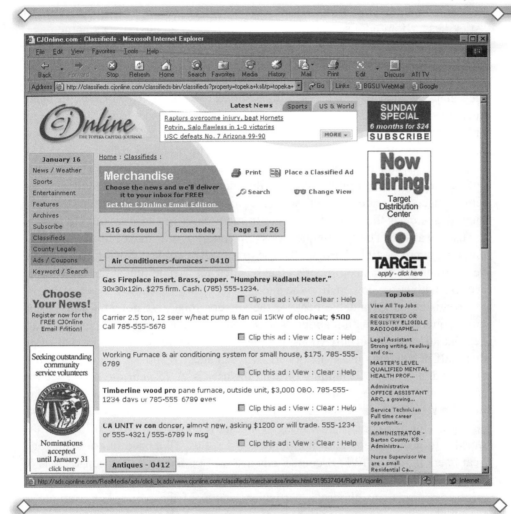

From CJOnline.com. Reprinted with permission.

its virtual space to advertisers. The determinants of how much a Web site charges for its advertising are also much like traditional media. Larger ads and more prominent positioning on the page (such as above the site's **nameplate**) cost more. The cost of advertising on a given page is also a function of the number of page views, or **hits,** for a given page. The more times a page is viewed, the more a site can charge for advertising on that page.

Through the use of specialized software, an organization can keep track of how many hits each page on its site gets and, in some cases, how many of those hits are from unique visitors. In other words, they can tell not only the total number of hits but how many different people viewed the page. Software can also keep track of how long users stay on a given page, a concept Web producers call "stickiness." If an ad also contains a link, such as to an advertiser's home page, the advertiser can in turn keep track of the number of **click-throughs,** visitors who come to its page through the ad link.

This ability to track both the number of visitors to a given page and how long they stay can also have editorial implications. For example, will editors make decisions about certain kinds of content merely because they draw lots of users or because the users stay on the pages for a long time? Already, many online journalists pay strong attention to the number of hits their stories receive.

An increasing number of online journalism sites require users to register before they can access information on the site. Some sites, such as nytimes.com, require users to create accounts with user names and passwords before they can view pages other than the home page. In other cases, a site may merely require the user to answer a couple of questions (zip code, sex and date of birth, for example) before proceeding. Through the use of browser **cookies,** this information can be saved on the user's computer so that he does not have to repeat the registration process with every new visit to the site.

Registration is valuable because the site can then give potential advertisers more concrete information about its users. For example, a cola company that targets its advertising toward young people may be interested to know that more than half of a certain site's visitors are between ages 18 and 35. Registration also allows ads to change depending on who the user is. A 15-year-old might see the cola ad, for example, while a 50-year-old would see an ad for a luxury car. Enrique Dans of Spain's Instituto de Emprese says this is the kind of specific targeting online journalism sites need to take advantage of. "We can't divide the world into just 'readers' and 'non-readers,'" he says. "We need to go further and treat users *individually*." Of course, ads also can be targeted to specific areas of a site, just as television advertisers can run their ads during particular shows or print advertisers can choose a particular section of the paper. For example, a financial services company might want to buy an ad on a site's business page.

One area where online advertising offers great potential is in reaching an audience during the day. Before the advent of the Web, many desirable potential consumers were available only during early morning (with the morning paper or drive-time radio) and evening (with radio and prime-time television) hours. Now, with so many people working in front of a computer terminal with Internet access, advertisers can reach consumers, often very well-to-do ones, from nine to five as well. As one observer points out, "the time between commutes is no longer an advertising wasteland."[3]

Despite the potential for online advertising, many online journalism sites have had a difficult time selling enough ads to make their sites profitable. While nearly every online journalism site has some ads, a much smaller number have been able to really take advantage of online as an advertising medium. Small-town newspapers, for example, often have a hard time convincing local advertisers to spend money on online ads. In other cases, local media organizations may not understand how to design and create effective online advertising. A media organization's sales staff may hesitate to concentrate on online sales, seeing more potential for making money with traditional print- or broadcast-based ads. Some media organizations now offer advertisers package deals that include both traditional ads and online ads.

Charging Subscription Fees

Another potential economic model involves charging users directly for access to the site. However, while many observers predicted that subscription fees would become the dominant model for online journalism, only a few sites have made it work. The most notable success has been *The Wall Street Journal* (http://online.wsj.com),whose unique content and predominantly wealthy audience have made it possible to charge its users directly.

Some newspapers are beginning to experiment with allowing subscribers to the printed paper to access online content for free while charging nonsubscribers. This addresses directly the potential problem of free online content cannibalizing the printed paper. Still, it is unclear whether online sites can make the subscription model work in large numbers. Users became accustomed to free Internet content during the boom times of the late 1990s and thus are particularly reluctant to start paying for it now. "It's really easy to persuade people that everything should be free," says Jack Fuller, president of Tribune Publishing Company. Giving away content during the early days of online journalism, Fuller contends, "may have been our biggest mistake."

Offering Value-Added Services

A more popular model provides varying levels of access to a site based on subscriptions or other fees. Anyone may be able to access the home page, for example, but subscribers might get access to special features, such as video clips or multimedia content (see Exhibit 11.2). Sites may also charge for content on a per-use basis. Many sites, for example, charge users a fee (normally a few dollars) to access archived material. Salon.com offers several levels of user access; users who pay less have to click through more ads to see content and also have access to less material.

On the Web

More information about targeted advertising, ad tracking software and other economic issues, plus cookies:

Under Chapter 11, select **The Economic Structure of Online Journalism.**

Exhibit 11.2   A number of sites, such as CNN.com, charge users for advanced content or video clips.

From CNN.com. Reprinted with permission.

The downside is that it is difficult for an online site to make money on value-added services alone, because such services usually appeal to only a small percentage of total users. Industry analysts estimate, for example, that charging for archived stories provides less than 5 percent of total online revenue.[4]

THE ROLE OF ONLINE JOURNALISM IN SOCIETY

Many of the economic issues may be determined to a large extent by the role that online journalism plays in society. In other words, how important will online journalism be to consumers of news, and will it spark an interest in news for people who don't read newspapers or watch television news?

It is already clear that online journalism has become an important source of information for many people. As author Philip Seib notes, September 11, 2001, "marked a true coming of age of Web-based news" as an estimated 30 million people went online to get news about the terrorist attacks and their aftermath.[5] While newspaper circulation has been declining slowly for years and the audiences for network television news have been shrinking, traffic at online news sites has generally been increasing.[6]

The Internet itself is becoming more and more transparent, allowing people to use it without having to think much about it. In the future, technological advances are likely to make the processes of browsing, bookmarking, linking and integrating information easier. Consider, for example, the difference between connecting to the Internet using a traditional dial-up modem and connecting using a more advanced cable modem. The user of the dial-up modem must sit and wait as the modem beeps and buzzes its way to a connection and then will have to wait for information to slowly fill the page as it downloads. The cable modem connection, on the other hand, is "always on," and all the user needs to do is sit down and start working. The cable modem user also gets a more transparent experience throughout the browsing process because information downloads much more quickly. **Wireless-fidelity (wi-fi)** systems will allow people to have the Internet "always on" as they travel (see "Delivery to Other Devices" later in this chapter). These kinds of advances are also coming in other areas of Internet use; eventually, Seib points out, people will use the Internet "much like making telephone calls or switching on the television."[7]

At present, users are increasingly relying on online journalism for both breaking news and more in-depth information. For breaking news, online journalism's speed is unmatched by any other medium, and it can (as discussed in Chapter 7) provide both the latest developments and the larger context for a story simultaneously. The key, of course, is making sure we don't lose sight of journalistic standards—posting unverified information to the Web site quickly just because we can. "The problem for serious journalists," Seib warns, "is the relegation of news judgment to a secondary status while technological capabilities become determinative."[8]

Online journalism also has become an important source for in-depth and contextual information. A growing number of people are looking to the Internet when they want information about *old* news stories. Here again, online journalism offers unmatched potential for storing information, linking it together by keyword or contextual relationship and making it easily accessible. Want to learn the process behind the tax abatements that led to the new factory on the edge of town? If your local media site has a well-designed archival system, you can look the topic up and read past stories. Permanent storage and indexing of a media organization's daily output provide a valuable tool for casual users, "news junkies," researchers and others.

Throughout this book, we have seen that the Internet offers significant potential for journalism. We have also seen that very few online sites take full advantage of this potential, instead relying in large part on **shovelware** content repurposed from print or broadcast. The question is whether shovelware will be enough to continue to attract and keep an audience for online journalism in the future.

Online journalism, of course, can be much more than shovelware. Consider the potential of virtual reality simulations and other immersive experiences that could engage the user at a level that is impossible with print or broadcast. We have seen that some sites are producing this kind of product, but it is only a start. We also have seen the potential for informed linking of information as a journalistic function. In this way, online journalism sites can help users make sense of the daunting array of information the Internet offers. Here, too, however, we have only scratched the surface. What if instead of going to a search engine like Google to look up information, a user's first inclination was to check out an online journalism site that had developed a reputation for culling the best links from the Internet? Will this be the way journalistic Web sites compete on the Internet, or will they work to develop a sense of ownership of the most accurate, up-to-date and reliable *news* coverage?

The challenge in all of this, of course, is economics. While, after an initial investment, a media organization can operate a shovelware site with very little additional expense, creating enhanced content takes more resources and requires the kind of resources that media organizations, increasingly part of larger conglomerates, are often less likely to invest in: additional employees. It takes people to create immersive multimedia content, to index and maintain a truly useful archiving system or to research and present links. Media organizations are unlikely to hire dedicated employees to do these things unless they know they will attract users and revenue.

But providing this type of content, or perhaps new types of content we haven't thought of yet, may be crucial to ensuring online journalism's future—and perhaps the future of journalism itself. A significant number of young people, who are raised with interactive media such as video games and who are increasingly computer-savvy at an early age, simply aren't engaged by traditional media forms. A Kaiser Family Foundation study found that very young children spend much more time using screen media (computer games, for example) than they do reading. "It's not just teen-agers who are wired up and tuned in," the study noted. "It's babies in diapers as well."[9]

The Internet offers the best hope of engaging these young people, but only if the content goes beyond shovelware. Here it may be that online journalism will be pressured by other types of sites to provide more immersive and engaging content. Already, many Internet commerce sites (which have a much more direct business model) are far ahead of their journalistic counterparts when it comes to compiling and linking related information. Sites such as amazon.com provide links based on books the user has already purchased or inquired about, and users can compile their own lists of "favorites" to share with other users (see Exhibit 11.3). Most of this type of information linking is done by automation, but journalists—given the time—could create the same kinds of information pathways for users. As commerce and other nonjournalistic sites increase multimedia and immersive content, online journalism sites may *have* to follow suit to remain relevant.

Again, the key question will be whether the technology is allowed to overrun the journalistic principles. Journalistic sites shouldn't just provide "toys" for

Commercial sites such as amazon.com, shown here, can provide users with personalized information based on past purchases or other information.   **Exhibit 11.3**

users to play with; they should make available features that engage the user while informing or educating. Journalistic principles *can* be applied to linking, multi-media and immersive content, and they should be. Indeed, all of these features can be valuable tools in the repertoire of online journalism.

Delivery to Other Devices

This book has concentrated on delivering journalistic content to full-size desktop or laptop computers. However, the proliferation of various types of handheld portable devices is creating a new target for journalistic content. For example, portable digital assistants (PDAs) and a growing number of wireless (cellular) telephones have text capability or built-in browsers.

The challenge with these kinds of devices is that they have much lower screen resolution than full-size computers. As such, they can't easily display Web pages designed for an 800- by 600-pixel screen size. Thus, online sites must design pages specifically for low-resolution devices or simply make text-only content available for them. The **short message system (SMS)** is one format that allows textual information to be transmitted to wireless telephones, PDAs and other devices. As discussed in Chapter 4, the use of cascading style sheets (CSS) allows a Web site to change content presentation based on what kind of browser a user has. These style sheets can also be used to tailor content to PDAs and other devices.

An increasing number of online sites are targeting users of PDAs and advanced wireless telephones. The advantage is that users can access information anytime, nearly anywhere. Users can also choose to automatically have news "alerts" sent to their portable devices or to receive regularly scheduled updates. The *Lawrence (Ks.) Journal-World* Web site, for example, can automatically call users' cell phones when certain bands are playing in town.

Wireless-fidelity network service, in which a device such as a laptop computer or PDA can connect to the Internet without plugging in, is available in a growing number of areas. This means that in such places as airports, hotels, coffee shops and universities, a user can maintain nearly constant contact with the Internet through her own computer. Clearly, this is a potentially valuable audience for online journalism providers.

News reader software such as RSS, which stands for either "Rich Site Summary" or "Really Simple Syndication," is also becoming increasingly popular. RSS allows users to subscribe to various Web sites and have the "headlines" from those sites sent to their PDAs (or to desktop or laptop computers) automatically.

On the Web

Online journalism and the September 11 attacks plus more on PDAs, SMS and the Kaiser Family Foundation:
Under Chapter 11, select **The Role of Online Journalism in Society.**

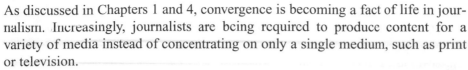

CONVERGENCE

As discussed in Chapters 1 and 4, convergence is becoming a fact of life in journalism. Increasingly, journalists are being required to produce content for a variety of media instead of concentrating on only a single medium, such as print or television.

Convergence presents both opportunities and challenges for online journalism specifically and for journalism in general. By requiring that journalists not concentrate on a single medium, convergence offers the opportunity for journalists to think outside the box, developing new ways to tell stories unconstrained by the limitations of a single medium. Converged newsrooms also offer the potential for improved communication and cooperation among journalists with strengths in various areas. The online component of journalism has been a significant aspect of most converged newsrooms, lending additional clout to the Internet as a journalistic medium.

But critics worry that convergence weakens journalism by putting fewer journalists on the street covering stories and in the newsroom. While a separate local television station and newspaper newsroom may have 50 employees each, the same converged newsroom might have only 70 total. Having fewer journalists means that journalistic organizations may be less likely to cover difficult stories, and certainly less likely to cover difficult stories well. It also means less competition among journalists and less inherent pressure to uncover stories that certain people might not want uncovered.

The economic pressure for convergence is likely to build in the future. As journalistic organizations are increasingly consumed by media conglomerates, pressure on the bottom line is likely to favor profits over quality journalism. For many decades, the Federal Communications Commission (FCC) would not allow a

> ## *On the Web*
>
> More about convergence, media conglomerates and the FCC's ownership rules:
> Under Chapter 11, select **Convergence.**

company that owned a newspaper to own a television station in the same city, although many existing cross-ownership situations were "grandfathered in." In recent years, however, the FCC has attempted to relax these and other ownership restrictions. Although Congress has reversed or weakened some of these FCC decisions, there is clearly a trend toward allowing bigger companies to own more media outlets. You need only look at the situation in radio, where over the past decade a handful of corporations has swallowed up the overwhelming majority of formerly independent stations, to the detriment of local news operations. Clearly, relaxing ownership restrictions—especially those that deal with cross-ownership of newspapers and television stations in the same city—will encourage further convergence of newsrooms.

SERVICE TO UNDERREPRESENTED COMMUNITIES

A common (and justifiable) criticism of journalism is that it ignores voices and issues outside the mainstream. Most mainstream news, critics point out, is told from the perspective of males, whites, heterosexuals and the rich (or at least the upper-middle class). There are alternative voices available in some cases, but they can hardly compete with the mainstream media outlets.

The Internet offers the potential for these voices to be heard. Because the Internet has no space limit, mainstream media organizations can devote coverage to alternative points of view without pushing aside something else. Alternative organizations also can set up Web sites that reach a national and international audience at a fraction of what it would cost to achieve such coverage in print or broadcast.

The question, as always, for the mainstream media outlets is whether they will respond to this opportunity. Again, news coverage of alternative points of view can be more effective when journalists have alternative points of view, but mainstream media outlets might not devote the necessary resources to hiring such journalists.

In the meantime, independent sites have cropped up to serve diverse, non-mainstream audiences. Hispanicvista.com, for example, provides news and commentary about issues of concern to the Hispanic community (see Exhibit 11.4). Among the site's goals are encouraging Hispanic participation in the political process and promoting an understanding of Hispanic culture among all Americans. Similarly, blackvoices.com provides news, commentary and information targeted to African-American users as well as an online forum with more than 800,000 active members (http://new.blackvoices.com).

At the same time, however, it is feared that minority communities are being left behind by the Internet. The United States, for example, is becoming a community stratified between the information "haves" and the information "have-nots," creating what is often called the "Digital Divide." A significant number of minorities and poor people lack computers, computer training and access to the Internet. Thus, as the Internet becomes an increasingly important part of everyday life, those without access are excluded socially and politically as well as economically. Although recent years have brought signs that the situation is improving, the full potential of the Internet and its content will be realized only when people are not prevented access because of economic or educational disadvantage.

Service to Users with Disabilities

Another area where the Internet can offer a valuable service is in providing information to people with disabilities. Visually impaired persons, for example, can use specialized browsers that read Web content aloud or convert textual information to Braille. This means that a massive amount of journalistic content is potentially available to people who could not access it before.

Sites such as Hispanicvista.com can serve specialized audiences.   **Exhibit 11.4**

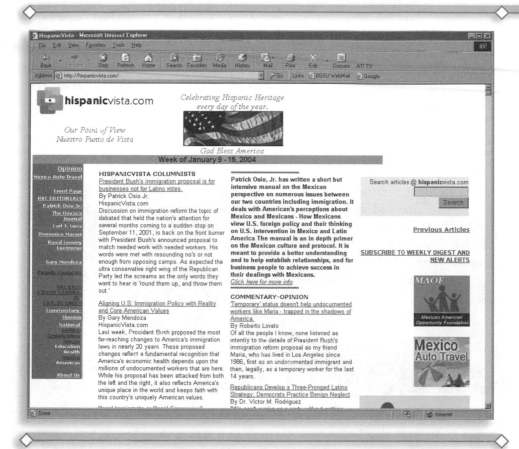

From hispanicvista.com. Reprinted with permission.

However, to be truly useful, Internet content must be designed with **accessibility** in mind, meaning that it must be accessible by persons who are disabled. This means, for example, that photographs and other graphic information should be accompanied by descriptions and that pages with tables should make sense when the content is read linearly. Unfortunately, researchers who have looked at online journalism content have found that most sites are not fully accessible and, in fact, that many are decidedly not accessible.[10] Once again, a new potential audience is available to online journalism as long as media organizations respond to its needs.

> ### On the Web
>
> More about serving niche audiences, the Digital Divide and accessibility resources, including software you can use to see how accessible your site is.
>
> Under Chapter 11, select **Underrepresented Communities.**

WHAT'S NEXT

This book's first chapter ended by pointing out that today's generation of new journalists could play a significant role in shaping online journalism for many generations to come. It is true. Online journalism is still in a nascent stage, and the chance exists for people like you to have a significant impact on how it develops.

As this final chapter has noted, both opportunities and challenges exist. The online journalists of today and those of the immediate future can significantly influence whether online journalism takes advantage of the opportunities or succumbs to the challenges. Certainly, as seen in this chapter, many of the issues facing online journalism (and journalism in general) are beyond the power of one individual to change. However, if online journalism is to reach something approaching its full potential, it will take individuals who are dedicated to *journalism* and who understand the ways online media can be put to use. Will online journalism remain a mere appendage (or direct replacement for) traditional media, or will it rise to greater things? The answer to this question will be determined by people like you.

Again, welcome to the exciting world of online journalism!

Activities

11.1 Examine the Web site of a local media organization in your region or hometown. What economic model does it appear to be using? Is it selling advertising, requiring users to register or subscribe, providing value-added services or using some combination of these?

11.2 Think about ways that online journalism could be made more relevant and interesting to you. What are the things that attract you to your favorite Web sites (both journalistic and nonjournalistic)? How could these things be used for journalism?

11.3 Look at the Web site for a big-city newspaper or a national television news organization. What features, if any, does it provide for underrepresented groups? Does it provide services for PDAs and other portable devices?

ENDNOTES

1. Doug Brown, "Searching for Online Gold," *American Journalism Review,* June/July 2003, p. 54.

2. See Brown, "Searching for Online Gold," p. 55; and Michael Learmonth, "Online Reloaded," *Folio,* July 2003, p. 22.

3. Doug Brown, "How Stand-Alone Sites Cope," *American Journalism Review,* June/July 2003, p. 59.

4. Brown, "Searching for Online Gold," pp. 54–55.

5. Philip Seib, *Going Live: Getting the News Right in a Real-Time, Online World* (Lanham, MD: Rowman and Littlefield Publishers, Inc., 2002), p. 175.

6. Tim Race, "Most Wanted: Drilling Down/Web Sites," *The New York Times,* May 12, 2003, p. C-12.

7. Seib, *Going Live,* p. 122.

8. Seib, *Going Live,* p. 40.

9. Kaiser Family Foundation Study, http://www.kff.org/content/2003/3378/ (accessed November 18, 2003).

10. See Joel J. Davis, "The Accessibility Divide: The Visually-Impaired and Access to Online News," *Journal of Broadcasting and Electronic Media* 47, no. 3 (September 2003): pp. 474–481; and James C. Foust, "Access for Everyone? Analyzing the Accessibility of Newspaper Web Sites" (paper presented to the Association of Internet Researchers International Conference, Minneapolis, Minn., October 2001).

COMMON TEXT-FORMATTING SELECTORS IN CASCADING STYLE SHEETS (CSS)

You can find examples of these selectors on this book's Web site.

Color. Sets the foreground color for an object. In the case of text, this will be the color of the lettering. The color can be designated by name, hexadecimal or other methods (see Web site).

> *Examples:* h1 {color: blue;}
>
> h1 {color: #FFFFCC;}

Font-family. Sets the font for the text. Can use generic or specific names, or set multiple choices. Enclose names with spaces in double quotes.

> *Examples:* h1 {font-family: serif;}
>
> h1 {font-family: "Times New Roman";}
>
> h1 {font-family: Arial, Helvetica, sans-serif;}

Font-size. Sets the size of the font. Can designate size in pixels (px) or other methods.

> *Example:* h1 {font-size: 24px;}

Font-style. Sets the style of the font. Choices are normal or italic.

> *Example:* h1 {font-style: italic;}

Font-weight. Sets the weight (boldness) of a font. Can be set numerically (100, 200, 300, 400, 500, 600, 700, 800, 900) or using bold, bolder, lighter or normal.

> *Examples:* h1 {font-weight: 900;} Sets boldest.
>
> h1 {font-weight: bold;}

Margin. Sets the top, right, bottom and left margins around an element.

> *Example:* h1 {margin: 10px 5px 10px 5px;} Sets top and bottom margins to 10 pixels and top and bottom margins to 5 pixels

Text-align. Sets the horizontal alignment of text. Choices are left, right, center or justify.

Examples: h1 {text-align: center;}

h1 {text-align: justify;}

Text-indent. Sets the indentation of the first line of a paragraph.

Example: h1 {text-indent: 10px;}

COMMON POSITIONING AND DESIGN SELECTORS IN CASCADING STYLE SHEETS (CSS)

You can find examples of these selectors on this book's Web site.

Background-color. Sets the background color for an object. Can be applied to text, the page itself or other elements.

> *Examples:* h1 {background-color: blue;}
>
> body {color: #FFFFCC;} Sets the background color of the page.

Border-color. Sets the color of the border around an element.

> *Example:* h1 {border-color: red;}

Border-style. Sets the style of the border around an element. Choices are dotted, dashed, solid, double, groove, ridge, inset, outset and none.

> *Example:* h1 {border-style: dashed;}

Border-width. Sets the width of the border around an element.

> *Example:* h1 {border-width: 5px;} Sets the border width to 5 pixels.

Position. Sets how an element is to be positioned on the page. Normally, it is set to static, but it can be used to achieve other effects. Used in combination with top, left, right and bottom selectors.

> *Example:* h1 {position: static;}

Top, right, bottom, left. Set the top, right, bottom and left positions of an element. Can use one or more and in combination with height or width elements.

> *Examples:* h1 {top: 10px; right: 100px; bottom: 200px; left: 10px;}
>
> h1 {top: 10px; left: 10px; height: 190px; width: 90px;}
>
> Both of the above statements do essentially the same thing. They create a content block for the h1 element that begins 10 pixels from the left edge of the page and 10 pixels from the top of the page and is 190 pixels high and 90 pixels wide.

above the fold   A newspaper layout principle mandating that the top half of the newspaper's front page contain its most important information and most attractive elements.

accessibility   Provision of convenient use of or access to interactive media to persons with a disability.

accuracy   Getting the facts right.

analog   Data that travels and is stored in continuously varying "waves" and cannot be stored, manipulated or transmitted without some degradation of the original information.

animation   A moving graphic image.

ASCII   A text format in which each individual character takes up one byte of space.

associative linking   Linking that can be controversial because it associates the content of one Web site with that of another.

attribute   A means to modify HTML tags and set specific values.

attribution   The reporting of not only the facts but also the source of those facts.

audio interchange file format (AIFF)   A standard format for sound in digital form.

AVI (audio-video interleaved)   A standard format for video in digital form.

bandwidth   The amount of digital data that can flow across a given connection.

binary   A numbering system made up of only two digits, normally zero (0) and one (1). A binary numbering system is used by computers and other digital devices.

bit depth   The range of high frequencies (treble) to low frequencies (bass) that are included in digitized sound.

bitmap (BMP)   A standard format for graphics in digital form.

bit   A computer unit of data having a value of either zero or one.

block left   A way to align text horizontally on the screen with alignment to the left margin, thus leaving a ragged right margin.

block right   A way to align text horizontally on the screen with alignment to the right margin, thus leaving a ragged left margin.

blog   A Web log (i.e., an electronic journal or diary).

bloggers   Individuals who create Web log (blog) sites.

body   The section of an HTML document containing the main content displayed in the browser.

Boolean connectors   Key words (such as AND, OR and NOT) used to perform more specific online searches.

broadband   A high-bandwidth Internet connection capable of transferring data at very high speed. Broadband connections are usually made of coaxial or fiber optic cable.

browser   A computer program used to interpret HTML coding and reconstruct Web pages on the user's screen.

browser sniffing   A process whereby an HTML document contains code that determines what kind of browser the user has.

browser-safe palette   The group of 216 colors recognized by both Macintosh and PC platforms and, thus, properly displayable on both types of machines.

bulletin board system (BBS)   A computer-based system that allows users to post messages that other users can access.

byte   A series of eight bits.

cable modem   A means by which Internet access is obtained through a cable television service.

capture   To bring audio or video information into a computer.

cascading style sheets (CSS)   A way of formatting text in HTML documents. Using CSS, content information can be kept separate from presentation information.

CD-ROM   A removable storage device for digital data.

cell   An individual "box" in an HTML table.

cell padding   The space between a cell's content and its border in an HTML table.

cell spacing   The space between individual cells in an HTML table.

centered   A basic way to align text horizontally on the screen with alignment to an imaginary center line, creating ragged margins on both the left and right sides of the text.

central processing unit (CPU)   The "brain" of a computer.

chat   A process allowing two or more computer users to communicate in real time by typing information on their keyboards.

chronological   A basic way to structure journalistic stories that tells what happened in the order it happened.

chunk   An individual piece of a story that has been divided into parts.

chunking   A method of presenting a whole story in parts, with each part (or chunk) corresponding to one of the story's main points.

click-through   A term referring to visitors who come to a Web page through a link on another page.

clip   An individual segment of digital sound or video.

comments   Notes to Web page developers or technical information appearing in the HTML document but not showing on the page itself.

compression   Methods using mathematical codings to make video or audio files smaller.

computer-assisted reporting (CAR)   Using computers to enhance journalism.

consistency   Use of the same design elements within a single page and across all pages in a Web site.

content management system (CMS)   Computer software designed to create Web pages from raw content.

context   Related information that helps give a journalistic story meaning and significance.

contrast   The process of making individual elements on a page distinguishable from one another quickly and easily.

convergence   The act of two or more media "partnering" to produce a Web site.

cookie   Data stored in a user's browser that can be read by individual Web sites.

copyright   Law that protects original works of authorship.

country-code top-level domain (ccTLD)   A top-level domain that identifies the country in which the host computer is located, such as .ca for Canada.

cropping   Cutting an image to retain only its most compelling parts.

database   A collection of digital information organized into parts called *records* and *fields*.

database control   A software function that allows individual pieces of data to be stored and accessed via automation.

dayparting   Tailoring Web content to different readers at different times of the day, creating, in effect, different online editions.

deep linking   The practice of bypassing an organization's home page to link to a page within the Web site.

deprecation   The process of deleting commands in HTML standards.

digital   Data in binary form, meaning it is made up entirely of zeros and ones. Digital data can be manipulated, stored and transmitted without any degradation of the original information.

digitize   To convert analog data to digital form.

direct subscriber line (DSL)   A service that transmits data over telephone lines at fast speeds.

directory   A Web site in which Web content has been organized by topic.

discussion board   A means to facilitate continuing conversation. It involves users contributing information that is compiled and made available to future users.

domain name system (DNS)   A text-based addressing scheme used to identify different computers on the Internet.

dots per inch (dpi)   A measurement for the level of detail or resolution of an image.

DVD (digital versatile disc)   A removable storage device for digital data.

e-mail (electronic mail)   A system allowing one user to send text messages to another user.

encapsulated PostScript (EPS)   A standard format for graphics in digital form.

end tags   Entries that "turn off" an HTML command. End tags begin with a backslash (/).

external style sheet   A document that defines text and other formatting characteristics for one or more HTML documents.

fair use   The concept under copyright law that allows others to use part of a copyrighted work in certain situations.

fairness   The ability to approach information without bias and report it the same way.

field   An individual data unit of a record in a database; for instance, a data record about a book might contain fields for author, title and ISBN number.

file transfer protocol (FTP)   Programs allowing a user to transfer files to and from remote computers.

Firewire   A type of digital connection often used to transport video between cameras and computers. Also referred to as IEEE-1394.

floppy disk   A removable storage device for computer files.

frame   An individual still picture that makes up moving video.

frame rate   A measurement for the number of individual still images (frames) that make up each second of video.

frame size   The size of a video picture measured in pixels.

frames   An HTML feature that allows the browser window to be divided into different sections.

framing   Surrounding someone else's content using HTML frames, thus making it look as if you produced the framed content.

GIF (graphics interchange format)   A graphic format used on the Web that is well-suited to high-contrast artwork such as logos.

gigabyte   A billion bytes.

gigahertz   One thousand megahertz.

graphical interface   A computer system that allows users to perform tasks using icons and a mouse without having to type in commands.

grid   The basic layout structure of a page (print document or Web page); comprised of a series of lines and boxes into which the content fits.

hard drive   A computer data storage device.

head   The section of an HTML document containing basic structural information about the document.

hexadecimal   A base 16 numbering system that uses the digits 0 through 9 and the letters A through F. Hexadecimal numbers are indicated by a pound sign (#) at the beginning, as in #99FF00. Also known as *hex*.

hierarchy   The priority ordering of elements on a page according to importance.

hits   The number of page views for a given Web page.

hyperlinking   Linking two or more Web pages together.

hypertext markup language (HTML)   A computer markup language used to create Web pages. It is the standard interface for the Internet.

hypertext transfer protocol (HTTP)   A uniform method of transferring HTML documents over the Internet.

indecency   Certain words, nudity or other things of a sexual or nonsexual nature that could offend manners or morals.

inline linking   Placing a copy of an image on a Web page without actually copying the file.

instant messaging   Systems that allow users to send text messages, pictures and other information to one another in real time.

integrated services digital network (ISDN)   A service that transmits data over telephone company lines at fast speeds.

interactivity   Audience participation.

Internet   The worldwide network, or connection, of computers that allows any user on the network to access information from anywhere else on the network.

Internet protocol (IP)   An address that allows a computer to be accessed by others on the Internet.

Internet service provider (ISP)   A company that charges a fee for providing Internet access.

inverted pyramid   A way to structure journalistic stories so that the most important information is at the beginning and progressively less important information appears as the story proceeds.

JPEG (joint photographic experts group)   A graphic format used on the Web that is best suited for images with subtle tonal variations, such as photographs.

justified   A way to align text so that both left and right margins line up.

kilobyte   A thousand bytes.

layering   Dividing a story into parts by level of detail or by topic.

libel   The publication of false information that is defamatory, or likely to harm someone's reputation.

line length   The horizontal length (width, actually) of text lines.

link   An HTML feature that allows a user to move to a new Web page or to perform a function such as playing a video clip. Also called a *hyperlink*.

listserv   A system that sends out identical e-mail messages to everyone who subscribes to it.

main story   The primary textual story on the Web site that can either stand on its own or be supplemented with other types of media and other stories.

megabyte   A million bytes.

moblog   A blog created using portable devices such as cellular phones or personal digital assistants.

mode   The aural form of a digital sound recording, mono or stereo.

modem   A device that allows computers to communicate over telephone lines.

monitor   The screen used to display information on a computer.

monospace   A type of lettering in which each character is given the same amount of horizontal spacing regardless of its width. For example, the letters *w* and *i* would both receive the same amount of space (see also *proportional*).

MP3   A standard format for sound in digital form that uses compression to make files significantly smaller.

MPEG (moving picture experts group)   A compression format for digital video.

multimedia   Online provision of text, pictures, sounds and video.

musical instrument digital interface (MIDI)   A standardized method of controlling musical instruments or other digital audio devices.

nameplate   The name and logo of a newspaper or Web page, normally placed at the top of the screen or front page.

narrative   A way to structure journalistic stories that relies on using vivid descriptions of people and places to "set scenes" and involve the reader the way a novel or short story might.

navigation bar   A part of a Web page that contains links to other portions of the Web site.

network   An interconnection of computers allowing them to share data.

newness   The act of providing information that has not been given before.

newsgroup   A system that allows users to "post" e-mail messages where others can read them.

novelty   A category of font using stylized representations of letters.

obscenity   Depiction of sexual activity in a manner designed to cause arousal and lacking artistic, literary or scientific value and regulated or prohibited by laws enacted by federal, state and local governments.

parameter   A value given to an attribute in an HTML command.

pixel   A tiny "dot" of colored light.

pixels per inch (PPI)   The unit of measurement for the resolution of computer screens.

plug-in   Additional software added to a browser to allow access to specialized content, such as audio, video or rich content.

PNG (portable network graphics)   A graphic format designed to replace GIF that has been slowly gaining acceptance on the Web.

portable digital assistant (PDA)   A handheld computer that has graphics capabilities and the ability to connect to networks.

portable document format (PDF)   A programming format designed for storing print-based documents and making them available online.

print plus   The most basic type of story form that can be produced "from scratch" relatively quickly and that can also be converted to and from other forms—print, broadcast or wire copy—with minimal effort.

processor   A chip in a computer or other digital device that can perform electronic calculations.

proportional   A lettering style that assigns horizontal spacing to letters based on their individual width. The letter "w," for example, would receive more space than narrower letters such as "i." Proportional lettering is usually easier to read and looks neater than monospace lettering.

public domain   Material that is outside the boundaries of copyright ownership and available for anyone's use.

query   A search question for a database.

QuickTime   A standard format for digital video.

random access memory (RAM)   The part of the computer where programs are stored while they are running and where data is stored while it is being used.

RealAudio   A streaming audio format.

RealVideo   A streaming video format.

record   An individual part of a database. For example, a database of U.S. presidents would have individual records for George W. Bush, Jimmy Carter and so forth.

relevance   Importance to the audience.

removable storage   Digital storage devices that can be physically removed from the computer.

resolution   The level of detail in an image.

rich content   Web-based content, created with Java, Flash or other programming, that is more interactive than individual HTML pages.

sampling rate   A measurement of how often an original sound or other analog source is analyzed as it is converted to digital.

sans serif   A category of font not using protrusions (serifs) on the ends of the letters.

scan   To pick out individual words and other points of interest instead of reading word for word.

search engine   A Web site designed to search the Internet for other Web sites containing key words, phrases or other criteria.

serif   A category of font using small protrusions (called *serifs*) on the tips of the letters.

server   A computer used to store HTML documents and other data for access by others.

shell   A collection of related links and information organized onto a Web page.

short message system (SMS)   A format that allows textual information to be transmitted to wireless telephones, portable digital assistants (PDAs) and other devices.

shovelware   Content taken from the newspaper, wire services or other media and placed onto a Web site with little or no modification.

sound card   A device in a computer that allows it to record and play digital sounds.

standalone tag   An HTML command that works by itself, with no need for end tags.

start tag   An HTML tag used to turn on a command.

streaming   A technology in which users can listen to a file as it is downloaded onto their computer.

superjournalist   One who gathers information and produces stories for more than one type of media.

table   An HTML feature that divides a page into individual parts called *cells*. A table can be used to present technical information in chart form or to create a basic design grid for a Web page.

tag   A basic HTML command.

tagged image file format (TIFF)   A standard format for digital graphics.

TCP/IP (transmission control protocol/Internet protocol)   A method of breaking messages into small chunks called "packets" that are "addressed" to specific computers and, upon reaching their destinations, are reassembled to re-create the original message.

telnet   A program allowing a user to log onto and control a remote computer.

template   A basic page design that can be used as the starting point for one or more pages on a Web site. For example, a designer could create one template for the various news sections, then fill in the content of those pages using the basic template design.

thematic   A news story arranged according to various themes in the story.

title   The HTML tag that inserts text into a user's title bar.

title bar   The very top of the browser's window.

top-level domain (TLD)   A code that identifies the type of entity that is publishing the Web site.

uniform resource locator (URL)   A Web site address.

Unity   A quality of a well-designed Web page that creates the impression of a coherent whole.

universal serial bus (USB)   A connector on a computer that allows devices such as printers, scanners, storage devices and cameras to be plugged in.

usability   The concept of how easy it is for users to navigate Web pages to achieve their desired goals.

users   People actively engaged in seeking online information.

video capture   The act of bringing video information into a computer.

video card   A device that allows a computer to play back—and, in some cases, capture—digital video.

virus   A program created by computer hackers to damage data or slow down or disable networks.

waveform audio file format (WAV)   A standard format for sound in digital form.

Web extras   Additional features added to a main story Web page.

Windows Media   A standard format for digital audio and video.

wireless-fidelity (wi-fi)   A network service in which a device, such as a laptop computer or portable digital assistant (PDA) can connect to the Internet without plugging into a telephone or cable line.

World Wide Web (WWW)   The set of technologies that places a graphical interface on the Internet and allows users to explore the network using a mouse, icons and other visual elements rather than having to type obscure computer commands.

World Wide Web Consortium (W3C)   An organization that develops and implements Web standards.

WYSIWYG   An acronym for "What you see is what you get." Refers to a feature of Web page creation programs in which the finished page appears on-screen exactly as it was arranged in the design program. The software automatically creates HTML coding to represent the design (pronounced "wissy wig").

XHTML (extensible hypertext markup language)   The next generation of HTML.

zip disk   A removable storage device for digital data.